OECD Studies on SMEs and Entrepreneurship

SME and Entrepreneurship Policy in Indonesia 2018

OECD
BETTER POLICIES FOR BETTER LIVES

This document, as well as any data and any map included herein, are without prejudice to the status of or sovereignty over any territory, to the delimitation of international frontiers and boundaries and to the name of any territory, city or area.

Please cite this publication as:
OECD (2018), *SME and Entrepreneurship Policy in Indonesia 2018*, OECD Studies on SMEs and Entrepreneurship, OECD Publishing, Paris.
https://doi.org/10.1787/9789264306264-en

ISBN 978-92-64-30625-7 (print)
ISBN 978-92-64-30626-4 (pdf)

Series: OECD Studies on SMEs and Entrepreneurship
ISSN 2078-0982 (print)
ISSN 2078-0990 (online)

The statistical data for Israel are supplied by and under the responsibility of the relevant Israeli authorities. The use of such data by the OECD is without prejudice to the status of the Golan Heights, East Jerusalem and Israeli settlements in the West Bank under the terms of international law.

Corrigenda to OECD publications may be found on line at: *www.oecd.org/publishing/corrigenda*.

Foreword

This publication presents the OECD country review of small and medium-sized enterprise (SME) and entrepreneurship policy in Indonesia. The report is part of the series of OECD Studies on SMEs and Entrepreneurship undertaken by the OECD Centre for Entrepreneurship, SMEs, Regions and Cities. In addition to Indonesia, country reviews have covered Canada, Israel, Italy, Kazakhstan, Mexico, Poland, the Russian Federation and Thailand.

The series provides a tool for assessing and improving the design and implementation of SME and entrepreneurship policy and for sharing policy experiences among OECD member and partner countries. The reviews are based on a standard methodology, which includes a diagnostic questionnaire completed by national government authorities, a fact-finding mission by an OECD team to hold detailed interviews with policy and business stakeholders and discussion of a draft report at a peer review session in the OECD Working Party on SMEs and Entrepreneurship (WPSMEE). The final report of the Indonesia review of SME and entrepreneurship policy (CFE/SME(2018)4/REV1) was approved by the WPSMEE through written procedure on 31 August 2018.

The report highlights that the Indonesian government recognises SMEs as key drivers of economic growth and social inclusion. Indonesia has a Micro, Small and Medium Enterprise (MSME) Law (Law 20/2008) and a dedicated Ministry for the development of co-operatives and SMEs. SMEs also feature prominently in the National Medium-Term Development Plan, 2015-2019, which sets out the development priorities of the executive in office. As a result, many ministries operate programmes supporting SMEs, which is good for the overall development of SMEs but also poses a co-ordination challenge to ensure that programmes are coherent, complementary and have sufficient scale. The report recommends that the government prepare an SME Strategy document with the aim of strengthening the overall coherence of national SME policies.

The government of Indonesia has also undertaken important reforms in specific policy areas, such as improving the ease of doing business and enhancing access to finance for SMEs. This report suggests that these policy measures are helpful for SMEs, but it also recommends placing stronger attention in the future on measures that foster firm-level productivity through increased innovation activity in SMEs, and increased participation of SMEs in global markets and global value chains.

This report is funded by the Government of Canada as part of the Canada-OECD Project for ASEAN SMEs (COPAS), which aims to support SME development in the Association of Southeast Asian Nations (ASEAN) Member States.

Acknowledgements

This review was undertaken by the OECD Centre for Entrepreneurship, SMEs, Regions and Cities (CFE) led by Lamia Kamal-Chaoui, Director, in co-operation with the Ministry of Co-operatives and SMEs of the Government of Indonesia.

The project was led by Marco Marchese, Policy Analyst, under the supervision of Miriam Koreen, Deputy Director of CFE and Head of the SME and Entrepreneurship Division. The report was drafted by Marco Marchese, Marco Bianchini (Policy Analyst), Sandra Hannig (Policy Analyst) and Jonathan Potter (Head of Unit), with written contributions from Lois Stevenson (independent consultant), Anders Johansson (Stockholm School of Economics) and Andy Pike (Newcastle University). Important local support and inputs were provided by Eugenia Mardanugraha (Universitas Indonesia).

Within the Indonesian Ministry of Co-operatives and SMEs, project organisation and report development contributions were made by I-Wayan Dipta, Deputy Minister for Production and Marketing; Meliadi Sembiring, Secretary of the Minister of Co-operatives and SMEs; Rosdiana V. Sipayung, Secretary of the Deputy-Minister for Production and Marketing; Destry Anna Sari, Head of the Planning Division; and Hilman M. Firdaus, supporting staff.

A Steering Group was formed for this review composed of delegates of the OECD Working Party on SMEs and Entrepreneurship (WPSMEE), involving Mattia Corbetta (Ministry of Economic Development, Italy) who also provided written inputs, Veronika Michalkova (Ministry of Economy, Slovak Republic), Eoghan Richardson (Department of Business, Enterprise and Innovation, Ireland), and Karl Woodhead (Ministry of Business, Innovation and Employment, New Zealand).

The report benefitted from comments from Christine Lewis (Senior Economist) and Patrice Ollivaud (Economist) from the Indonesia Country Desk of the OECD Economics Department and from Max Bulakovskiy (Policy Analyst) and Annie Norfolk Beadle (Policy Analyst) from the Southeast Asia Division of the OECD Global Relations Secretariat.

Many individuals and organisations in Indonesia provided important information for the review, including the Ministry of Co-operatives and SMEs, the Ministry of National Development Planning/National Development Planning Agency (BAPPENAS), the Co-ordinating Ministry for Economic Affairs, the Ministry of Industry, the Ministry of Trade, the Ministry of Research, Technology and Higher Education, the Ministry of Manpower, the Ministry of Communication and Informatics, the Ministry of Youth and Sports, the Ministry of Social Affairs, the Ministry of Home Affairs, the Ministry of Education, the Ministry of Women's Empowerment and Child Protection, the Central Bureau of Statistics (BPS), the Indonesia Investment Co-ordinating Board (BKPM), the Agency for the Creative Economy (BEKRAF), the Public Procurement Agency (LKPP), the Antitrust Authority (KPPU), the Agency for the Assessment and Application of Technology

(BPPT), Bank Indonesia, the Financial Services Authority (OJK), Credit Guarantee Indonesia (JAMKRINDO), the Indonesia Stock Exchange (IDX), Indonesia Eximbank, the Indonesia Chamber of Commerce and Industry (KADIN), the Indonesian Co-operative Council (DEKOPIN), the Indonesia Business Women Association (IWAPI), the Association of Business Development Services of Indonesia (ABDSI), the Association of Business Incubators (AiBI), and Presisi Research and Consultancy.

Table of contents

Tables

Figures

Boxes

Follow OECD Publications on:

http://twitter.com/OECD_Pubs

http://www.facebook.com/OECDPublications

http://www.linkedin.com/groups/OECD-Publications-4645871

http://www.youtube.com/oecdilibrary

http://www.oecd.org/oecddirect/

This book has...

StatLinks
A service that delivers Excel® files from the printed page!

Look for the *StatLinks* at the bottom of the tables or graphs in this book. To download the matching Excel® spreadsheet, just type the link into your Internet browser, starting with the *http://dx.doi.org* prefix, or click on the link from the e-book edition.

Main abbreviations

ABDSI	Association of Business Development Services Indonesia
AiBI	Association of Indonesian Business Incubators
APEC	Asia-Pacific Economic Co-operation
AEC	ASEAN Economic Community
ASEAN	Association of South-East Asian Nations
BAPPENAS	*Badan Perencanaan Pembangunan Nasional* (Ministry of National Development Planning/National Development Planning Agency)
BDS	Business Development Services
BIK	*Biro Informasi Kredit* (Public credit bureau)
BPPT	*Badan Pengkajian Penerapan Teknologi* (Agency for the Assessment and Application of Technology)
BPS	*Badan Pusat Statistik* (Indonesian Central Bureau of Statistics)
BEKRAF	*Badan Ekonomi Kreatif* (Creative Economy Agency)
BEP	Beginner Entrepreneur Programme (*Program Bantuan Dana Bagi Pengembangan Wirausaha Pemula*)
BKPM	*Badan Koordinasi Penanaman Modal* (Indonesia Investment Co-ordinating Board)
BPKP	*Badan Pengawasan Keuangan dan Pembangunan* (Finance and Development Supervisory Agency)
BRI	*Bank Rakyat Indonesia* (People's Bank of Indonesia)
CCCs	Commercial Credit Circuits
CERNE	Reference Centre for Support of New Ventures (Brazil)
CGCs	Credit Guarantee Companies
CPNE	Coaching Programme for New Exporter
GDP	Gross Domestic Product
GEM	Global Entrepreneurship Monitor
IBT	*Inkubasi Bisnis Teknologi* (Technology and Business Incubator)
IDX	Indonesia Stock Exchange
IMK	*Survei Industri Mikro dan Kecil* (BPS Survey of Micro and Small Enterprises)
IPO	Initial Public Offering
IPR	Intellectual Property Rights
IUMK	Micro and Small Business License Programme
IWAPI	Indonesian Women's Business Association
KADIN	*Kamar Dagang dan Industri* (Indonesia Chamber of Commerce and Industry)
KKU/KKN-PP	Business Lecture Programme
KUR	*Kredit Usaha Rakyat* (People's Business Credit Programme)
KURBE	KUR Financing for Export-Oriented SMEs Programme
LAKU-PANDAI	Inclusive Finance Framework (under the responsibility of OJK)
LKPP	*Lembaga Kebijakan Pengadaan Barang/Jasa Pemerintah* (Government Goods and Services Procurement Agency)
LGUs	Local Government Units
LPDB	*Lembaga Pengelola Dana Bergulir* (Revolving Fund Management Agency)
MCA	Millennium Challenge Account (Indonesia Procurement Modernisation Project)
M-CORE	Micro-enterprise Competitiveness Rating for Enhancement (Malaysia)
MKU	Youth Entrepreneurship Apprenticeship Programme
MNEs	Multinational Enterprises
NCs	Negosyo Centres (Philippines)
NPLs	Non-Performing Loans
NSDC	National SME Development Council (Malaysia)

OECD	Organisation for Economic Co-operation and Development
OJK	*Otoritas Jasa Keuanga* (Financial Services Authority)
PELAKU	Centres for Education, Consumer Services and Financial Access (under the responsibility of OJK)
PKBL	Partnership Programme with Small Business
PLUT-KUMKM	*Pusat Layanan Usaha Terpadu Koperasi & UMKM* (Integrated Business Services Centres for Co-operatives and SMEs)
PMR	Product Market Regulations
PPBT-PT	*Perusahaan Pemula Berbasis Teknologi – Perguran Tinggi* (University-based business incubator)
PPP	Purchasing Power Parity
SCORE	SME Competitiveness Rating for Enhancement (Malaysia)
SDBS	Structural and Demography Business Statistics (OECD)
SEBRAE	Brazilian Micro and Small Enterprise Agency
SKP	*Sentra Kewirausahaan Pemuda* (Youth Entrepreneurship Centres)
SME Corp. Malaysia	SME Agency (Malaysia)
SMEs	Small and Medium-sized Enterprises
SMI	Industry-based Small and Medium-sized Enterprises
SOEs	State-Owned Enterprises
STRI	Service Trade Restrictiveness Index (OECD)
SYB	Start Your Business Programme (ILO)
TEA	Total Early-stage Entrepreneurship Activity (GEM database)
TNP2K	*Tim Nasional Percepatan Penanggualangan Kemiskinan* (National Task Force for the Acceleration of Poverty Reduction)
VET	Vocational and Educational Training
WBES	World Bank Enterprise Survey
WMP	*Wirausaha Muda Pemula* (Young Entrepreneur Programme)
WPSMEE	Working Party on SMEs and Entrepreneurship

Basic statistics of Indonesia

Land, people and electoral cycle

	Indonesia	OECD average		Indonesia	OECD average
Population					
Population (million) (2017)	264.0		Population density per km² (2017)	145.725	37.73
Under 15 (%)	27.4	18.0	Life expectancy (years, 2015)	69.1	80.4
Over 65 (%)	5.3	16.8	Men	67.0	77.7
Latest 5-year (2013-2017) average population growth (%)	1.3	0.6	Women	71.2	83.1
			Population of largest metropolitan areas (million people, 2018)		
			Jakarta	10.86	
			Surabaya	2.95	
			Bandung	2.47	
			Latest general elections	April 2014	
Economy					
Gross Domestic Product (GDP) (volume, 2017)			Value added shares of GDP (%, 2017)		
In current prices (trillion IDR)	13 589		Primary sector (including mining)	21.5	2.5
In current prices (billion USD)	1 016		Industry including construction	33.1	26.9
Latest 5-year (2013-2017) average GDP growth (%)	5.1	2.1	Services	45.4	70.6
Per capita (000 USD PPP)	11.7	42.2			
General government					
Revenue (% of GDP, 2016)	15.3	39.1	Government net borrowing (% of GDP, 2016)	2.4	1.6
Expenditure (% of GDP, 2016)	17.7	40.7	Net government interest payments (% of revenue, 2016)	6.64	4.62
External accounts					
Exchange rate (IDR per USD, 2017, average)	13 381.5		Main merchandise exports (balance-of-payments basis) (% of total, 2016)		
Value in USD of 1 million IDR (2017 FX rate)	7 473.0		Mineral products	21%	
Value in USD of 1 billion IDR (2017 FX rate)	74 730.0		Animal and vegetable products	13%	
PPP for GDP (national currency for USD, 2017)	4 190.5		Machines	12%	
Exports of goods and services (% of GDP, 2017)	20.4	27.9	Main merchandise imports (balance-of-payments basis) (% of total, 2016)		
Imports of goods and services (% of GDP, 2017)	19.2	27.3	Machines	27%	
Current account balance (% of GDP, 2017)	-1.7	0.4	Mineral products	14%	
			Chemical products	10%	
Labour market, skills and innovation					
Employment rate for 15-64 year olds (%, 2017)	66.1	67.8	Unemployment rate (age 15 and over, %, 2017)	5.6	5.9
Men	80.0	75.5	Youth (age 15-24, %, 2017)	17.8	11.9
Women	52.1	60.1	Tertiary educational attainment 25-64 year olds (%, 2015)	9.8	35.7
Participation rate for 15-64 year olds (%, 2017)	70.0	72.1	Gross domestic expenditure on Research and Development (R&D) (% of GDP, 2013)	0.1	2.3
Men	84.8	80.2			
Women	55.1	64			

Executive Summary

Indonesia is the largest economy of Southeast Asia (the 16th largest worldwide) and has experienced sustained rates of growth over the last ten years. The government of Indonesia recognises SMEs as key drivers of economic growth and social inclusion, and has enshrined SMEs as a policy priority through a national Micro, Small and Medium Enterprise (MSME) Law and a Ministry specifically devoted to SMEs (i.e. the Ministry of Co-operatives and SMEs). SMEs also feature prominently in the main government development strategies, such as the five-year National Medium-Term Development Plan that sets out the development priorities of the executive in office.

Key findings

SMEs in Indonesia have scaled-up in recent years

There has been a significant scaling-up process in recent years in which small and medium-sized enterprises have come to account for a larger share of national employment and investment compared with micro-enterprises. Nonetheless, Indonesia's average enterprise size is still small by international standards. Labour productivity gains have also been modest across all enterprise size classes, pointing to the importance of stronger labour productivity growth in the future if Indonesia is to reach higher levels of income. Indonesian data on SMEs are affected by the large domestic informal sector, which is estimated to account for about 70% of national employment and more than 90% of total business enterprises.

The business environment presents strengths and weaknesses for SME and entrepreneurial development

Indonesia's business environment offers mixed conditions for SME and entrepreneurial activity. Macroeconomic conditions are generally healthy and include a stable political system, a prudent fiscal policy framework and steady economic growth. Indonesia has also made significant progress in the ease of doing business during the last five years. On the other hand, the national tax base is narrow, which restrains spending on public policies, and employment and education statistics point to skills gaps in the labour market. More business-friendly product and labour market regulations (e.g. on business licenses and permits and regulations on dismissal) hold the potential to foster business formalisation and enterprise productivity growth.

An SME Strategy would help strengthen the coherence of national SME policies

Many ministries play an active role in SME policy, which poses a co-ordination challenge to ensure that existing programmes are coherent and complementary and have sufficient scale. The development and implementation by the government of an SME Strategy document that outlines policy objectives, policy targets, detailed policy measures and government departments responsible for implementation would help improve the overall coherence of SME and entrepreneurship policies by helping reduce overlaps among programmes and fill policy gaps where necessary.

Most programmes for SMEs are aimed at self-employed and micro-enterprises

Indonesia has a large number of programmes for SMEs and entrepreneurs, although most of them are targeted at necessity-driven entrepreneurship, while relatively few address productivity growth in SMEs. Stronger spending on productivity-enhancing programmes – such as those aimed at the upgrading of workforce and managerial skills and strengthening of innovation in SMEs – are warranted if Indonesia is to improve its productivity performance.

The largest programme for SMEs is Kredit Usaha Rakyat (KUR) (i.e. People's Business Credit), a government-backed loan guarantee with an interest rate subsidy. Support for innovation in SMEs consists principally of grants and advisory services, whereas common fiscal incentives such as R&D tax credits are underdeveloped. Policies targeting SME internationalisation comprise both traditional measures (e.g. export finance, market and export information, and export training) and innovative approaches (e.g. the use of state-owned enterprises as trading houses for small firms); however more could be done to build stronger linkages between foreign investors and local SMEs, including through targeted tax incentives.

Subnational authorities are well empowered to enable the tailoring of national policies to the local context

Indonesia exhibits significant diversity in SME and entrepreneurship activity and in the quality of the business environment across its provinces, calling for the tailoring of national policies to the local context. The major devolution process of the early 2000s has provided local authorities with the flexibility needed to adjust national policies to the local context, although there are co-ordination challenges related to the large number of national and local government institutions involved in SME and entrepreneurship policy. Furthermore, a recent law (Law 23/2014) that assigns to each level of government policy responsibility for a respective firm size class is a potential source of complexity for the design and implementation of appropriate SME policies.

Stronger synergies could be established among existing programmes in the field of business development services

Many ministries operate programmes that provide business development services (BDS) to entrepreneurs and SMEs in Indonesia. The Ministry of Co-operatives and SMEs has recently launched the Integrated Business Services Centres for Co-operatives and SMEs to improve the standardisation and accessibility of BDS nationwide. This is a good initiative which should help reduce the current fragmentation of the BDS offer, especially if further synergies are sought with similar programmes operated by other ministries.

Key policy recommendations

- Improve data collection on SMEs by adopting and using more frequently an employment-based definition to allow better international comparison of the structure and performance of the SME sector between Indonesia and OECD countries.

- Develop and implement an SME Strategy that outlines the main SME policy objectives, targets and support measures and that defines roles and responsibilities of implementing ministries and agencies.

- Explore opportunities for integrating and merging programmes offering similar services with a view to streamlining the national SME policy offer. In the field of business development services, for example, consider merging some of the existing initiatives under the framework of the new Integrated Business Services Centres for Co-operatives and SMEs (PLUT-KUMKM Centres).

- Increase the focus on productivity-enhancing policies for SMEs through targeted measures aimed at strengthening workforce and managerial skills and innovation activity in SMEs and through business-friendly product and labour market reforms.

- Monitor the implementation of SME loan set-asides in commercial banks to ensure that they do not result in an increase of non-performing loans and/or in reduced competition in the banking sector.

- Develop stronger FDI-SME linkages through tax incentives for multinational companies that invest in the upgrading of local suppliers through training, mentoring or staff secondment.

- Consider amending Law 23/2014 regarding the responsibility for the development of specific business size classes by specific levels of government (micro-enterprises to regencies/cities, small enterprises to provinces, and medium-sized enterprises to the national government); this provision is difficult to implement and risks widening the development divide between more and less prosperous regions.

1. Overall assessment and recommendations

SME and entrepreneurship characteristics and performance

There has been a recent consolidation process in the Indonesian SME sector, but the average enterprise size is still small

Indonesia has a large number of small and medium-sized enterprises (SMEs). In 2014, according to data from the Ministry of Co-operatives and SMEs which include the agricultural sector and follow a turnover and asset-based SME definition, there were 59.3 million enterprises: 98.75% were micro-enterprises, 1.15% were small enterprises and 0.1% were medium-sized enterprises.

Data from the Ministry of Co-operatives and SMEs point to an important consolidation process in the period 2006-2014 whereby the share of micro-enterprises in private-sector employment shrunk from 91% to 87%, while small enterprises increased their employment share from 3.5% to 5.7% and medium-sized enterprises from 3% to 4%.

Despite the recent consolidation, internationally comparable data from the last Indonesian Economic Census (2016) and the OECD Structural and Demographic Business Statistics (SDBS) database, both of which follow an employment-based SME definition, show that Indonesian SMEs are still small by international comparison. Small companies employing less than 20 people accounted for 76.3% of Indonesian employment in 2016, more than any OECD country.

Indonesian data on SMEs are affected by a large informal economy: about 70% of national employment and more than 90% of total businesses enterprises are estimated to be informal. Widespread informality reduces the average size and performance of Indonesian SMEs, since informal enterprises need to operate under the radar of public authorities and are reluctant to engage in long-term investments.

Given that larger SMEs tend to have higher productivity levels, the Indonesian government should encourage the ongoing consolidation process and help domestic SMEs to further scale up, including through product and labour market regulatory reforms which can favour business formalisation and enterprise productivity growth.

Average labour productivity is low, but there are strong variations within the SME sector

According to data from the Asian Labour Productivity Organisation (APO), Indonesia's average labour productivity (GDP per worker) was slightly higher than the ASEAN average in 2016: USD 24 300 compared with USD 21 900. However, this aggregate figure hides strong variations within the Indonesian SME sector. According to data from the Ministry of Co-operatives and SMEs, GDP per worker in micro-enterprises was only 3% of GDP per worker in large enterprises, while GDP per worker in small enterprises and medium-sized enterprises was respectively 16% and 31% that of large companies. Productivity growth over the period 2006-2013 was modest across all business size classes, with average annual rates of 1.1% among micro-enterprises, 0.3% among small enterprises, and 0.6% among medium-sized enterprises (World Bank Enterprise Survey data).

Comparable data on the specific subset of industry-based small companies (1-19 people employed) show that Indonesia's labour productivity (measured as turnover per worker) in this business segment is about one-quarter of the OECD median value.

Export activity is driven by large companies

Export activity is mostly driven by the large corporate sector in Indonesia. This has become increasingly the case in recent years. Between 2006 and 2013, the share of medium-sized enterprises in total exports (excluding oil and gas) declined from 12.2% to 11.5%, the share of small enterprises from 4% to 2.8%, and the share of micro-enterprises from 1.7% to 1.4%. Survey data from the World Bank also indicate that Indonesian SMEs are less integrated into global markets, either through direct exports or as suppliers of exporters, than those of Cambodia, Malaysia and Vietnam, but more integrated than those of Myanmar, the Philippines and Thailand in the ASEAN region.

Indonesian SMEs actively invest in tangible assets, but less so in intangible assets

SMEs account for an important share of aggregate investment in Indonesia, 56.2% of the total in 2013 (data from the Ministry of Co-operatives and SMEs). The share of total investment by medium-sized enterprises, in particular, leapt from 22.4% to 30.9% between 2006 and 2013.

Conversely, Indonesian SMEs are less engaged in investments in intangible assets. According to World Bank survey data, only 2% of Indonesian firms invest in R&D, although the proportion goes up to 10% in the case of companies employing more than 100 employees. Low R&D investments are also reflected in innovation outcomes: only 5% of small enterprises (5-19 employees) and 9.7% of medium-sized enterprises (20-99 employees) have introduced a new product and/or service in Indonesia in the last three years. The large informal sector of Indonesia is likely to drag down business investment activity, both in the form of tangible and intangible assets.

Entrepreneurship culture is healthy and business ownership is widespread

Entrepreneurial attitudes are generally healthy in Indonesia. Nearly half (47.7%) of the Indonesian adult population (aged 18-64) see good opportunities to start a business in the area where they live; perceived levels of entrepreneurship capabilities to exploit such opportunities are also high (Global Entrepreneurship Monitor -GEM- data).

However, GEM data also show that risk aversion (i.e. the proportion of people perceiving good opportunities in the local market who indicate that fear of failure would prevent them from seizing such an opportunity) is relatively high in Indonesia, at 47%, compared with the OECD median value of only 37%. The rate of nascent or new entrepreneurship, captured by the GEM Total Entrepreneurial Activity (TEA rate), is also low by international standards.

On the other hand, business ownership is widespread and is a contributing factor to the average small size of Indonesian SMEs. Women represent about 37% of total self-employed people; however, only 6% of them are employers with permanent paid workers, compared with 12% of the male self-employed.

Recommendations on SME and entrepreneurship characteristics and performance

- Design a wide range of productivity-enhancing policies which encompass targeted approaches aimed at upgrading workforce skills, managerial skills and business innovation in SMEs, as well as business-friendly product and labour market regulations such as further ease of business licensing procedures and less strict but better-enforced labour market regulations.
- Encourage further consolidation in the SME sector through the development of co-operatives and business consortia, and through a network approach to SME policy in which programmes are delivered to groups of companies rather than to individual companies.
- Consider the launch of a campaign to strengthen entrepreneurial attitudes in the Indonesian adult and youth population. This could include initiatives to raise awareness about social and growth-oriented entrepreneurship and to improve the quality of entrepreneurship training, entrepreneurship education and business incubation.
- Improve data collection on SMEs by adopting and using more frequently an employment-based definition to allow better international comparison between Indonesia and OECD countries with respect to the structure and performance of the SME sector.
- Renew the partnership between the Ministry of Co-operatives and SMEs and the Central Bureau of Statistics which had allowed annual SME data collection until 2015.

The business environment for SMEs and entrepreneurship

Macroeconomic conditions are healthy

Indonesia's macroeconomic conditions are supportive of SME and entrepreneurship development and include a young and growing population, a large domestic market, abundant natural resources, a stable political system, a prudent fiscal policy framework and steady economic growth. However, the development of a strong manufacturing sector able to tap into global value chains has been hindered by Indonesia's strong dependence on imported raw materials and, more recently, by the depreciation of the Indonesian rupiah against the US dollar.

Labour market conditions could be improved

Indonesia's main employment indicators (employment rate, unemployment rate and labour market participation rate) are similar to the OECD averages, but domestic working conditions are, on average, poor. Informal employment is estimated at 70% of total employment and vulnerable employment (e.g. own account workers and unpaid family workers) at 58% of total employment, higher than in China (45%), the Philippines (37%) and Malaysia (22%).

There are also signs of skills deficits in the Indonesian labour market. Twenty-seven percent of the total labour force has only completed primary education and 17% has not attended or has not graduated from primary school. Furthermore, Indonesian employers consider 20% of new hires with vocational education and training (VET) qualifications to be of poor quality and claim they would hire more workers if they could find those with the right skills.

Indonesia has made progress in the ease of doing business, but the licensing system remains complex

The OECD Product Market Regulation index shows that Indonesia is in line with key comparator countries on measures such as the level of barriers to entrepreneurship and to trade and investment. Indonesia performs better than Brazil, China and India on barriers to entrepreneurship, while it has a higher level of state control in the economy compared to other major emerging-market economies. Indonesia has also made significant progress in the World Bank's ease of doing business indicator, gaining 48 positions (from 120th to 72nd) between 2015 and 2018 thanks to a wide range of reforms in areas such as property registration and tax compliance.

However, Indonesia's business license and permit system remains fairly complex and contributes to Indonesia's low position (144th) in the specific World Bank Doing Business indicator of "starting a business". The Indonesian government is currently developing an online single submission system to centralise licensing procedures from all levels of government in one single website. This is a positive development that will help simplify the business licensing process, although it typically takes some time to make such websites fully operational and commonly used by the intended beneficiaries.

A special tax regime has been introduced to reduce small business informality

Since 2013, Indonesia has operated a revenue-based tax regime for small businesses with annual revenues below IDR 4.8 billion, whereby small business owners are only asked to pay taxes corresponding to 0.5% of their monthly revenues. The aim of this special tax regime is to attract small informal businesses into the formal sector and to expand the national tax coverage. As of 2018, 1.5 million small enterprises had joined this regime, 1.2 million of which were individual companies.

A special micro-enterprise tax regime to reduce the size of the informal economy is common to other emerging-market economies with large informal sectors (e.g. Mexico). However, the revenue threshold for eligibility seems to be high in the case of Indonesia, which implies the risk of exempting large numbers of small companies from paying more significant taxes and of further hollowing out Indonesia's narrow tax base. The revenue threshold of this special tax regime could be lowered, while additional benefits could be offered to participants in the regime such as access to book-keeping assistance and government support programmes.

Important reforms have been introduced to strengthen SMEs' access to finance

In 2015, only 27.4% of Indonesian firms had a bank loan or a credit line and only 12.8% of business investment was financed by bank loans. The government has taken significant measures to increase access to finance for SMEs, the most important of which has been the requirement for all banks to allocate 20% of their business loans to SMEs. The 20% target seems reasonable based on the experience of OECD countries, although fully comparable statistics on small business loans are not available. Nonetheless, given the existence of other major measures to foster SME lending in Indonesia, such as the People's Business Credit Programme (*Kredit Usaha Rakyat*, KUR), the government should monitor whether these policies lead to a higher rate of non-performing loans. The Indonesian government has also encouraged access to loan finance for SMEs through other policies such as the development of credit bureaus, collateral registries and financial education.

The government is also actively supporting the development of alternative sources of finance for SMEs. It has taken regulatory measures to facilitate peer-to-peer lending for small businesses, has simplified procedures for SMEs to make initial public offerings (IPOs), and has introduced financial incentives for private equity investors. Nonetheless, the number of investment ready SMEs is still limited, which reins in the impact of these policies.

ICT adoption by SMEs is a government priority, but other aspects of the knowledge economy require further development

The Indonesian government has placed a strong emphasis on ICT development and ICT adoption at the firm level, notably by ramping up spending on broadband infrastructure and by implementing an E-commerce Roadmap that involves several ministries and government agencies.

However, other aspects of the knowledge economy require further attention. R&D expenditure, in particular, accounts for only 0.08% of GDP in Indonesia, compared with an OECD average of 2.5%. While a number of government documents acknowledge the importance of building a stronger national innovation system, frequent innovation policies such as competitive grants and R&D tax breaks are not common in Indonesia. Increased R&D activity would reinforce opportunities for innovative entrepreneurship and SME innovation and would contribute to productivity growth.

Stronger FDI inflows could become a lever for SME development

Foreign Direct Investment (FDI) is a key lever for SME development, especially in emerging-market economies. Over the last ten years, FDI inflows as a share of GDP have not been as large in Indonesia as in some other BRICS and ASEAN economies. Indonesia shows stricter FDI regulatory restrictions than both the OECD average and the ASEAN-9 average, which is the result of a relatively long list of sectors that are either closed or only partly open to foreign investors. Indonesia's negative investment list was simplified in 2016, but still remains relatively complex to navigate with six different investment categories.

Trade openness in the services sector is also important to attract FDI. The OECD Service Trade Restrictiveness Index (STRI) shows that, in all 22 sectors considered, Indonesia exceeds the average restrictiveness of the 44 countries (37 OECD countries plus 7, including the 5 BRICS) covered by the index.

Indonesia's main policies to attract FDI include tax breaks for foreign investments which have high value, are labour intensive or have high local content, as well as the recent creation of an "investment one-stop" online service that intends to reduce the time to process foreign investment applications.

Recommendations on the business environment for SMEs and entrepreneurship

- Simplify regulatory protection in the labour market with the aim to reduce the size of the informal sector and to favour the scale-up of existing businesses. Possible pilot measures could include simpler procedures and circumstances for individual dismissals, the replacement of the high severance pay with a form of government-backed unemployment insurance and quarterly payments (instead of monthly payments) of social contributions for small firms.

- Improve literacy and numeracy skills in the labour force, a precondition for on-the-job training and skills development, by increasing participation rates in secondary and tertiary education and by strengthening efficiency in public spending on education (e.g. through an improvement in teacher competencies).

- Reform the existing VET system by strengthening dialogue and collaboration between private-sector companies and schools in VET provision and by increasing the proportion of teachers who also have an industry, rather than only academic, background.

- Move forward with current plans to integrate (across levels of government) and digitalise the national business license and permit system, drawing inspiration from consolidated international good practices in this field.

- Lower the income threshold (currently set at IDR 4.8 billion) to which the special 0.5% turnover-based business tax rate currently applies to better target micro-enterprises. Consider combining this tax measure with additional support in terms of access to book-keeping assistance and to government support programmes for enterprises that join this tax regime.

- Improve tax collection by investing in the tax administration system, particularly staff, electronic services and databases; using technology to strengthen monitoring and detect non-compliance, including through the use of risk-based assessments for conducting tax audits; and building capacity at the subnational level through training.

- Monitor the implementation of SME loan set-asides in commercial banks to ensure that they do not result in a rise in non-performing loans and/or in reduced competition in the banking sector.

- Apply international good-practice principles to the work of public and private credit bureaus and consider extending collateral registries to moveable assets (beyond fixed assets) to reduce information asymmetries in credit markets and boost SME lending.

- Strengthen junior equity markets through the scale-up of existing investment readiness programmes for medium-sized firms and growth-oriented SMEs.

- Strengthen R&D tax credits to encourage more R&D spending in SMEs while paying attention to the design and implementation of this policy to ensure that it is not abused, for example carefully considering which eligible costs to include.

- Continue to support the development of broadband infrastructure, making sure that it reaches not only government offices but also private-sector premises, including SMEs.

- Simplify the current FDI negative investment list by reducing the number of investment categories and opening up more sectors to foreign direct investment.

- Open up more domestic services sectors to international trade with a view to attracting more FDI and improving Indonesia's performance in the OECD Service Trade Restrictiveness Index (STRI).
- Develop stronger FDI-SME relationships, including through tax incentives for multinational companies that invest in the upgrading of local suppliers through training, mentoring or staff secondment.

The strategic framework and delivery system for SME and entrepreneurship policy

Law 20/2008 and the National Medium-Term Development Plan set a clear framework for national SME and entrepreneurship policy

SME development is a priority of the Indonesian government that is enshrined in Law 20/2008, also known as the Micro, Small and Medium Enterprise (MSME) Law. Law 20/2008 sets to strengthen the participation of SMEs in economic growth, job creation and poverty reduction, with the aim of making Indonesia an equitable economic democracy. This law covers different policy areas relevant to SME and entrepreneurship development, including access to finance, business information, business support infrastructure and business licensing. The MSME Law also makes it clear that SME policy is not the prerogative of only one government ministry, and that it falls within the remit of both the national and subnational governments.

The national SME policy agenda is further detailed by the National Medium-Term Development Plan 2015-2019, which is the main planning document of the executive in office. The Plan includes national targets to increase the contribution of SMEs to the economy and sets five main SME development priorities: improving human resource quality; enhancing access to finance; increasing the value added of SME products and their international presence; strengthening partnerships and networks; and improving rules and regulations affecting the life of SMEs.

Policy emphasis on entrepreneurship has increased

The government's emphasis on entrepreneurship development has also recently increased. In 2017, the Ministry of Co-operatives and SMEs, in collaboration with other ministries and national stakeholders, prepared a Draft Law on National Entrepreneurship to foster social entrepreneurship, innovative entrepreneurship, entrepreneurship education and easier business licensing for micro and small enterprises. The Draft Law also refers to the future creation of an Inter-Ministerial National Entrepreneurship Task Force and to the preparation of a National Entrepreneurship Masterplan.

Several ministries are involved in SME and entrepreneurship policy

Given the central role of SMEs in national development strategies, many ministries are involved in SME policy, including sector-focused ministries such as industry, agriculture, fisheries, tourism, and communication and informatics. The Ministry of Co-operatives and SMEs has a mandate for SME policy co-ordination that is mentioned in Law 20/2008, but important co-ordinating roles are also played by the Ministry of National Development Planning-National Development Planning Agency (BAPPENAS) and the Co-ordinating Ministry for Economic Affairs. BAPPENAS, through the Medium-Term

Development Plan, sets outs five-year development priorities and targets that also affect SMEs, while the Co-ordinating Ministry for Economic Affairs prepares "SME Policy Packages" for the relevant ministries and agencies. Despite these co-ordination mechanisms, there are not always strong synergies among SME support programmes on the ground, which has led on occasion to programme duplications and to some programmes lacking sufficient scale.

Many countries have an Inter-Ministerial SME and Entrepreneurship Policy Committee to improve cross-government policy co-ordination. The Draft Law on National Entrepreneurship includes provisions for the creation of a National Entrepreneurship Task Force, which could perform this role if its mandate were to include SME development. One of the first tasks of the Task Force could be the preparation of a National SME and Entrepreneurship Strategy Document to rationalise the offer of existing support measures and clarify existing policy objectives and policy targets. This could build on the existing plan for a National Entrepreneurship Masterplan.

A policy portfolio analysis could help steer decisions about the best SME policy mix

An SME policy portfolio consists of an analysis of the distribution of government spending by main policy area (e.g. access to finance, export development, entrepreneurship training, etc.) and main target population (e.g. potential entrepreneurs, new start-ups, existing SMEs, etc.). This approach involves mapping all SME policy measures across ministries and agencies, assigning programmes to a specific policy category and main target group, and attaching budgets to each policy measure. An SME policy portfolio analysis can help identify policy gaps or duplications across ministries and agencies and determine the extent to which the policy mix corresponds to the government's overall strategic objectives and to the perceived needs of businesses.

A full policy portfolio analysis is hindered in Indonesia by two main factors. First, a large number of ministries and agencies are in charge of SME programmes. Second, there is currently no co-ordinating mechanism to detail total spending allocation by programme activity and category. Based on a simple and preliminary assessment of budget figures from existing programmes, a portfolio analysis could, for example, reveal large government spending on the KUR Programme (i.e. *Kredit Usaha Rakyat*, or People's Business Credit Programme), which favours access to finance for micro and small companies, and relatively little spending on programmes to enhance SME productivity, for example through increased R&D and innovation.

There is scope for streamlining the policy offer in certain programme areas

There are some policy areas, such as business incubators and business development services, where a large number of ministries and agencies are concurrently active. In such cases, there is scope for simplifying the current offer of programmes, including by integrating and merging similar policy initiatives operated by different ministries.

In addition, access to information on the range of programmes could be improved by creating a unified online business portal for entrepreneurs and SMEs. This could present information on available programmes by type, stage of development, delivering organisation, and location. Many Indonesian small business owners are, in fact, unaware of existing support programmes and, even when they are aware, find it difficult to use them.

Recommendations on the strategic framework and delivery system for SME and entrepreneurship policy

- Prepare an SME Strategy document that outlines the main SME policy objectives, targets and support measures and that defines roles and responsibilities of implementing ministries and agencies.
- Establish an Inter-Ministerial State Council on SME Policy to strengthen cross-government co-ordination on SME policy. The newly created National Entrepreneurship Task Force could play this role if its mandate were extended to encompass existing SMEs and not only new entrepreneurs and start-ups.
- Adopt an SME policy portfolio approach to better assess whether spending on SMEs adequately reflects government priorities and the perceived needs of SMEs.
- Explore opportunities for integrating and merging programmes offering similar services with the aim to rationalise the national SME policy offer.
- Create a national web portal and mobile phone application to collate and display business regulations and SME assistance programmes in an accessible way for small business owners and entrepreneurs.

National SME and entrepreneurship programmes

KUR is the largest SME programme in Indonesia

Kredit Usaha Rakyat (KUR, i.e. People's Business Credit) is the largest SME programme in Indonesia by budget. It is a microcredit programme which combines a loan guarantee with an interest rate subsidy that allows banks to lend to SMEs at a capped interest rate. Several institutions are involved in the implementation of the KUR Programme (Ministry of Finance, Bank Indonesia, Ministry of Co-operatives and SMEs), which also falls under the responsibility of the National Task Force for the Acceleration of Poverty Reduction.

Together with other policies (e.g. the 20% SME loan set-aside requested of commercial and state-owned banks), the KUR Programme has succeeded in increasing the credit flow to SMEs and is contributing to poverty alleviation and social inclusion through economic activity. However, there are also some concerns surrounding its high opportunity cost (i.e. some of the resources committed to this single large programme could be spent on other policy initiatives), the sustainability of the initiative (i.e. the cost has increased by ten times since the interest rate subsidy was added to the loan guarantee in 2015), the possible crowding out of unsubsidised lending, and potential misuse of programme-backed loans.

There are also smaller-scale access to credit programmes

There are also smaller-scale programmes which promote access to credit for SMEs and entrepreneurs. The Ministry of Finance has recently launched a microcredit programme for firms that are too small to qualify for the KUR Programme. The Revolving Fund Management Agency offers credit to co-operatives, SMEs and to financial intermediaries for SME lending. Although the agency has five local branch offices, loan decisions are centralised at the headquarters in Jakarta, which is likely to contribute to an over-representation of the island of Java in the distribution of loans. The Beginner Entrepreneur Programme provides loans for new entrepreneurs. This programme has experienced significant budget fluctuations over the years, but has only reached an annual average of 2 000 beneficiaries.

Equity investment in SMEs could be further encouraged

Equity investment in SMEs is still at an early stage of development in Indonesia. The Indonesia Stock Exchange (IDX) operates a Development Board which has less strict listing requirements for small companies with net tangible assets of less than IDR 100 billion. However, there have been few offerings to date on this board (only seven between 2003 and 2015), making trading on this platform very thin. IDX is in the process of launching a third board – the Acceleration Board – which will have even less strict listing requirements than the Development Board and will be mostly aimed at young start-ups.

In 2017 there were 61 licensed venture capital firms operating in Indonesia, but the size of aggregate investments by venture capital firms in the country is still modest. Out of USD 90 billion in venture capital investments across Asia in 2016, only 1.29 billion (2%) were made in Indonesia. As of 2017, Indonesia did not have a large government programme (e.g. government-sponsored venture capital funds or funds of funds) in place to develop the domestic venture capital sector, although a strong government intervention has often proven important in other countries to kick-start the domestic venture capital industry.

The government has a roadmap in place for the development of business incubators

Business incubation activity has not yet reached its full potential in Indonesia. Most incubators are small in scale (with 3-5 tenant enterprises) and do not offer a full range of services in the form of consulting, technical support, mentoring/coaching, and linkages to sources of finance for tenant enterprises. Furthermore, only 10-20% of incubated enterprises are estimated to graduate from the incubator and move on to become sustainable companies.

The government has launched the Roadmap for Incubator Development, 2014-2029, to increase the number of incubators and improve their performance. The Roadmap assigns responsibility for incubator development to 17 different ministries and agencies and sets the target of reaching 732 incubators by 2029 from 75 in 2014. These growth projections are based on the assumption that the current plan to build 100 science and technology parks unfolds as envisaged. As part of the Roadmap, operating standards for business incubators and a certification programme for managers of incubators are being developed.

SME digitalisation is a priority of the national government

Only 18% of Indonesian SMEs are currently engaged in e-commerce through the use of a website or social media, and only 9% adopt more sophisticated e-commerce strategies. The national government is enacting an E-Commerce Roadmap to boost the use of e-commerce by SMEs. Three main programmes in the E-Commerce Roadmap, all of them operated by the Ministry of Communication and Informatics, are the SME Go Online Programme, the One Million id. Domain Programme, and the 1 000 Digital Start-up Programme. These programmes complement each other: the first two help SMEs to expand their markets by building an online presence, while the third encourages the development of digital start-ups. An important challenge facing these interventions will be not only to meet the ambitious targets they have set, but also to make sure that the outcomes they achieve are sustainable after the phase-out of government support and have a real impact on business growth.

SME internationalisation policies include both traditional and innovative approaches

Indonesia encourages business internationalisation through both traditional and innovative policies. Export financing services (i.e. credit, guarantees and insurance) are managed by Indonesia Eximbank, the national export financing agency, which also delivers targeted training for new exporters. Indonesia Eximbank also operates the KURBE Programme (*Kredit Usaha Rakyat Berioritentasi Ekspor*, i.e. Export-Oriented People's Business Credit), a spin-off of the KUR Programme mostly aimed at suppliers of large exporters and large employer companies. The Ministry of Trade, by contrast, supports business internationalisation through non-financial services, such as market information, product development, export information and export training.

The Ministry of State-Owned Enterprises (SOEs) also encourages small business internationalisation through an innovative programme (i.e. Business Aggregator Programme) by which SOEs act as trading houses for small enterprises which want to export but find it difficult to deal with export regulations and documentation. This is a good initiative that helps small businesses to export by passing the export-related regulatory burden on to SOEs. One downside, however, is that this approach prevents small companies from gaining first-hand experience in the export process. One complementary government strategy could consist in supporting export-oriented consortia or co-operatives through which small enterprises can learn to cope with the export process in a collective and direct manner.

Workforce training in SMEs is still relatively sporadic

The main government institution in the field of workforce training is the Ministry of Manpower and Transmigration, which operates 22 SME Productivity Centres that deliver technical training to improve the productivity of SME workforces. Nonetheless, workforce training in SMEs remains sporadic: only about 5% of Indonesian firms offer formal training to their workers.

Many ministries deliver entrepreneurship and management training

More than 100 entrepreneurship and management training programmes are conducted annually by various ministries and government agencies in Indonesia, although the effectiveness and outcomes of these programmes is often not measured. Many of these training programmes are undertaken in collaboration with chambers of commerce and business associations. One example is the National Entrepreneurship Movement, which is operated by the Ministry of Co-operatives and SMEs and which supports 1 000 nascent entrepreneurs every year through a range of skills development activities, including peer learning from successful entrepreneurs.

The government is actively supporting entrepreneurship education in universities

Indonesia is well advanced in the field of entrepreneurship education in higher education thanks to several learning opportunities offered by the Ministry of Research, Technology and Higher Education and the Ministry of Education and Culture. The Ministry of Research, Technology and Higher Education supports Entrepreneurship Campus Centres (*Pusat Kewirausahaan Kampus*), which offer advisory services, mentoring and lectures to encourage student entrepreneurship, and the Student Entrepreneurial Programme (*Programme Mahasiswa Wirausaha*), which offers funding to students who develop a business plan for the commercialisation of an innovative product. The Ministry of Education and Culture has developed the Entrepreneurship Lecture Programme, which nurtures entrepreneurial attitudes among students, and the Business Lecture Programme, a practical course that helps students to apply their learning to solve a social problem in a local community.

Corporate social responsibility is encouraged as a tool for SME development

Support for social entrepreneurship is still limited in Indonesia, but corporate social responsibility is commonly used to encourage SME development. For example, through the Partnership Programme with Small Business (PKBL), state-owned enterprises (SOEs) are asked to reserve 4% of their net profit after tax for programmes fostering small business development and community development. This can include small business loans for equipment and working capital or grants to participate in productivity-enhancing activities (training, coaching, etc.).

There is dedicated support for women and young entrepreneurs

There are multiple government programmes for women entrepreneurship, including vocational training, technical assistance and microloans. However, most of these programmes are small in scale and primarily targeted at self-employed and micro-enterprises. Conversely, there is little support for larger and growth-oriented women-owned businesses, although one notable exception is access to public procurement. The Indonesia Procurement Modernisation Project, *inter alia*, seeks to better integrate women-owned businesses into public procurement through the hire of more female procurement officers and the organisation of workshops to educate local procurement officers on gender-sensitive procurement and to train women entrepreneurs on bidding for government contracts.

The Ministry of Youth and Sport operates two main youth entrepreneurship programmes. The Young Beginner Entrepreneur Programme (*Wirausaha Muda Pemula*) offers grants to young entrepreneurs who have run a business for less than three years to purchase new equipment, participate in training courses or improve the production process. The Youth Entrepreneurship Centres (*Sentra Kewirausahaan Pemuda*) are established locally with support from the central government to provide training, mentoring and networking opportunities for young entrepreneurs.

SMEs are recognised in public procurement policies

Access by SMEs to government contracts is promoted through a regulation that mandates government ministries and agencies to allocate small working packages of up to IDR 2.5 billion to SMEs. The government also gives preferential treatment to micro and small enterprises in terms of the percentage of the contract that can be paid in advance (30% versus 20%) and hosts an online SME vendor directory at the National Procurement Agency. These initiatives facilitate the participation of SMEs in public procurement: in 2017, 97.5% of procurement contracts were granted to micro and small enterprises, accounting for 28.3% of total public procurement value.

Recommendations on national SME and entrepreneurship programmes

- Increase spending on programmes that aim to improve SME productivity (e.g. innovation, internationalisation, managerial and workforce skills) by augmenting the overall SME policy budget or, alternatively, by transferring some of the existing resources from other more socially-driven programmes.

Financing programmes

- Consider increasing the focus of the KUR Programme on certain target groups of disadvantaged borrowers, such as first-time borrowers, enterprises in lagging regions, and sectors experiencing more constrained access to finance.
- Monitor possible misuse of the KUR Programme as well as the rate of KUR-backed non-performing loans.
- Consider decentralising the loan evaluation process in the LPDB Agency's Revolving Fund Programme, with the aim of improving capital allocation efficiency and favouring better geographical representation in the programme.
- Support the growth of the domestic venture capital industry through the establishment of a government venture capital fund and investment readiness programmes for growth-oriented SMEs.

Innovation programmes

- Reduce the number of ministries involved in the development of business incubators with the aim of simplifying the co-ordination of the National Roadmap for Incubator Development and increasing the size of existing incubators.
- Ensure that incubators are well integrated into the local entrepreneurial ecosystem by building relationships with external business support service providers, universities, research organisations and sources of equity finance.
- Open up university-based business incubators to applicants outside of the university hosting the incubator with the aim of making the selection process more competitive and improving the quality of tenant companies.
- Consider shifting the focus of the Indonesia Stock Exchange incubator from start-ups to existing high-growth firms, as the latter are typically closer to the stage of an initial public offering (IPO), which is one of the aims of the programme.
- Ensure that the location of science and technology parks is mostly driven by economic considerations, including the presence of a local base of innovative firms and knowledge-based workers.
- Support business accelerators, whose focus is on scaling up existing growth-oriented SMEs.
- Ensure that the targets of digitalisation support measures, such as the One Million id. Domain Programme, are not only met, but are also sustainable after government support comes to an end, and that they generate a real economic impact (e.g. in terms of increased revenues, profits and export at the firm level).

- Consider the development of a new intervention which fosters the adoption of digital technologies in SMEs beyond e-commerce, notably the use of hardware and software programmes supporting the professionalization of small business management.

Internationalisation programmes

- Increase budgetary resources for business internationalisation, including training measures to improve the export-related skills of SMEs and programmes such as export-oriented consortia or co-operatives that enable SMEs to gain direct exposure to export activity.
- Improve the involvement of SMEs in the KURBE Programme (i.e. the Export Oriented People's Business Credit Programme), for example by targeting not only Tier-I but also Tier-II suppliers of large exporters or SMEs which have the potential to become Tier-I suppliers.
- Strengthen existing programmes to improve the participation of Indonesian SMEs in global value chains, including by facilitating co-operation between multinationals and local SMEs.

Entrepreneurship and management training

- Initiate an evaluation of the main entrepreneurship and management training programmes with a view to assessing the outcomes (e.g. rate of business start-ups by trained participants) and identifying best-practice approaches and curricula.
- Expand the Youth Entrepreneurship Apprenticeship Programme to benefit a larger number of apprentices and SMEs. Ensure that businesses offering internships within this programme focus on the learning process of students and possibly on creating employment opportunities for them.

Entrepreneurship education

- Establish a National Commission on Entrepreneurship and Education, represented by relevant ministries and all levels of the education system, to review the entrepreneurship-related curriculum and learning outcomes at each educational level and to ensure a building-block approach (path) to the progression of entrepreneurial attitudes and competencies across the different levels of education.
- Allocate resources to the capacity building and professional development of teachers in the primary and secondary education systems to improve their competencies and abilities in the teaching of entrepreneurship content.

Social entrepreneurship and corporate social responsibility

- Establish government support for the development of social entrepreneurship and social enterprises in the form of dedicated capacity-building actions and access to finance.
- Develop a clear definition of social entrepreneurship and social enterprise in order to substantiate eligibility for government support programmes.

Programmes for specific target groups

- Consider increasing the size of the grant in the Young Beginner Entrepreneur Programme (and as a result the overall budget) to foster the creation of employer enterprises. Consider making job creation one of the requisites of the programme.
- Give stronger attention to supporting growth-oriented women-owned enterprises through appropriate programmes providing mentoring, training and access to domestic and international markets.
- Consider establishing goals or legal set-asides in terms of the proportion of procurement contracts to be awarded to women-owned businesses, whose definition and eligibility requirements should be set by the law.

Public procurement

- Strengthen SME access to public procurement through enhanced information on existing government contract opportunities and through targeted training to increase the ability of SMEs to bid for government contracts.

The local dimension of SME and entrepreneurship policy

There is strong heterogeneity in socio-economic conditions across Indonesian provinces

As many as 17 500 islands comprise the archipelago of Indonesia, about 1 000 of which are inhabited by a population of 261 million. Over half of the Indonesian population live on the island of Java, which also hosts the capital city Jakarta. There is strong heterogeneity across Indonesian provinces in terms of population density, GDP per capita and industry structure. Variations in local GDP per capita are primarily the result of geography and natural resource endowments, with the richest provinces found on the island of Java and in resource-rich places such as East Kalimantan (oil and gas), Papua (copper and gold) and Riau (palm oil), and the poorest provinces mostly located in remote southern and eastern islands of the archipelago.

Local economic conditions (e.g. the presence of natural resources and large employers, the size of the informal sector, etc.) affect business density (i.e. the number of enterprises per thousand people) at the local level. Densely populated areas such as Central Java, Bali and East Java have comparatively high business-to-population ratios, while the lowest ratios are found in the Special Region of West Papua, Papua, North and East Kalimantan.

The ease of doing business and the way of financing business also vary widely across the country

There are also notable local differences in the ease of doing business. The sub-national World Bank Doing Business Survey finds significant variations across Indonesian cities with respect to the burden of business regulations. Similarly, the Indonesia Governance Index reveals high heterogeneity in the quality of local government.

The way local businesses finance their operations also changes by province: bank loans are the main source of loans for 65% of industry-based small enterprises (1-19 people employed) in the Special Region of West Papua, but for only 7% in the province of

Banten in West Java. Loans from co-operatives are mostly used in more remote provinces such as North Maluku and East Nusa Tenggara.

An extensive devolution process has contributed to variations in the quality of the local business environment

Regional variations in the ease of doing business are, in part, the result of the extensive and rapid devolution process which the Indonesian government undertook in the early 2000s and which has led to strong differences in local business regulations and licensing regimes.

Variations in the quality of the local business environment could be further widened by Law 23/2014 on the role of local governments, which assigns responsibility for supporting firms of different sizes to different tiers of government. The national government is mandated to support co-operatives and medium-sized firms, as well as training for all firm size classes; provincial governments are responsible for developing policies for small enterprises; and cities and regencies are responsible for supporting micro-enterprises. Such neat distinctions of responsibilities are not easily enforceable and are likely to cause confusion among both policy makers and entrepreneurs. Furthermore, if fully implemented, this provision could increase regional disparities to the extent that richer provinces and cities will have more resources to support their own micro and small enterprises.

Local financial resources and institutional capacity for policy design and implementation are uneven

Although local governments have a high degree of autonomy, lack of financial resources constrains the ability of many subnational governments to finance adequate policies for SMEs and entrepreneurs, especially at the city and district levels. In addition to lacking resources, local governments may lack the capacity to analyse the local situation and develop appropriate policy responses, particularly in less developed regions. This means that the range of SME and entrepreneurship policy support is somewhat narrow in some places; for example, there are very few local programmes that encourage productivity growth at the firm level.

National SME and entrepreneurship programmes are generally well-tailored to local conditions

National programmes for SMEs and entrepreneurs are generally well-tailored to local conditions, which is also a result of the decentralised governance system of Indonesia. Several ministries use local tailoring of national SME programmes as a means to focus policy support on local priority areas. The One Village, One Product Programme, for example, provides support for the development of a product that is unique to its local area. Clear local tailoring is also evident in programmes for specific groups such as women and youth, for sectors and key products (e.g. food, furniture, garments), and for geographical areas, such as lagging and border regions.

National-local policy co-ordination mechanisms are flexible but struggle with the large number of institutions involved

National-local policy co-ordination mechanisms mostly stem from the national strategic plans (long-term, medium-term, and annual) which are prepared by BAPPENAS and reflect priorities set out at the Presidential level. The local governments at province, regency and city, and district levels each have medium-term development plans that are used to adapt national plans to local conditions. In addition, elected local governors can introduce their own policy priorities in local development plans. Despite such flexible arrangements, national-local co-ordination in SME policy is complicated by the large number of national ministries and subnational entities involved in SME and entrepreneurship policy and by uneven policy capacity at the local level.

Policy recommendations on the local dimension of SME and entrepreneurship policy

- Build capacity among local policy makers to develop local SME and entrepreneurship policies, including through information and awareness raising, training and guidance material, and mentoring and peer learning networks between stronger and weaker local governments.
- Encourage local-level reviews of the range of SME programmes in place to ensure an appropriate policy mix, which should also include programmes aimed at upgrading SME productivity through the use of new technologies, workforce training and/or managerial skills upgrading.
- Match quantity with quality targets for SME and entrepreneurship policy outcomes at the local level. This will require changing targets from focusing solely on the total numbers of SMEs and entrepreneurs created and/or sustained to a wider focus on their quality in relation to indicators such as value added, wage levels and employment.
- Consider amending Law 23/2014 where it assigns responsibility for the development of specific business size classes to specific levels of government (micro-enterprises to regencies or cities, small enterprises to provinces, and medium-sized enterprises to the national level) since this is a source of complexity and risks widening the development divide between more and less prosperous regions.
- Further streamline business regulation procedures and limit the negative impact of administrative fragmentation caused by the increase in the number of local government units.
- Develop and enhance mechanisms to improve co-ordination between government institutions at national and local levels, and among local governments, through more regular co-ordination meetings and policy dialogue on SME and entrepreneurship policies.
- Strengthen policy monitoring and evaluation systems and better align national and local-level monitoring and evaluation approaches and activities.

Business development services (BDS)

Many SMEs are still unaware of existing BDS institutions and programmes

Despite the presence of many government institutions involved in BDS provision, most SMEs are unaware of existing BDS programmes and, even when they are aware, find it difficult to obtain information on how to participate. Data from the Indonesian Central

Bureau of Statistics show that over 95% of small industry-based businesses (1-19 people employed) have never received business advisory services, and that the main reason for this is lack of awareness. These figures suggest the importance of promoting increased opportunities for access to BDS, including by consolidating the existing offer of programmes, creating a clear and visible entry point into the national BDS system, and extending the outreach of BDS nationwide.

Many national ministries are currently engaged in the provision of BDS

A number of ministries are involved in the provision of BDS in Indonesia, such as the Ministry of Trade, the Ministry of Industry, the Ministry of State-Owned Enterprises (SOEs) and the Ministry of Co-operatives and SMEs. The Ministry of Trade started the "SME Business Clinics" model in 2006 to provide free training and advisory services to SMEs, although this BDS model has now been mostly decentralised to local governments and universities. The Ministry of Industry operates a network of 40 Small and Medium Industry (SMI) Technical Services Units through approximately 500 technology extension workers who reach out to local SMEs to offer free technical assistance in areas mostly related to product development. The same ministry operates the SMI *Sentra* Programme, where *sentras* are groups of at least five industry-based SMEs which share similar raw material needs, production processes or end products, and which come together to receive technical assistance. The Ministry of SOEs has more recently launched the so-called "Creative Houses", a corporate social responsibility policy to provide SMEs with technical guidance and assistance in product development, access to finance and marketing. In addition, there are about 1 000 independent BDS providers across Indonesia, some of whom are represented by the Association of Business Development Services Indonesia (ABDSI).

The Integrated Business Services Centres have been established to improve the standardisation and accessibility of BDS nationwide

BDS provision sees the concurrent presence of different national ministries offering similar services and support activities to SMEs. In 2013, with the aim of improving the standardisation, co-ordination and accessibility of BDS nationwide, the Ministry of Co-operatives and SMEs launched the Integrated Business Services Centres for Co-operatives and SMEs (PLUT-KUMKM Centres). These centres intend to provide a more standardised level of services in areas such as management advice, assistance with legal affairs, marketing and adoption of digital technology. As of mid-2017, 51 PLUT-KUMKM Centres were active in different locations across Indonesia.

The PLUT-KUMKM Centres build on a close collaboration between the Ministry of Co-operatives and SMEs, provincial governments and, in some cases, local authorities (regencies and cities). The Ministry has issued technical guidelines on the design, organisational structure and technical responsibilities of the centres to ensure homogeneity in services delivery across the country. On the other hand, local governments are asked to provide the premises of the centres and to assume full responsibility for the management of the centres after the first three years of central government support.

There is scope for building synergies between the Integrated Business Services Centres and other institutions providing similar services

The objective of the government is to have 200 PLUT-KUMKM Centres by the end of 2019, which is a relatively moderate target given the population size and geographical expanse of Indonesia. At the same time, the large number of government institutions involved in BDS suggests that there is scope for building stronger synergies between the PLUT-KUMKM Centres and other similar government programmes, including through mergers as appropriate.

The development of rural and remote areas would also profit from mobile BDS centres, which could operate out of the PLUT-KUMKM Centres in collaboration with the Ministry of Villages, Disadvantaged Regions and Transmigration. In order to serve the needs of SMEs and entrepreneurs in more remote districts, mobile units could provide regularly scheduled visits to peripheral areas to provide initial advice and information to aspiring and existing entrepreneurs.

A national competency standard to certify BDS providers has been developed

In an attempt to ensure good quality services, the Ministry of Co-operatives and SMEs has developed, together with ABDSI, a national competency standard and curriculum for certifying BDS providers. This will be complemented by a national training programme for future business advisors and coaches, which is currently under development. An essential component for the management of the certification programme will be the establishment of a national certification body.

The development of an online diagnostic tool could help better assess the advisory and training needs of SMEs

To be able to deliver the most appropriate training for small enterprises, the Indonesian government could develop a diagnostic tool to help SMEs to assess their current strengths and weaknesses and business advisors to identify the areas in greatest need of improvement at the firm level. Adopting such a diagnostic service would allow the PLUT-KUMKM Centres to better tailor programme assistance to individual needs, including referrals to consultancy advice and technical assistance in areas not covered by the range of services of the centres. This effort should be complemented by the mapping of government support available at the national and local levels and by the publication of such information in an online portal accessible to the PLUT-KUMKM staff.

Recommendations on the national business development services (BDS) system

- Improve the take-up of BDS among SMEs by raising local awareness about the existence of such services and by ensuring that BDS are available across the whole country.
- Consolidate the offer of BDS in Indonesia through the integration, co-location and merger of some of the existing government-backed BDS programmes into the new PLUT-KUMKM Centres.
- Develop mobile business development services centres operating out of the PLUT-KUMKM centres to serve the needs of SMEs and entrepreneurs in more remote districts.
- Fully implement the national competency standard for business advisors through the development of a national training programme and the establishment of a certification body to attest the qualifications of professionals completing the training.
- Develop a diagnostic tool enabling SMEs to assess their performance and business counsellors to tailor the nature of advisory and consultancy services, based on the results of the diagnostic assessment.
- Ensure that business counsellors attached to the PLUT-KUMKM Centres are fully aware of existing government support programmes and local BDS consultants to be able to provide appropriate referral services to SME clients.
- Convene an annual conference for managers and business advisors of the PLUT-KUMKM Centres for the purpose of competency enhancement, sharing of good practices, and exchange of information and experience.
- Enhance the monitoring and evaluation system of the PLUT-KUMKM Centres by collecting and assessing data from users on their characteristics, types of services received, and level of satisfaction with the assistance received. Implement an electronic system to centralise this information for the purposes of aggregate analysis.

2. SME and entrepreneurship characteristics and performance in Indonesia

This chapter first presents information on the structure of the Indonesian SME sector and its performance in terms of productivity, export, investment and innovation. Second, it offers an overview of entrepreneurial attitudes, entrepreneurship performance and business ownership in Indonesia. The chapter shows that the average Indonesian SME is small by international standards, but that there has been a recent consolidation by which larger SMEs (e.g. medium-sized firms) have come to account for a larger share of total employment and total investment. However, Indonesian SMEs continue to be poorly integrated in global markets and do not undertake much R&D or other forms of innovation. Entrepreneurial attitudes are generally positive in Indonesian society, but risk aversion is still high and contributes, together with other factors, to low entrepreneurial activity (i.e. the act of being in the process of creating a business). On the other hand, business ownership is widespread and one of the contributing factors to the small size of Indonesian SMEs.

The structure of the Indonesian SME sector

This section adopts a two-pronged approach. First, it uses data from the Indonesian Ministry of Co-operatives and SMEs, which include the agricultural sector and are based on estimates from co-operative membership, to provide a domestic overview of trends in firm size distribution and employment distribution in the Indonesian SME sector. Second, it combines data from the OECD Structural and Demography Business Statistics (SDBS) Database and the 2016 Indonesian Economic Census to present comparable information for OECD and Indonesia on the proportion of small companies (1-19 people employed) out of the total business population and the proportion of total employment in such small companies.

Two main SME definitions are used in this chapter, one based on turnover/assets which follows the provisions of Law 20/2008 (i.e. the so-called MSME Law) and which is used by the Ministry of Co-operatives and SMEs, and one based on employment which is used by the Indonesian Central Bureau of Statistics (*Badan Pusat Statistik*, BPS) (see Box 2.1).

It should be noted that data from the Ministry of Co-operatives and SMEs and from BPS mostly cover the informal sector. The economic census, owing to the universality of its sample, includes unregistered businesses, while data from the Ministry of Co-operatives and SMEs cover agriculture (i.e. farmers are considered entrepreneurs) where informality is very common.

Estimates of the informal sector in Indonesia vary, but universally point to a large sector. Rothenberg et al. (2016), after pooling the 2010-2013 waves of the BPS Survey of Micro and Small Enterprises (*Survei Industri Mikro dan Kecil*, IMK), found that 96% of micro firms (with less than 5 people employed) and 93.2% of small firms (5-19 people employed) were informal. In previous studies, using labour force surveys, researchers had found that the informal sector employed between 61% and 70% of the total labour force (Alatas and Newhouse, 2010). The most recent OECD Economic Survey of Indonesia estimates that about 70% of national employment is informal, and that informality is above the national average among women, youth and older people (aged above 55 years), as well as in certain sectors such as agriculture, construction and transport and storage (OECD, forthcoming).

Simulations by the OECD suggest that easing labour market regulation to the OECD average level over ten years could shrink Indonesia's informal sector by about 40 percentage points, and that simplifying product market regulation from its 2013 level to the OECD average could lower informality by almost 25 percentage points (OECD, forthcoming). This underscores the importance of product and labour market regulatory reforms to reduce informality.

Box 2.1. SME definitions in Indonesia

Law 20/2008 (Ministry of Co-operatives and SMEs)

The Ministry of Co-operatives and SMEs defines SMEs based on the National Law 20/2008 (Art. 6), by which micro, small and medium-sized enterprises are defined according to the following criteria:

- Micro-enterprises:
  - Enterprises which have maximum net assets of IDR 50 million, not including the land and buildings used by the business; or
  - Enterprises which have maximum annual revenues of IDR 300 million.
- Small enterprises:
  - Enterprises which have net assets of more than IDR 50 million but less than IDR 500 million, not including the land and buildings used by the business; or
  - Enterprises which have annual revenues of more than IDR 300 million but less than IDR 2.5 billion.
- Medium-sized enterprises:
  - Enterprises which have net assets of more than IDR 500 million but less than IDR 10 billion, not including the land and buildings used by the business; or
  - Enterprises which have annual revenues of more than IDR 2.5 billion but less than IDR 50 billion.

This definition includes the agricultural sector and is, therefore, likely to result in an overestimation of the micro-enterprise segment through the inclusion of farmers.

Central Bureau of Statistics (*Badan Pusat Statistik*, BPS)

The Central Bureau of Statistics uses an employment-based definition of SMEs by which micro-enterprises are enterprises employing 1-4 people, small enterprises employ 5-19 people, medium-sized enterprises 20-99 people, and large enterprises above 100 people. This definition is used in the 2016 Indonesian Economic Census and in the BPS Survey of Micro and Small Enterprises (*Survei Industri Mikro dan Kecil*, or IMK), which were undertaken in collaboration with the Ministry of Co-operatives and SMEs until 2015.

Business distribution by size class

Based on data from the Ministry of Co-operatives and SMEs, Indonesia had nearly 59.3 million enterprises in 2014, up from 49 million in 2006, corresponding to an annual average increase of 2.4% over the period 2006-2014.[1] This upsurge is partly explained by demographic dynamics – the population in Indonesia increased by 1.3% between 2006 and 2014 – but also by the sustained growth of the Indonesian economy, which expanded at an annual rate of 5.8% over the same time period (see Table 2.1).

Table 2.1. Business establishments by firm size in Indonesia, 2006-2014

Number of units and percentage values

NUMBER OF ESTABLISHMENTS									
ENTERPRISES	2006	2007	2008	2009	2010	2011	2012	2013	2014
A. MSME	49 021 803	50 145 800	51 409 612	52 764 750	54 114 821	55 206 444	56 534 592	57 895 721	59 262 772
- Micro-enterprises	48 512 438	49 608 953	50 847 771	52 176 771	53 504 416	54 559 969	55 856 176	57 189 393	58 521 987
- Small enterprises	472 602	498 565	522 124	546 643	568 397	602 195	629 418	654 222	681 522
- Medium-sized enterprises	36 763	38 282	39 717	41 336	42 008	44 280	48 997	52 106	59 263
B. Large enterprises	4 577	4 463	4 650	4 676	5 150	4 952	4 968	5 066	4 987
TOTAL (A+B)	49 026 380	50 150 263	51 414 262	52 769 426	54 119 971	55 211 396	56 539 560	57 900 787	59 267 759
SHARE DISTRIBUTION									
ENTERPRISES	2006	2007	2008	2009	2010	2011	2012	2013	2014
A. MSME	99.99	99.99	99.99	99.99	99.99	99.99	99.99	99.99	99.99
- Micro-enterprises	98.95	98.92	98.90	98.88	98.86	98.82	98.79	98.77	98.74
- Small enterprises	0.96	0.99	1.02	1.04	1.05	1.09	1.11	1.13	1.15
- Medium-sized enterprises	0.07	0.08	0.08	0.08	0.08	0.08	0.09	0.09	0.10
B. Large enterprises	0.01	0.01	0.01	0.01	0.01	0.01	0.01	0.01	0.01
TOTAL (A+B)	100.00	100.00	100.00	100.00	100.00	100.00	100.00	100.00	100.00

Note: Data from the Ministry of Co-operatives and SMEs refer to establishments, rather than to enterprises, and include the agricultural sector which, depending on the year, accounted for 48-52% of the total number of businesses between 2006 and 2010. The SME definition of Law 20/2008 is used for this table (see Box 2.1).
Source: Ministry of Co-operatives and SMEs.

StatLink https://doi.org/10.1787/888933823888

Micro-enterprises represent the overwhelming majority of business enterprises in Indonesia, accounting for 98.75% of the total in 2014, 0.2 percentage points less than in 2006 (98.95%). Small and medium-sized enterprises accounted for 1.15% and 0.10% of the total stock of companies in 2014, respectively 0.2 and 0.3 percentage points more than in 2006. There has therefore been a consolidation process in the Indonesian SME sector over the period 2006-2014, to the extent that the proportion of micro-enterprises inched down and the proportions of small and medium-sized enterprises inched up. However, the share of large enterprises remained unchanged, pointing to the presence of barriers to further business growth.

Despite the recent consolidation, the Indonesian SME sector is still dominated by very small enterprises, as shown by Figure 2.1 which indicates the share of companies employing less than 20 people across OECD countries and Indonesia.[2] These companies make up 98.5% of the total enterprise population in Indonesia, one of the highest percentage values in comparison with OECD countries and a much higher figure than, for example, that of another emerging-market economy like Brazil (93.6%).[3]

On the whole, therefore, structural business data show that the Indonesian SME sector, despite some recent consolidation, is still dominated by very small companies. Further consolidation, through the scale-up of existing SMEs, could play an important role in driving national economic growth and poverty reduction strategies, in that a smaller number of larger SMEs are expected to offer better jobs (i.e. more productive and with better working conditions) and better access to public services than a very large number of own-account workers and micro-enterprises.

Figure 2.1. Share of small companies (1-19 people employed) in Indonesia and OECD countries, 2014

Percentage values

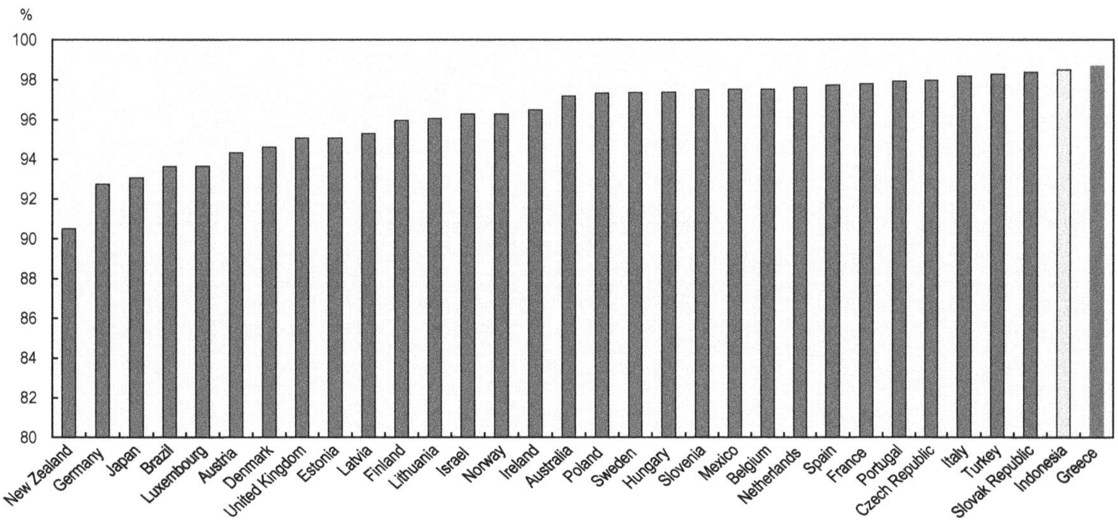

Note: Data refer to enterprises, except for Indonesia, Korea and Mexico where data refer to establishments. For countries which use establishments as the measurement unit, this may lead to an overestimation of small size classes such as the one taken into consideration in this figure. However, since when compared with the total business population most enterprises consist of only one establishment, problems in comparability are not expected to be significant. Data for Indonesia are from 2016, data for most OECD countries refer to 2014. Data from the Indonesian Economic Census exclude agriculture, forestry, fishery, government administration, defence and social security sectors, and household activities. Unregistered businesses are included.
Source: OECD (2017), *Entrepreneurship at a Glance 2017*, OECD Publishing, Paris, https://doi.org/10.1787/entrepreneur_aag-2017-en and Indonesian Economic Census 2016.

StatLink https://doi.org/10.1787/888933823603

Employment distribution by size class

Data from the Indonesian Ministry of Co-operatives and SMEs show that the private sector, including agriculture, employed nearly 127.5 million people in 2014, i.e. nearly three-quarters of the economically active population of Indonesia (170.5 million). The proportion of people employed in SMEs hovered around 97% (between 96.7% and 97.3%) over the period 2006-2014; however, this aggregate figure hides some important changes which occurred within the SME sector during this period. In particular, micro-enterprises employed 87% of the private-sector workforce in 2014, down from nearly 91% in 2006, whereas small enterprises employed 5.7% in 2014, up from 3.5% in 2006, and medium-sized enterprises employed 4% in 2014, up from 3% in 2006. On the other hand, the share of private-sector employment for large companies only changed by about half a percentage point between 2006 and 2014 (see Table 2.2). These data, therefore, corroborate the hypothesis of a recent consolidation process by which larger SMEs (small and medium-sized companies to the disadvantage of micro-enterprises) have come to account for a larger share of the economy.

Table 2.2. Employment by firm size in Indonesia, 2006-2014

Number of units and percentage values

NUMBER OF UNITS									
Establishments	2006	2007	2008	2009	2010	2011	2012	2013	2014
A. MSME	87 909 598	90 491 930	94 024 278	96 193 623	98 238 913	101 722 458	107 657 509	114 144 082	123 229 386
- Microenterprise	82 071 144	84 452 002	87 810 366	89 960 695	91 729 384	94 957 797	99 859 517	104 624 466	110 807 864
- Small enterprise	3 139 711	3 278 793	3 519 843	3 520 497	3 768 885	3 919 992	4 535 970	5 570 231	7 307 503
- Medium-sized enterprise	2 698 743	2 761 135	2 694 069	2 712 431	2 740 644	2 844 669	3 262 023	3 949 385	5 114 020
B. Large enterprise	2 441 181	2 535 411	2 756 205	2 692 374	2 753 049	2 891 224	3 150 645	3 537 162	4 194 051
TOTAL (A+B)	90 350 778	93 027 341	96 780 483	98 885 997	100 991 962	104 613 681	110 808 154	117 681 244	127 423 437
SHARE DISTRIBUTION									
Establishments	2006	2007	2008	2009	2010	2011	2012	2013*	2014**
A. MSME	97.3	97.3	97.2	97.3	97.3	97.2	97.2	97.0	96.7
- Microenterprise	90.8	90.8	90.7	91.0	90.8	90.8	90.1	88.9	87.0
- Small enterprise	3.5	3.5	3.6	3.6	3.7	3.7	4.1	4.7	5.7
- Medium-sized enterprise	3.0	3.0	2.8	2.7	2.7	2.7	2.9	3.4	4.0
B. Large enterprise	2.7	2.7	2.8	2.7	2.7	2.8	2.8	3.0	3.3
TOTAL (A+B)	100.0	100.0	100.0	100.0	100.0	100.0	100.0	100.0	100.0

Note: Data from the Ministry of Co-operatives and SME refer to establishments, rather than to enterprises, and include the agricultural sector which, depending on the year, accounted for 48-52% of the total number of businesses between 2006 and 2010. The SME definition of Law 20/2008 is used for this table.
Source: Ministry of Co-operatives and SMEs.

StatLink https://doi.org/10.1787/888933823907

Nonetheless, comparable data from the 2016 Indonesian Economic Census and the OECD SDBS database show that Indonesian SMEs are generally still much smaller in size than the OECD average. Small companies (1-19 people employed) accounted for 76.3% of Indonesian employment in 2016, more than in any OECD country (Figure 2.2). Based on data from the BPS IMK Survey, Rothenberg et al. (2016) also found that over two-thirds of such firms have no more than two people employed.

Figure 2.2. Share of total employment in small companies (1-19 people employed) across OECD countries and Indonesia, 2014 and 2016

Percentage of total employment

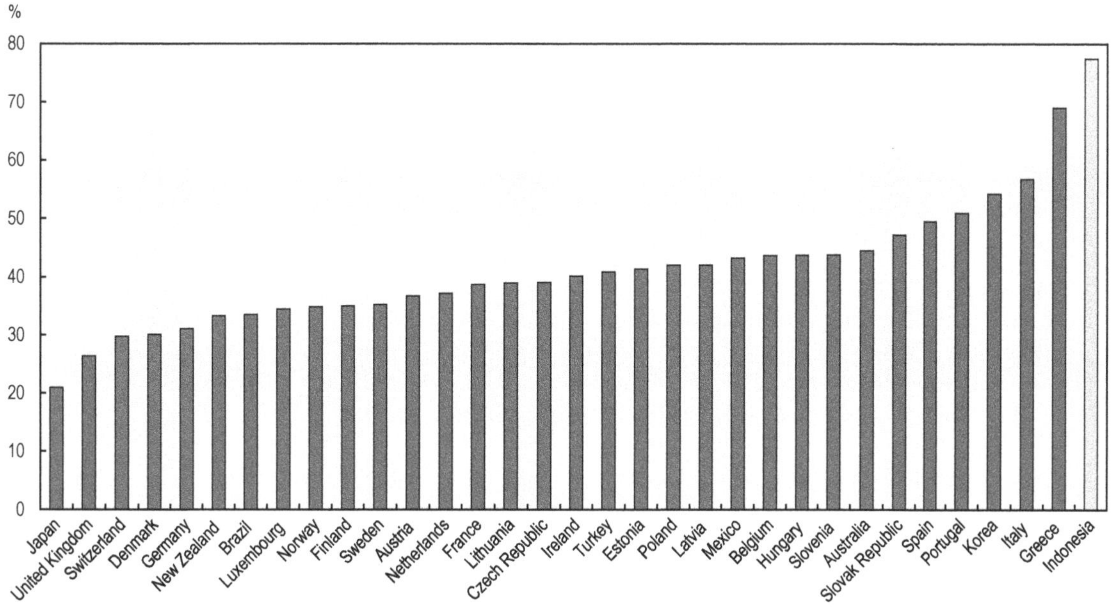

Note: Data refer to enterprises, except for Indonesia, Korea and Mexico where data refer to establishments. Data for Korea and Japan refer to employees, rather than to total people employed. For countries which use establishments as the measurement unit, this may lead to an overestimation of small enterprise size classes such as the one taken into consideration in this figure. However, since most small enterprises consist of only one establishment, problems in comparability are not expected to be significant. Data for Indonesia are from 2016, data for most OECD countries refer to 2014. Data from the Indonesian Economic Census exclude agriculture, forestry, fishery, government administration, defence and social security sectors, and household activities. Unregistered businesses are included.

Source: OECD (2017), *Entrepreneurship at a Glance 2017*, OECD Publishing, Paris, https://doi.org/10.1787/entrepreneur_aag-2017-en and Indonesian Economic Census 2016.

StatLink https://doi.org/10.1787/888933823622

The performance of Indonesian SMEs

This section follows a three-pronged approach. First, it draws on data from the Indonesian Ministry of Co-operatives and SMEs to show recent productivity trends in Indonesian SMEs (including the agricultural sector), as well as information on their export and investment activity. Second, it combines data from the OECD Structural and Demography Business Statistics (SDBS) database and the BPS IMK Survey to present comparable information for OECD countries and Indonesia on the productivity and export performance of small companies (1-19 people employed) within the manufacturing industry. Third, it uses data from the World Bank Enterprise Surveys (WBES) to offer a comparative perspective on SME performance across selected ASEAN (Association of Southeast Asian Nations) economies.

The productivity of Indonesian SMEs

Productivity is a key driver of long-term economic growth, especially as economies seek to move from a middle-income status in which labour utilisation still plays an important role, to a high-income status in which growth is mostly driven by productivity gains. Labour productivity (GDP per worker) in Indonesia was USD 24 300 in 2015, behind Singapore (USD 127 800), Malaysia (USD 55 700) and Thailand (USD 26 500), but above all other ASEAN economies and the ASEAN average (USD 21 900) (APO, 2017).[4] The government of Indonesia has set the target of increasing labour productivity by 40% by 2019, which implies a larger number of high-quality jobs in the formal economy and a structural transformation of the economy in which an increasing share of jobs is created in manufacturing and supporting services (OECD, 2016).

Data from the Indonesian Ministry of Co-operatives and SMEs, which include agriculture, provide a first estimate of recent productivity trends among Indonesian SMEs. GDP per worker (at current prices) in micro-enterprises was about USD 8 400 in 2013, only 3% of GDP per worker in large enterprises (USD 266 328), while GDP per worker in small and medium-sized enterprises was respectively 16% (USD 41 460) and 31% (USD 82 540) of that of large companies. This is in line with Rothenberg et al. (2016), who found that the median micro or small firm (up to 20 employees) had a value added per worker of less than 5% of the average value added per worker of large firms (100+ employees).

Productivity growth net of inflation (i.e. using GDP at constant prices) over the period 2006-2013 was modest across all business size classes, with average annual rates between 0.3% (small enterprises) and 1.1% (micro-enterprises) (Table 2.3), despite the fact that the Indonesian economy continued to expand rapidly over this period, with annual growth rates between 4.5% and 6.3%. This suggests that economic growth in Indonesia has mostly been driven by factors other than firm-level productivity, such as consumer spending, government spending and increased labour force utilisation.

Table 2.3. Annual growth rates in GDP per worker (constant prices) in Indonesia, 2007-2013

Percentage values

	Micro-enterprises	Small enterprises	Medium enterprises	Large enterprises
2007	2.5	3.2	4.6	2.6
2008	1.6	-1.0	9.0	-2.2
2009	1.6	3.3	3.8	7.8
2010	3.4	-0.4	4.9	4.4
2011	2.3	5.1	3.0	2.6
2012	-1.2	-2.7	-7.9	-2.2
2013	-2.5	-5.2	-12.9	-6.0
Annual average	1.1	0.3	0.6	1.0

Note: Data from the Ministry of Co-operatives and SMEs include agriculture and follow the SME definition set out in Box 2.1.
Source: OECD based on data from the Ministry of Co-operatives and SMEs.

StatLink https://doi.org/10.1787/888933823926

Comparable information on the labour productivity performance (turnover per person employed) of small companies (1-19 employees) in manufacturing can be drawn from Indonesian BPS data (IMK survey) and the OECD SDBS database. The average labour productivity of Indonesian small manufacturers was about USD 38 000 in 2015, higher than Mexico but lower than Brazil, two other large emerging-market economies (Figure 2.3).[5] This corresponded to one-quarter of the OECD median value (USD 146 000).

Figure 2.3. Labour productivity of small manufacturers (1-19 people employed) in OECD countries and Indonesia, 2014

Turnover per worker, USD PPP

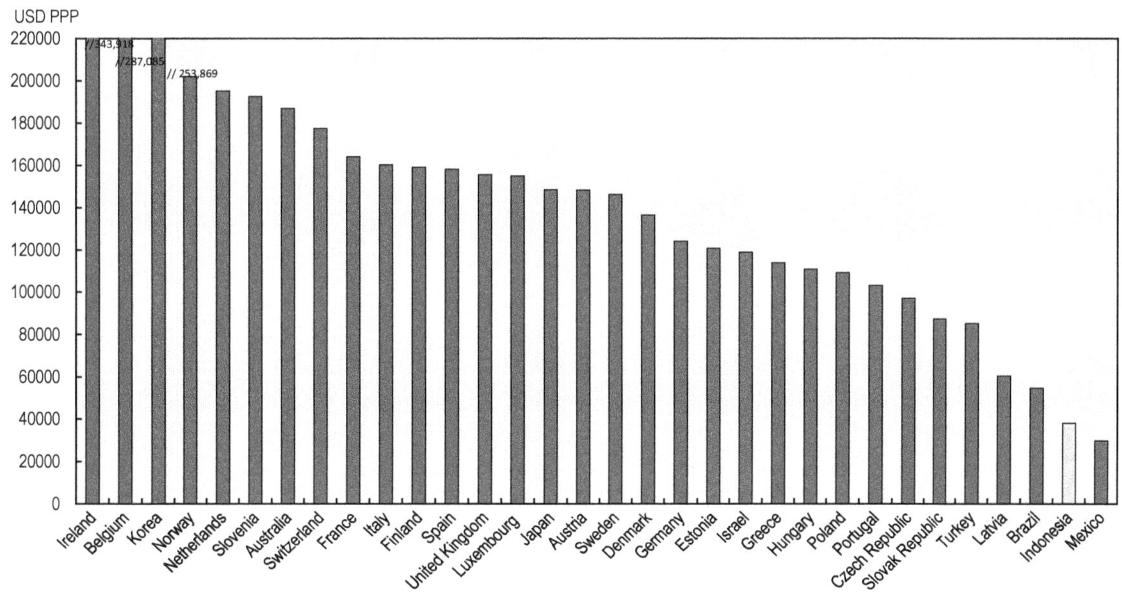

Note: Labour productivity is measured as turnover per worker (rather than as value added per worker) to enable the comparison between OECD countries and Indonesia. Data for Indonesia refer to 2015. Productivity levels in national currencies are converted to USD, using 2014 USD PPP conversion rates.
Source: OECD based on OECD Structural and Demography Business Statistics (SDBS) database, Indonesian Central Bureau of Statistics and OECD Purchasing Power Parity (PPP) statistics.

StatLink https://doi.org/10.1787/888933823641

Data from the World Bank Enterprise Survey (WBES) allow for a comparison of productivity growth trends across selected ASEAN economies. Altogether, average labour productivity growth (measured as turnover per person employed) over the three years preceding the national surveys has been modest across the whole ASEAN region. Indonesian small (5-19 employees) and large enterprises (100+ employees) experienced average negative growth over the period 2012-2015 (-1.2% and -2.4%), while medium-sized companies recorded slightly positive growth (+2%) (Figure 2.4).

To summarise, productivity levels in Indonesian SMEs are still low compared not only with OECD countries (one-quarter of the OECD median value in the case of small manufacturers), but also relative to other emerging-market economies such as Brazil. Enhancing SME productivity will be important not only to sustain economic growth, but also to reduce social inequalities by increasing the income of small business workers.

Figure 2.4. Average labour productivity growth in selected ASEAN countries by firm size, three years preceding the survey (2015 or 2016)

Turnover per person employed, Percentage values

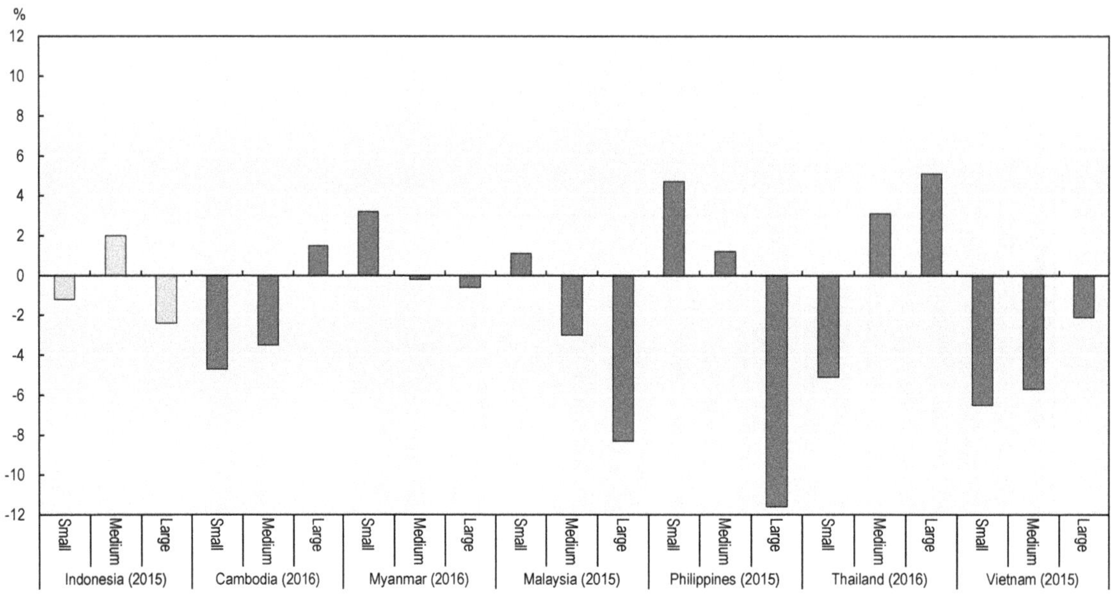

Note: Small companies are companies with 5-19 employees; medium-sized with 20-99 employees; large companies with 100+ employees. Average labour productivity growth in the WBES is measured over the three years preceding the national survey.
Source: World Bank Enterprise Survey (WBES) Database.

StatLink https://doi.org/10.1787/888933823660

The export performance of Indonesian SMEs

Exporting companies have typically already achieved levels of competitiveness which enable them to enter international markets. At the same time, exporting companies further improve their efficiency by being exposed to the competitive pressure and market knowledge of foreign markets. This self-reinforcing process makes exporting a key driver of SME performance.

Based on data from the Ministry of Co-operatives and SMEs, Indonesia's export activity (excluding the oil and gas sector) is strongly dominated by large companies. Large companies (as defined in Box 2.1) accounted for 84.3% of total exports in Indonesia, up from 82% in 2006. Conversely, the proportions of total exports by other firm size classes declined over the same period 2006-2013: from 12.2% to 11.5% for medium-sized firms; from 4% to 2.8% for small enterprises; and from 1.7% to 1.4% for micro-enterprises (Figure 2.5). Such statistics are affected by the large weight of commodities (e.g. palm oil, coal, rubber, etc.) in Indonesia's national exports, as well as by the large informal sector which undermines the contribution of SMEs to national exports (since companies need to operate in the formal economy to export).

Figure 2.5. Export volumes (excluding oil and gas) by firm size in Indonesia, 2006-2013

Percentage values

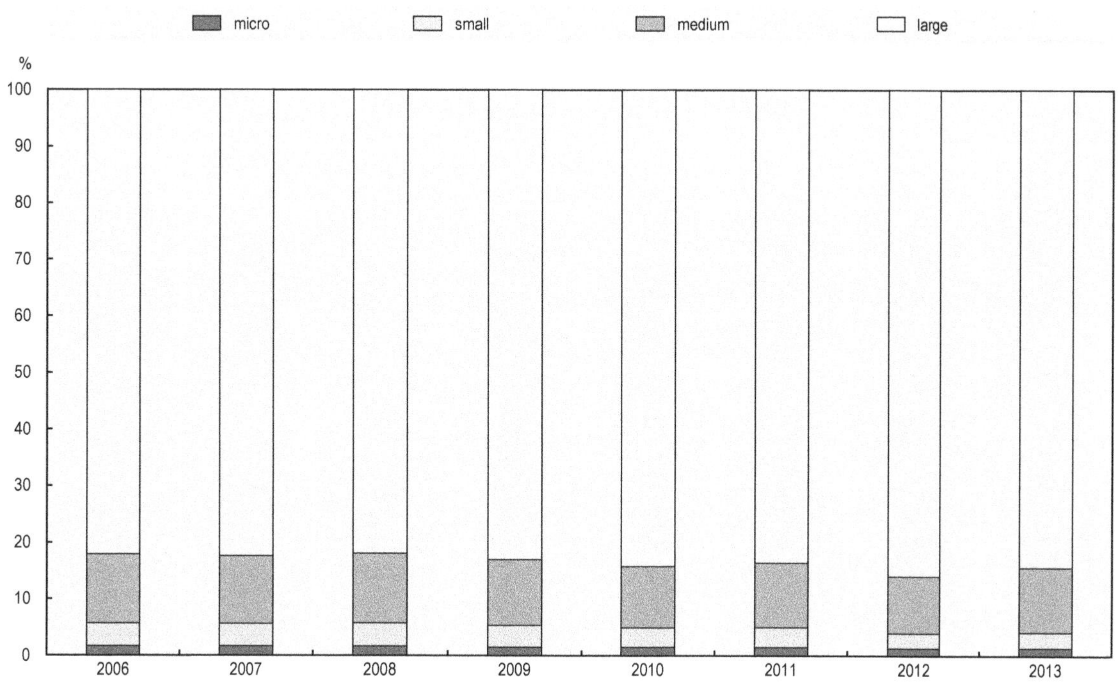

Note: The SME definition of Law 20/2008 is used in this graph.
Source: OECD based on data from the Ministry of Co-operatives and SMEs.

StatLink https://doi.org/10.1787/888933823679

By the same token, over the period 2006-2013, the average export performance (i.e. total export volume divided by the number of firms by firm size) increased by an annual rate of 6.9% for large companies, but only by 2.4% for medium-sized companies and 3% for micro-enterprises, whereas the average export performance of small enterprises declined at an annualised rate of 1.7%. The overall picture is, therefore, one in which export activity is mostly driven by the large corporate sector in Indonesia, and this feature has become even more prominent over the last seven years (2006-2013) for which data are available.[6]

Data from the World Bank Enterprise Survey (WBES) allow for a comparative analysis of export performance by firm size across selected ASEAN economies. Figure 2.6 shows the proportion of firms in each country exporting (at least 10% of total sales) either directly or indirectly (as suppliers of exporting companies). Both variables are affected by the size of the domestic economy since companies located in large countries (such as Indonesia) are under less pressure to export to be able to grow. Furthermore, the second variable (indirect exports) provides an indication of the ability of SMEs to tap into global supply chains.

Overall, as many as 10% of firms export directly (6.4%) or indirectly (3.6%) in Indonesia, which is less than in Malaysia (19.4%), Cambodia (14%) and Vietnam (12.8%), but more than in the Philippines (8.5%), Thailand (5.1%) and Myanmar (4.8%).

A break-down by firm size corroborates these aggregate figures. Indonesian small and medium-sized enterprises are less integrated into global markets than those of Cambodia, Malaysia and Vietnam (with the exception of small firms in Vietnam), but more integrated than those of the other three ASEAN economies taken into consideration (Myanmar, the Philippines and Thailand).

Figure 2.6. Percentage of firms exporting directly or indirectly (at least 10% of total sales) in selected ASEAN countries, 2015-2016

Percentage values

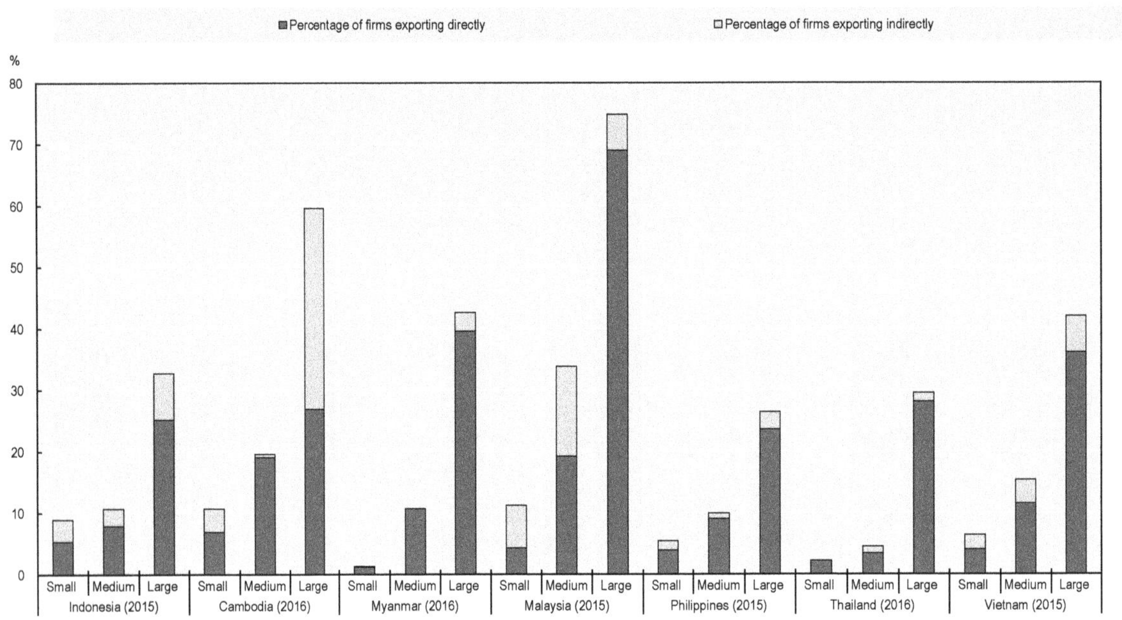

Note: Small companies are companies with 5-19 employees; medium-sized with 20-99 employees; large companies with 100+ employees. Only firms which export at least 10% of total sales are considered exporters.
Source: OECD based on World Bank Enterprise Survey database.

StatLink https://doi.org/10.1787/888933823698

On the other hand, the percentage of firms using foreign-origin inputs in the production process is lower in Indonesia than in all other ASEAN economies analysed (except Thailand) across all three business size classes, which may point to existing restrictions to imports (see chapter 3) (Figure 2.7).

Figure 2.7. Percentage of manufacturing firms using foreign-origin inputs by firm size in selected ASEAN countries, 2015-2016

Percentage values

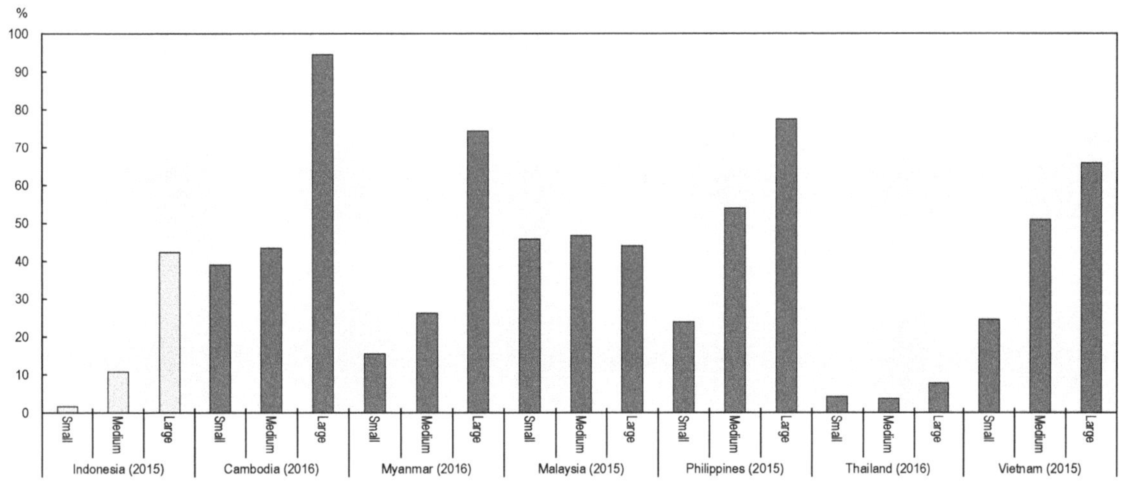

Note: Small companies are companies with 5-19 employees; medium-sized with 20-99 employees; large companies with 100+ employees. This graph only considers the manufacturing sector.
Source: OECD based on World Bank Enterprise Survey database.

StatLink https://doi.org/10.1787/888933823717

Tangible and intangible investments in Indonesian SMEs

Aggregate investment is also driven by the large corporate sector in Indonesia, albeit less than in the case of exports. Large companies accounted for 43.8% of total aggregate investments in 2013, down from 48.4% in 2006. Total investments by small and micro-enterprises also dropped over the same period, respectively from 20.7% to 18.4% and from 8.6% to 6.9%, to the advantage of medium-sized enterprises, whose shares of aggregate investments leapt from 22.4% in 2006 to 30.9% in 2013 (Figure 2.8). Average investment by firm size (i.e. total investment divided by the number of firms by firm size) has also increased considerably more for medium-sized companies (+7.8% on an annual basis) than for large (5.4%), small (1.6%) and micro-enterprises (2.6%), confirming the consolidation process by which larger SMEs (e.g. medium-sized firms) have assumed a greater role in the economy, especially in terms of aggregate investment and aggregate employment (export being an exception, as noted earlier).[7]

When compared to other ASEAN economies, the percentage of firms buying fixed assets in Indonesia is only 11.1% of the total, less than in the other benchmarked countries except for Malaysia (6.7%). On the other hand, there is not much difference in the investment propensity across different firm size classes in Indonesia, with the proportion of firms buying fixed assets ranging between 10.5% among small companies and 15.1% among large companies (Figure 2.9).

Figure 2.8. Investment volumes by firm size in Indonesia, 2006-2013

Percentage of total investment

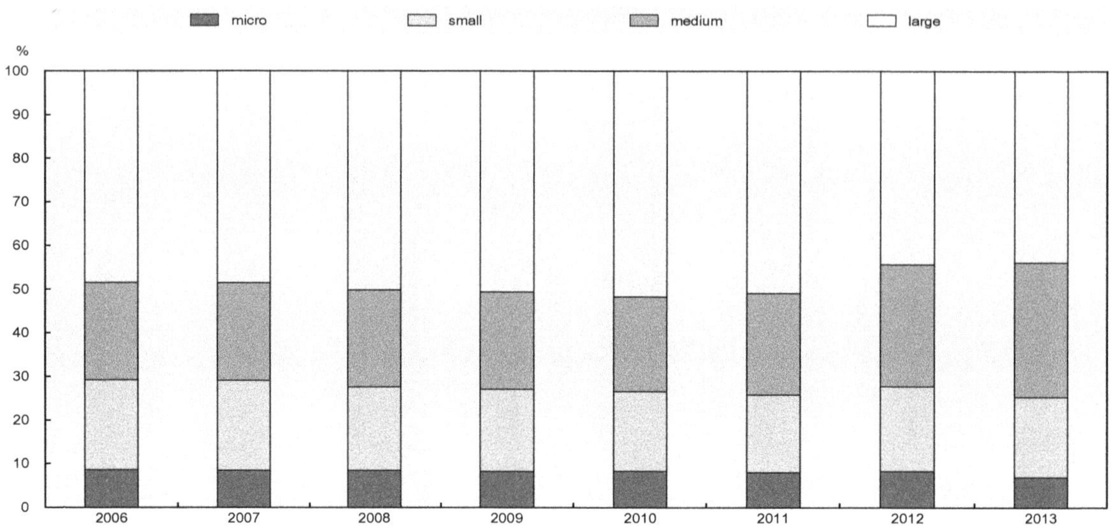

Note: Data in constant prices. The SME definition of Law 20/2008 is used in this graph.
Source: OECD based on data from the Ministry of Co-operatives and SMEs.

StatLink https://doi.org/10.1787/888933823736

Figure 2.9. Percentage of firms buying fixed assets by firm size in selected ASEAN countries, 2015-2016

Percentage values

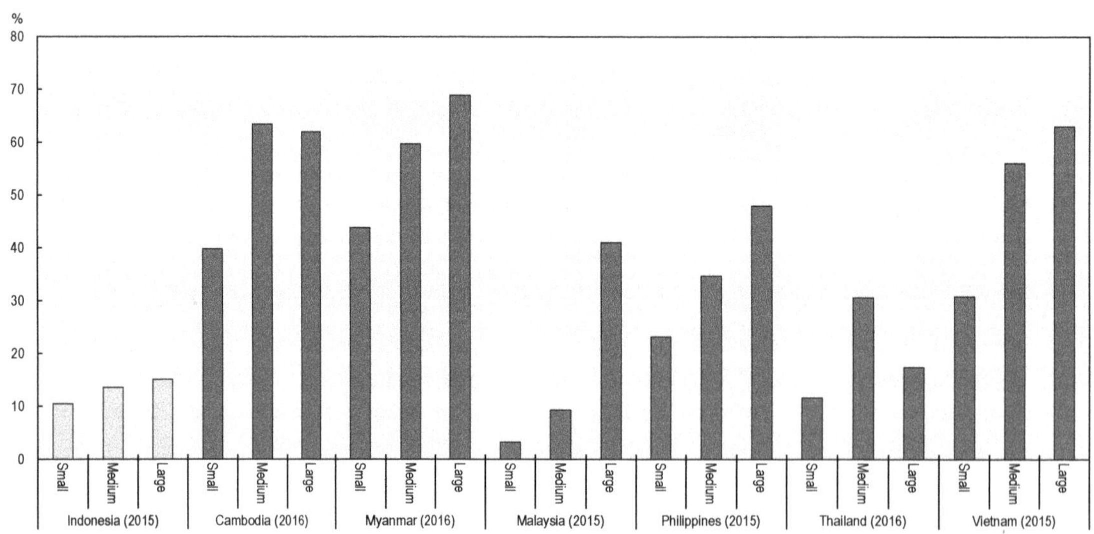

Note: Small companies are companies with 5-19 employees; medium-sized with 20-99 employees; large companies with 100+ employees.
Source: OECD based on World Bank Enterprise Survey database.

StatLink https://doi.org/10.1787/888933823755

Investments in intangible assets have also become a key driver of productivity growth (Haskel and Westlake, 2017). Based on survey data from the World Bank Enterprise Survey, the proportion of firms which invest in R&D, one of the most common forms of intangible asset and often a precondition of product development, is only about 2% in Indonesia, much less than in Vietnam (15.7%) and Malaysia (10.5%). There is, nonetheless, some heterogeneity in R&D performance in the Indonesian business sector, with only 1% of small firms (5-19 employees) but as many as 10% of large firms (100+ employees) investing in R&D (Figure 2.10).

R&D outcomes are affected by a number of structural conditions, including the weight of manufacturing (which is more R&D-driven than services or agriculture) in the economy, the average enterprise size (i.e. larger firms are more likely to engage in R&D) and the degree of informality in the economy (i.e. informal businesses are by definition reluctant to invest).

The proportion of firms which has introduced new products or services is also lower in Indonesia (6.2%) than in the other benchmarked ASEAN economies, again with the significant exception of Malaysia (3.5%), which also had a lower proportion of firms buying fixed assets. Only 5% of small enterprises (5-19 employees) and 9.7% of medium-sized enterprises (20-99 employees) have introduced a new product or service in Indonesia, which is more than in Malaysia (2% and 3.9% respectively), similar to Thailand (6.9% and 10.2% respectively), but less than in the other ASEAN economies (Figure 2.11).

Figure 2.10. Percentage of firms that spend on R&D by firm size in selected ASEAN countries, 2015-2016

Percentage values

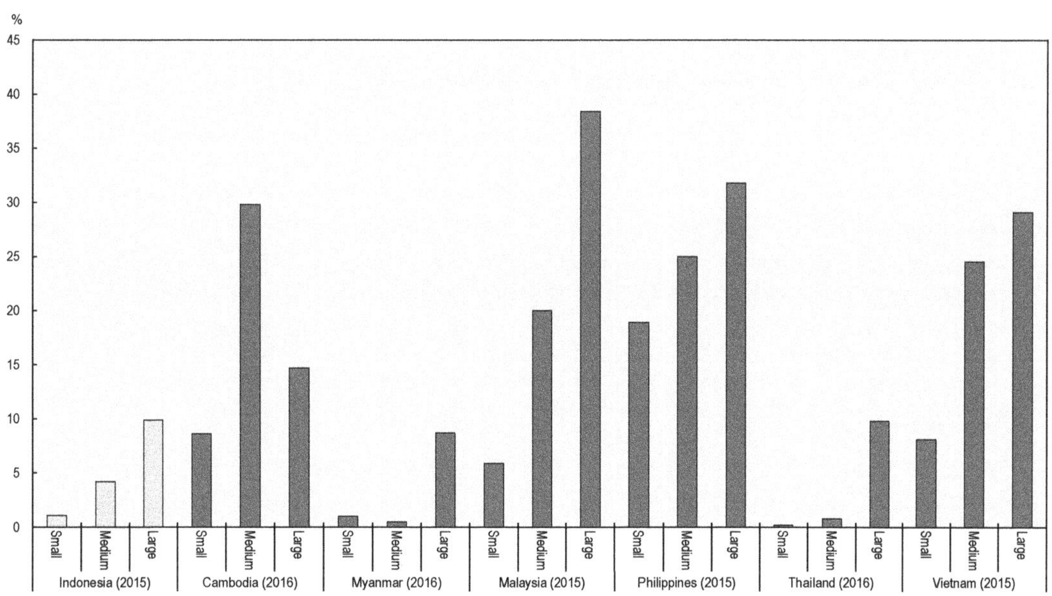

Note: Small companies are companies with 5-19 employees; medium-sized with 20-99 employees; large companies with 100+ employees.
Source: OECD based on World Bank Enterprise Survey database.

StatLink https://doi.org/10.1787/888933823774

Figure 2.11. Percentage of firms that introduced a new product or service by firm size in selected ASEAN countries, 2015-2016

Percentage values

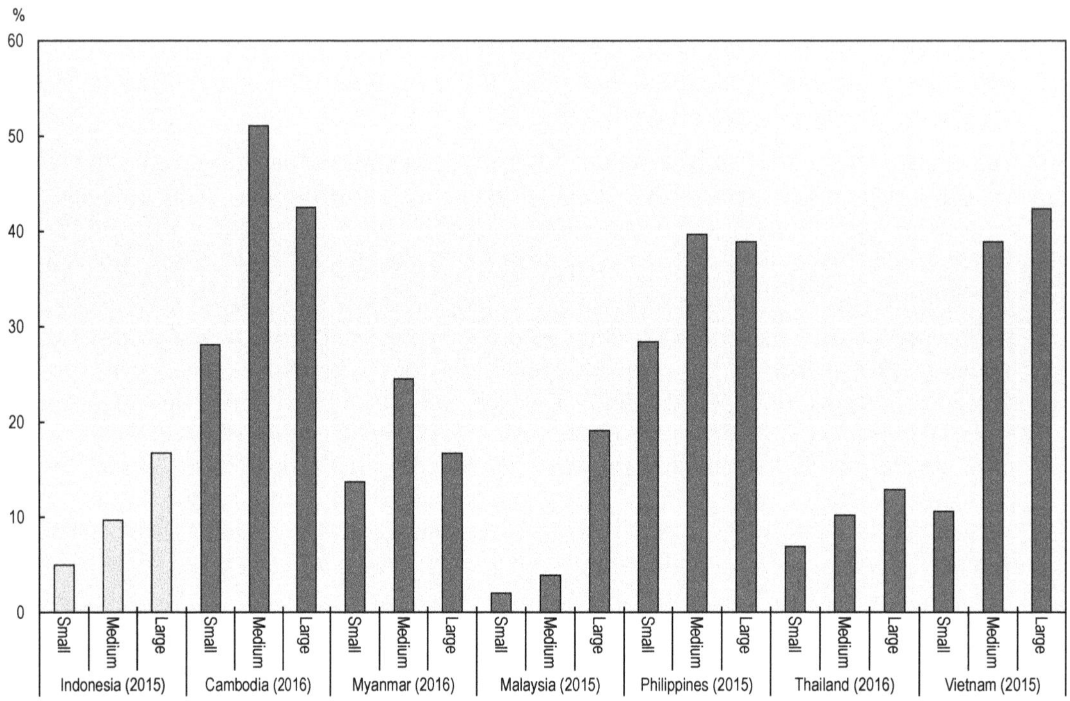

Note: Small companies are companies with 5-19 employees; medium-sized with 20-99 employees; large companies with 100+ employees.
Source: OECD based on World Bank Enterprise Survey database.

StatLink https://doi.org/10.1787/888933823793

Enhancing the innovation performance of Indonesian SMEs, both in terms of inputs (e.g. investments in R&D) and outcomes (e.g. new products), will be one of the vehicles to strengthen SME productivity and, thereby, improve the contribution of Indonesian SMEs to economic growth and social inclusion through the offer of better quality jobs.

Entrepreneurship performance in Indonesia

Entrepreneurial attitudes

Positive entrepreneurial attitudes (e.g. self-confidence and risk assessment) are important drivers of successful entrepreneurship. Data from the Global Entrepreneurship Monitor (GEM) research consortium show that nearly half (47.7%) of the Indonesian adult population (aged 18-64) see good opportunities to start a business in the area where they live, which is higher than the OECD median value (42.6%) and higher than all other BRICS economies. However, risk aversion, as measured by "fear of failure" (i.e. the proportion of people perceiving good opportunities in the local market who indicate that fear of failure would prevent them from setting up a business) is relatively high in Indonesia, at 47%, compared with the OECD median value of only 37%. Risk aversion is also higher in Indonesia than in all BRICS economies, and only second to Thailand among the ASEAN economies for which GEM data are available (Figure 2.12).

Figure 2.12. Entrepreneurial attitudes in selected ASEAN and BRICS economies, 2017

Percentage values

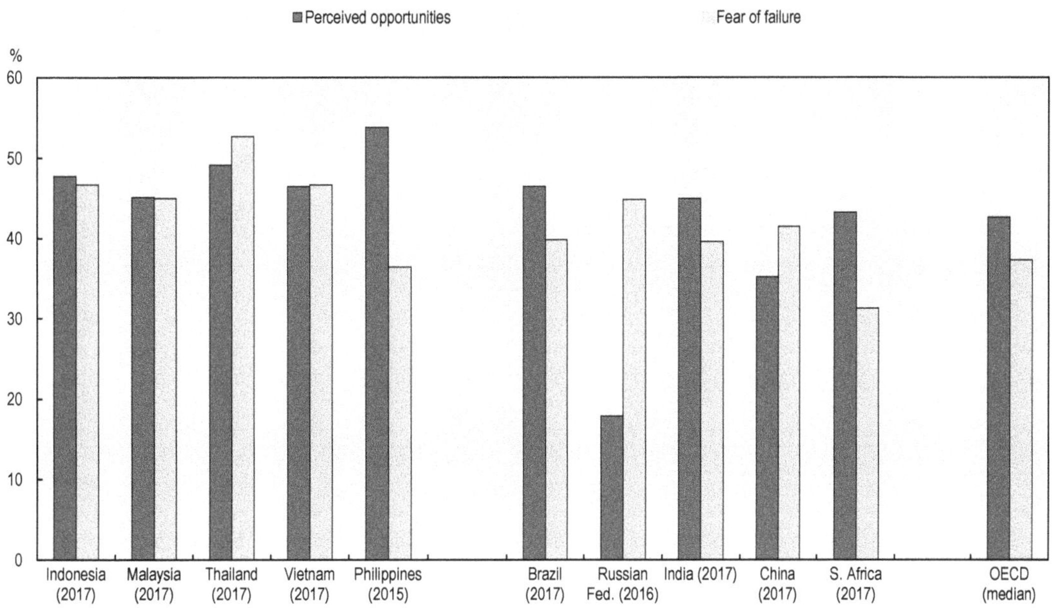

Note: Perceived opportunities: Percentage of total adult population (aged 18-64) who see good opportunities to start a business in the area where they live. Fear of failure: Percentage of total adult population (aged 18-64) with positive perceived opportunities who indicate that fear of failure would prevent them from setting up a business.
Source: OECD based on Global Entrepreneurship Monitor (GEM) database.

StatLink https://doi.org/10.1787/888933823812

Perceived entrepreneurial skills are strong in Indonesia: 57.3% of Indonesian adults believe they have the required skills and knowledge to start a business, which is higher than the OECD median value (43.8%) and all benchmarked BRICS and ASEAN economies, except for the Philippines (69%). Entrepreneurial intentions (i.e. people who intend to start a business within three years but have not yet taken any steps in this respect) are also robust in Indonesia, at 28%, which is nearly three times as high as the OECD median value (11%) and only second to the Philippines (37%) and Thailand (37%) among the benchmarked ASEAN economies (Figure 2.13).

Figure 2.13. Perceived capabilities and entrepreneurial intentions in selected ASEAN and BRICS economies, 2017

Percentage values

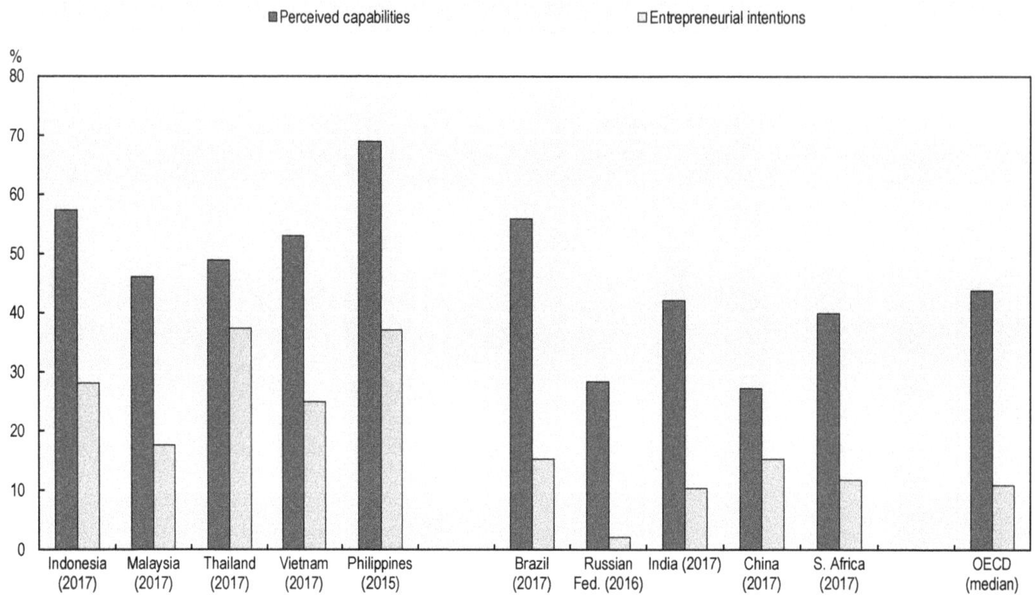

Note: Perceived capabilities: Percentage of total adult population (aged 18-64) who believe they have the required skills and knowledge to start a business. Entrepreneurial intention: Percentage of total adult population (aged 18-64) who intend to start a business within three years, excluding individuals already involved in any stage of entrepreneurial activity (i.e. those counted in the Total Entrepreneurial Activity rate, TEA rate)

Source: OECD based on Global Entrepreneurship Monitor (GEM) database.

StatLink https://doi.org/10.1787/888933823831

Despite strong perceived market opportunities, perceived entrepreneurial skills and entrepreneurial intentions, Indonesia's Total Entrepreneurial Activity (TEA) rate (i.e. the proportion of adults who are either a nascent entrepreneur or owner-manager of a new business which is less than 42 months old) is low by international comparison (7.5%), less than the OECD median figure (8.4%) and all other benchmarked ASEAN and BRICS economies (except for the Russian Federation) (Figure 2.14). There is, therefore, a significant gap between entrepreneurial attitudes and entrepreneurial activity in Indonesia, which is partly explained by some risk aversion (i.e. fear of failure) in the population but also by the wage job opportunities generated by sustained economic growth (e.g. Indonesia's employment rate rose by 4 percentage points between 2005 and 2017).

Figure 2.14. Total early-stage entrepreneurial activity (TEA) rate in selected ASEAN and BRICS economies, 2017

Percentage values

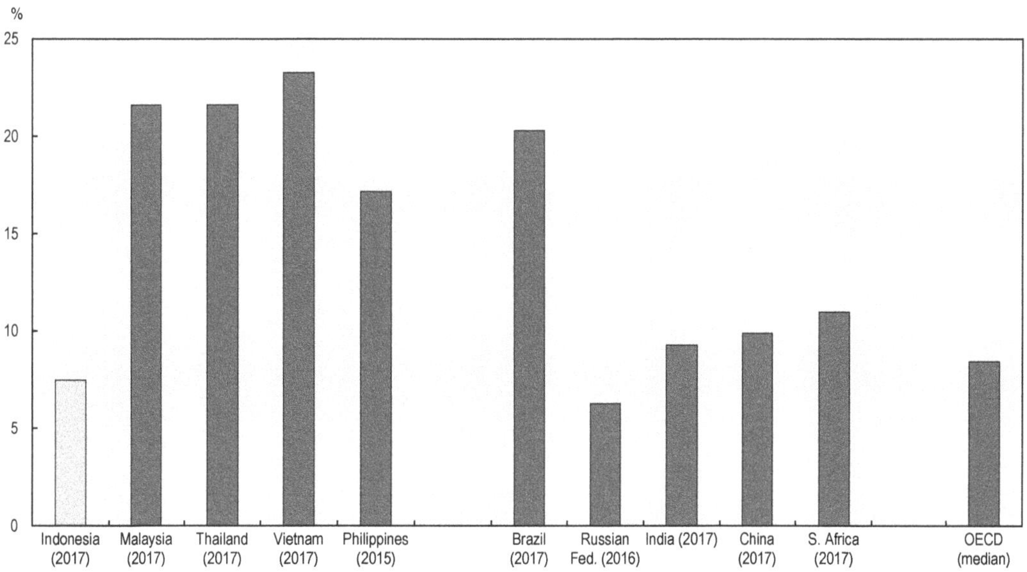

Note: The TEA rate provides estimates of the proportion of the adult population (aged 18-64) who have either been involved in a start-up for less than three months (i.e. nascent entrepreneurs), or who have been business owners for less than three-and-a-half years (i.e. new business owners).
Source: OECD based on GEM database.

StatLink https://doi.org/10.1787/888933823850

Business ownership

Based on GEM data, "established business ownership" (i.e. the proportion of adults who own and manage an existing enterprise) is relatively common in Indonesia at 10.4%, higher than the OECD median value (6.7%) and most benchmarked ASEAN and BRICS economies. By the same token, business density (i.e. the number of enterprises per 1 000 economically active people), an indicator which shows the spread of business ownership in the labour force, is particularly high in Indonesia, i.e. 174 companies for every 1 000 economically active people, compared with the OECD median value of 106 (Figure 2.15). Indonesia's Central Bureau of Statistics also calculates its own "entrepreneurship ratio" as the number of employer business owners over the total population: the ratio was 1.7% in 2017, up from 1.64% in 2014. Altogether, existing data indicate that business ownership is widespread in Indonesia and a contributing factor to the average small size of Indonesian SMEs.

There are 14.3 million self-employed women in Indonesia, corresponding to 37% of total self-employed people. About 94% of self-employed women are own-account workers, while only 6% are employers, compared with 12% of the male self-employed (BPS, 2016). Although the number of women entrepreneurs has been steadily rising, women-owned businesses are on average smaller than male-owned businesses and concentrated in sectors such as trade and services (World Bank, 2016).

Figure 2.15. Business density across OECD countries and Indonesia, 2014

Number of businesses per 1 000 economically active people (aged 15-64)

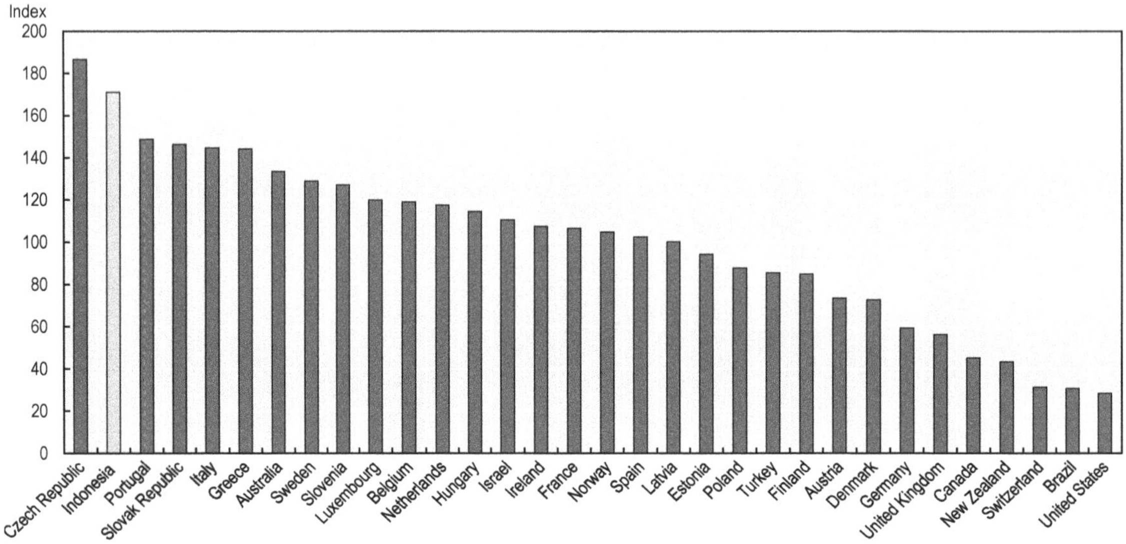

Note: Business density for OECD countries is measured based on information from the OECD Structural and Demography Business Statistics (SDBS) Database and the OECD Labour Force Database. For Indonesia business density is calculated based on data supplied by the Indonesian Ministry of Co-operatives and SMEs and the World Bank World Development Indicators (WDI). Data from the Ministry of Co-operatives and SMEs are net of firms from the agricultural sector (the percentage average, 50.5%, over the period 2006-2010 for which data are available from the Ministry) and from companies in finance and insurance to enable better comparison with OECD data. Comparative statistics on business densities should be taken with caution due to differences in the definition of what constitutes the creation of a new business across countries, resulting in a relatively wide range of values.

Source: OECD based on information from OECD SDBS database, OECD Labour Force database, World Bank World Development Indicators and Indonesian Ministry of Co-operatives and SMEs.

StatLink https://doi.org/10.1787/888933823869

A call for more and better data

The main aim of this chapter has been to highlight the key characteristics of the Indonesian SME sector. However, the chapter has also indirectly shown that data collection on SMEs could be improved in Indonesia in order to build a stronger evidence base for national policies.

At present, the Ministry of Co-operatives and SMEs and the Central Bureau of Statistics use different definitions of SMEs, the first of which is based on assets and/or turnover and the second on number of employees. Moreover, the current configuration of size classes is such that it does not allow for an in-depth comparative analysis of Indonesian SMEs with other regional groups, including ASEAN, or with OECD member countries. As seen earlier, a comparative analysis between Indonesian SMEs and SMEs in OECD countries has only been possible for the group of companies employing less than 20 people and, in some cases, only for the manufacturing sector. Collecting more granular information on SMEs across a larger number of employment size bands, and ensuring that these new size bands allow comparison with commonly used firm size bands at international level (e.g. 1-9; 10-19; 20-49; 50-99; 100-249; 250-499; and 500+ employees) would help enrich the analysis on the Indonesian business structure and provide stronger evidence for the decisions of policy makers.

In this respect, the collaboration between the Ministry of Co-operatives and SMEs and the Central Bureau of Statistics, which had allowed some regular SME data collection until 2015, should be renewed and revamped, collecting information not only based on the SME definition of Law 20/2008, but also on the aforementioned employment size classes. Key areas of analysis covered in the partnership could include business distribution by firm size as well as distribution of employment, investment and export by firm size. In addition, ad-hoc surveys could be developed to measure innovation activity in SMEs – similar to the Community Innovation Survey taking place in EU countries every three years – and to estimate size and trends of the informal sector.

Conclusions and policy recommendations

Indonesian structural business statistics reveal that the average domestic enterprise is small by international standards, but also that there has recently been a consolidation process by which larger SMEs have come to account for a larger share of national employment and investment. The large informal sector contributes to the average small size of Indonesian SMEs; estimates point out that it accounts for about 70% of national employment and more than 90% of total business enterprises.

Labour productivity gains have been modest across all business size classes, suggesting that economic growth in Indonesia has thus far been mostly propelled by other factors (e.g. increased labour utilisation and consumer spending) and making the case for productivity growth to become a more important objective of future SME policies. This shift will be especially important as the country approaches a stage of development where gains in efficiency, e.g. through increased industrialisation, will matter more than before.

Productivity-enhancing policies will span from encouraging the further scale-up of existing SMEs through targeted measures (e.g. aimed at upgrading workforce and managerial skills), through nurturing a business environment which favours experimentation and business entry-exit dynamics (e.g. via business-friendly product and labour market regulations), to designing national and local policies (e.g. cluster policies) which encourage economies of agglomeration and economies of specialisation. Enhancing SME productivity will not only encourage growth but will also reduce income disparities by improving the quality of jobs in SMEs. Less burdensome product and labour market regulations will also help reduce the size of the informal sector.

Business ownership is widespread in Indonesia and is a contributing factor to the small average size of Indonesian SMEs. However, nascent entrepreneurial activity, as measured by the Total Entrepreneurial Activity (TEA) rate, is not very high, which is also probably linked to growing job opportunities in the labour market.

Finally, there is a need to collect more and better (i.e. more granular and more internationally comparable) data on SMEs in Indonesia, including through stronger collaboration between the Central Bureau of Statistics and relevant ministries. This would allow the government to achieve a better understanding of recent trends in business dynamics and SME performance and would ultimately support better informed public policies.

Based on the analysis in this chapter, the following recommendations are put forward to improve SME and entrepreneurship performance in Indonesia.

Recommendations on SME and entrepreneurship characteristics and performance

- Design a wide range of productivity-enhancing policies which encompass targeted approaches aimed at upgrading workforce skills, managerial skills and business innovation in SMEs, as well as business-friendly product and labour market regulations such as further ease of business licensing procedures and less strict but better-enforced labour market regulations.
- Encourage further consolidation in the SME sector through the development of co-operatives and business consortia, and through a network approach to SME policy in which programmes are delivered to groups of companies rather than to individual companies.
- Consider the launch of a campaign to strengthen entrepreneurial attitudes in the Indonesian adult and youth population. This could include initiatives to raise awareness about social and growth-oriented entrepreneurship and to improve the quality of entrepreneurship training, entrepreneurship education and business incubation (see also chapter 5).
- Improve data collection on SMEs by adopting and using more frequently an employment-based definition to allow better international comparison between Indonesia and OECD countries with respect to the structure and performance of the SME sector.
- Renew the partnership between the Ministry of Co-operatives and SMEs and the Central Bureau of Statistics which had allowed annual SME data collection until 2015.

Notes

[1] The large number of companies (59.3 million) in a population of 261 million is primarily due to the inclusion of agriculture, which accounts for about 50% of the total number of companies estimated by the Ministry of Co-operatives and SMEs.

[2] Comparable information for Indonesia and the OECD is achieved through the use of data from the 2016 Economic Census of Indonesia and the OECD SDBS database. As noted earlier, the 2016 Indonesian Economic Census follows an employment-based classification of SMEs by which: micro-enterprises, 1-4 people employed; small enterprises, 5-19 people employed; medium-sized enterprises, 20-99 people employed; and large enterprises, 100+ people employed. The OECD SDBS database also collects information on firm size by employment, based on the following classes: 1-9 people employed; 10-19 people employed; 20-49 people employed; 50-249 people employed; and 250+ people employed. A common and comparable (small) firm size class of 1-19 people employed can, therefore, be used for both Indonesia and OECD countries.

[3] Due to the inclusion of agriculture, the SME definition used by the Ministry of Co-operatives and SMEs leads to an overestimation of the size of the SME sector compared with the definition of BPS. For example, micro and small enterprises are 99.9% of the total in the first case and 98.3% of the total in the second case. This can be better observed in employment terms. In the first case, micro and small enterprises account for 92.7% of total employment in the business economy, in the second case the proportion is 76.3%.

[4] The Asian Productivity Organization (APO) measures, in this case, labour productivity as "per-worker GDP", using GDP at constant basic prices per worker, based on 2011 USD purchasing power parities.

[5] The relatively large difference in labour productivity estimates for Indonesia in the case of APO calculations (USD 24 300) and calculations in this report (USD 38 000) can be attributed to different measurement methods. APO's labour productivity estimate is based on "GDP per worker for the whole economy", where the measurement of GDP only includes the value of final goods produced by a country within a certain period of time, thus excluding intermediate inputs to avoid double counting. The labour productivity estimate in this report is based on "turnover per worker in manufacturing", with the measurement of turnover which does not exclude intermediate inputs and with manufacturing which has productivity levels above the rest-of-the economy average.

[6] Average export performance by firm size can be affected by changes in the value of exports as much as by changes in the number of firms within the firm size band, which will also depend on business dynamics, including movements of companies which scale up and move to the next firm size band or which scale down and move to the previous firm size band.

[7] Average investment by firm size follows the same logic of average export by firm size, this indicator also being affected by business dynamics within the SME sector, i.e. companies which grow and move up to the next firm size band and companies which shrink and move down to the previous firm size band.

References

Alatas V. and D. Newhouse (2010), *Indonesia Jobs Report: Toward Better Jobs and Security for All*, World Bank, Washington, DC.

Asian Productivity Organization (APO) (2017), *APO Productivity Databook* 2017, Tokyo. http://www.apo-tokyo.org/publications/wp-content/uploads/sites/5/APO-Productivity-Databook_2017.pdf

Badan Pusat Statistik (Central Bureau of Statistics) (2016), *Labor Force Situation in Indonesia, August 2016*, Jakarta. https://www.bps.go.id/website/pdf_publikasi/Keadaan-Angkatan-Kerja-di-Indonesia-Agustus-2016--.pdf

Haskel J. and S. Westlake (2017), *Capitalism without Capital: The Rise of the Intangible Economy*, Princeton University Press, Princeton, NJ.

OECD (forthcoming), *OECD Economic Surveys: Indonesia 2018*, OECD Publishing, Paris.

OECD (2017), *Entrepreneurship at a Glance 2017*, OECD Publishing, Paris, https://doi.org/10.1787/entrepreneur_aag-2017-en

OECD (2016), *OECD Economic Surveys: Indonesia 2016*, OECD Publishing, Paris, https://doi.org/10.1787/eco_surveys-idn-2016-en.

Rothenberg A., A. Gaduh, N. Burger, C. Chazali, I. Tjandraningsihc, R. Radikun, C. Sutera and S. Weilant (2016), "Rethinking Indonesia's Informal Sector", *World Development*, Vol. 80, 96-113. https://doi.org/10.1016/j.worlddev.2015.11.005

World Bank (2016), *Women Entrepreneurs in Indonesia: A Pathway to Increasing Shared Prosperity*, World Bank Indonesia Office, Jakarta.

3. The business environment for SMEs and entrepreneurship in Indonesia

This chapter assesses the business environment for SMEs and entrepreneurship in Indonesia and, in particular, macroeconomic conditions, labour market regulations, the level of skills in the labour force, product market regulations, taxation affecting small business development, access to finance conditions, the innovation system and the ability of Indonesia to attract foreign investments. Indonesia's macroeconomic conditions are healthy and supportive of business growth, small business taxation is light, and access to finance for SMEs has been enhanced by a series of regulatory reforms, including the requirement on state-owned and commercial banks to devote at least 20% of their business loans to SMEs. On the downside, there are signs of skills shortages in the labour market, the business license and permit system is still fairly complex despite recent improvements, and the national innovation system should be further developed. Stronger SME development policies, however, are likely to require an enlargement of the national tax base by bringing more companies into the formal sector and by improving efficiency in tax administration.

Macroeconomic conditions

Indonesian macroeconomic conditions are generally healthy and supportive of business growth. They include a young and growing population, a large domestic market, abundant natural resources, a stable political system, and a prudent fiscal policy framework. National gross domestic product (GDP) has grown steadily over the past decade and has not been affected too negatively by the 2008-2009 global recession, with Indonesia's GDP growth rate having been higher than both the OECD average and the average of dynamic Asian economies since 2011 (Figure 3.1). Indonesia's GDP in current prices totalled IDR 13 589 trillion (about USD 1 016 billion) in 2017, making Indonesia by far the largest economy of Southeast Asia.

Figure 3.1. Annual GDP growth rates in Indonesia, OECD and dynamic Asian economies, 2007-2018

Year-on-year growth rates

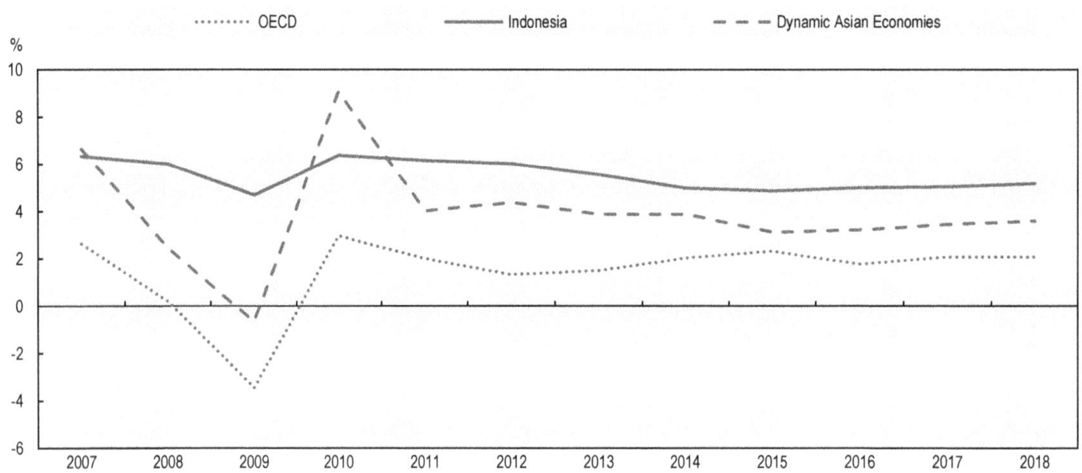

Notes: Gross domestic product in US dollars and constant exchange rates. Dynamic Asian Economies include Chinese Taipei, Hong Kong (China), Malaysia, the Philippines, Singapore, Thailand and Viet Nam.
Source: OECD Economic Outlook Database.

StatLink https://doi.org/10.1787/888933823945

The drop in commodity prices in 2011 and then, more severely, from mid-2014 onwards has had a serious impact on Indonesia's exports, since commodities (e.g. palm oil, coal, natural gas, crude oil, rubber and copper) account for about half of national export volumes. This has had an impact on the current account balance which has been in a deficit position since 2012 (Figure 3.2). Furthermore, the development of a strong national manufacturing sector has partly been hindered by Indonesia's strong dependence on imported raw material and, more recently, by the depreciation of the Indonesian rupiah against the US dollar.

Figure 3.2. Indonesia's current account balance, 2007-2017

Percentage of GDP

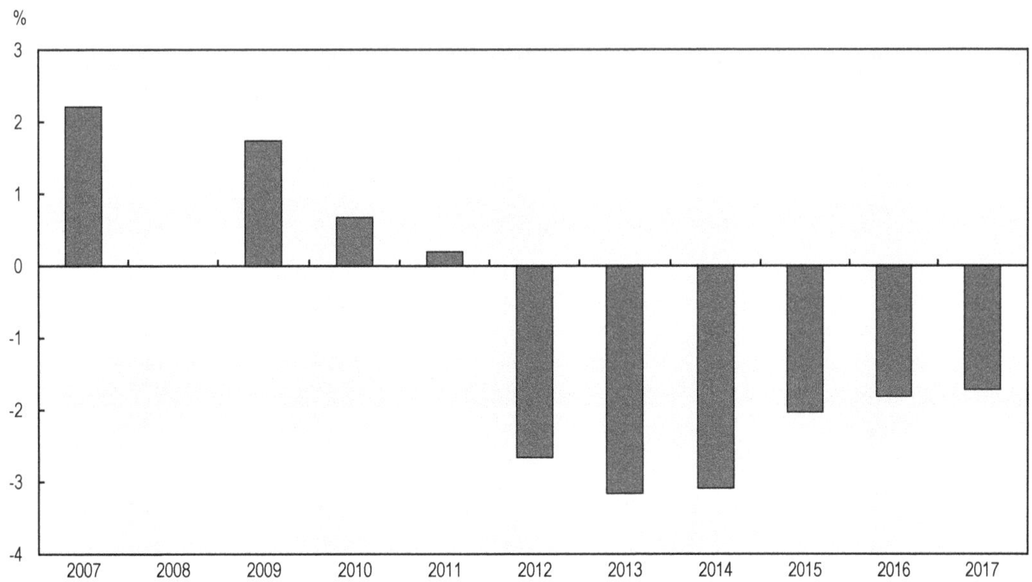

Source: OECD Economic Outlook Database.

StatLink https://doi.org/10.1787/888933823964

Indonesia's government budget position is solid, with low public debt (29% of GDP in 2017) and a budget deficit which is below the 3% limit set by national law: 2.5% in 2017 and 2.1% in 2018. The budget deficit is projected to drop further to 1.8% in 2019, with an increase in tax revenues driving the consolidation (OECD, forthcoming). Indonesia's government spending is moderate by international standards, at 21.6% of GDP, compared with the OECD average of 40.6%. The central government collects 89% of total tax revenues, but only accounts for 47% of total government expenditures, which is due to large cash transfers from the central government to subnational governments as a consequence of the extensive devolution process started in the early 2000s (OECD, 2016a) (see also chapter 6).

The Indonesian economy is still characterised by a low share of services in the economy, i.e. 45.4% of national value added, with industry (including construction) and the primary sector (including mining) accounting respectively for 33.1% and 21.5%. The services sector has grown faster than industry and the primary sector, at an annual average rate of 6.8%, but its weight in the economy is still much lower than in other middle-income economies, where it averages 60% of GDP (World Bank, 2017a). Policies to support the services sector, such as trade liberalisation of services, are likely to benefit the whole economy through the close linkages of the services sector with other industries.

The labour market

In 2017, Indonesia's labour market participation rate (70%) and employment rate (66%) were slightly lower than the respective OECD averages (72% and 68%), while the unemployment rate (5.6%) was similar to the OECD average (5.9%). However, youth unemployment is still high and women's labour market participation continues to be low. In 2017, Indonesia's youth unemployment rate was 17.8%, while women's labour market participation rate was nearly 30 percentage points below that of men (55.1% vs. 84.8%). Furthermore, about 70% of national employment is estimated to be informal (OECD, forthcoming; Rothenberg et al., 2016), and vulnerable employment (e.g. own account workers and unpaid family workers) is estimated at 58% of total employment, higher than China (45%), the Philippines (37%) and Malaysia (22%) (ILO, 2016).

Some rigidities in labour market legislation help to explain the large size of the informal economy. According to the OECD Employment Protection Legislation (EPL) dataset, Indonesia has the most restrictive legislation related to the protection of permanent workers against individual dismissals, including high severance pay, whereas regulations on temporary labour contracts are more relaxed, with Indonesia ranking 19th in this specific indicator (Figure 3.3).

Figure 3.3. Employment protection legislation in Indonesia, OECD, and selected emerging-market economies, 2013 or latest available year

Index from 0 (least restrictive) to 6 (most restrictive)

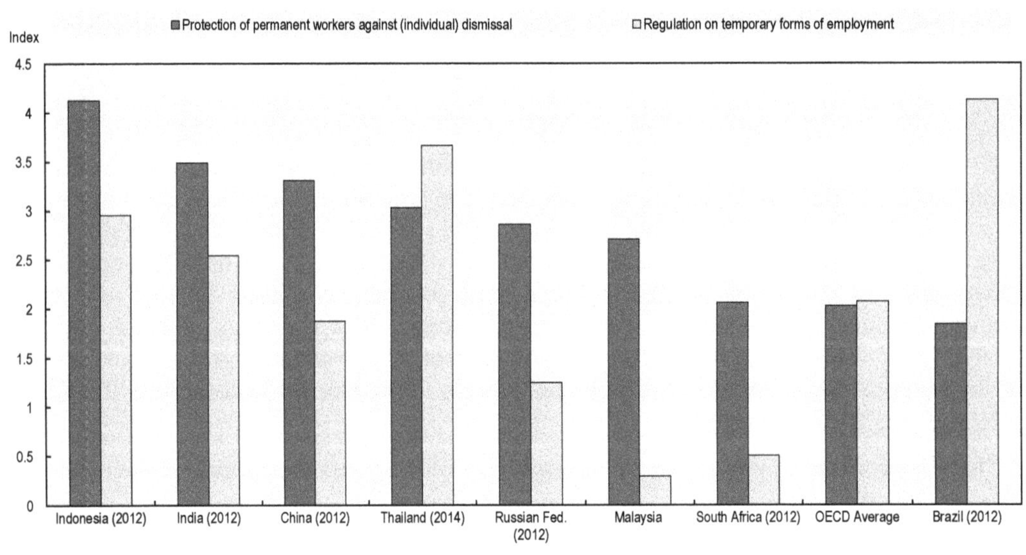

Note: The OECD indicators on Employment Protection Legislation measure the procedures and costs involved in dismissing individuals or groups of workers and the procedures involved in hiring workers on fixed-term or temporary work agency contracts. Data for Brazil, China, Indonesia, India, the Russian Federation and South Africa refer to 2012; data for Malaysia to 2013; data for Thailand to 2014.
Source: OECD Employment Protection Legislation Database.

StatLink https://doi.org/10.1787/888933823983

Indonesia's statutory minimum wage is also high in international comparison, at around the full-time national median wage (OECD, forthcoming). A high minimum wage mostly penalises vulnerable workers (e.g. low-skilled, unemployed, workers from socially disadvantaged groups), especially when a large informal sector provides an easy and cheaper alternative to employers.

Labour market reforms can play an important role in reducing the size of the informal sector and fostering the scale-up of existing SMEs. Pilot policy measures could include simpler procedures and circumstances for individual dismissals, the replacement of high severance pay with a form of government-backed unemployment insurance and quarterly payments (instead of monthly payments) of social contributions for small firms (OECD, forthcoming).

Human resources

Indonesia has achieved nearly universal literacy – 94% of the population was literate in 2014 – and its enrolment rates in secondary school for 15-19 year-olds (79% for men and 78% for women) are not too far from the OECD average (82.7% for men and 84.6% for women). However, Indonesia's enrolment rates drop considerably in the following age group (20-29 years old), where only 9% of both men and women are enrolled in education, compared with OECD averages of 26.5% for men and 29.8% for women (OECD, 2017a). This suggests that participation in tertiary education is still limited.

The composition of the labour force reflects education statistics. Those who did not attend school (4 million), did not graduate from primary school (16 million) or only completed primary school (32 million) account for 43.5% of the total labour force; those who graduated from junior high school (21 million), senior high school (21 million) and vocational high school (12 million) account for 45.2%; and those who obtained a diploma (3 million) or a university degree (10 million) make up the remaining 11.3% (Figure 3.4).

Data from the OECD Programme for the International Assessment of Adult Competencies (PIAAC), which conducts surveys of adult skills in OECD and non-OECD countries, also point to skills deficits in the Indonesian adult population (aged 16-64): almost 70% of the surveyed population did not reach proficiency Level 2 out of 5 in literacy and 60% did not reach Level 2 in numeracy.

People with higher levels of education show unemployment rates above the national average. This suggests limited returns from investment in education, which might be linked to an underperformance of the national education system (OECD/ADB, 2015) and to low-skilled workers being more willing to work in the informal sector.

OECD PIAAC data also show that as many as 14.5% of workers are considered over-skilled in their current job in Indonesia, against an OECD average of 10.8%, while more than half of Indonesian workers (54.6%, compared with an OECD average of 39.6%) work in industries unrelated to their field of study. This has important wage implications: wages for workers working in industries unrelated to their educational qualification are 19% lower than those of equally-skilled workers working in sectors related to their field of education (OECD, 2016b).

Figure 3.4. Indonesian workforce by educational attainment, 2016

Total number and Percentage of the total

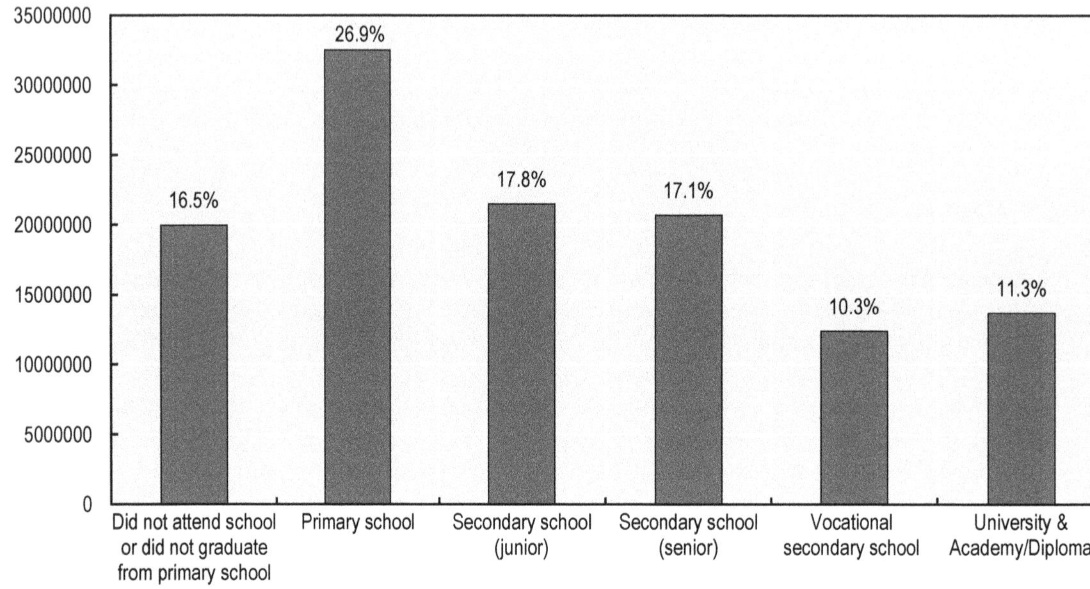

Source: Central Bureau of Statistics (*Badan Pusat Statistik*), https://www.bps.go.id

StatLink https://doi.org/10.1787/888933824002

Indonesia's Masterplan for the Acceleration and Expansion of Economic Development sets the objective of reaching 113 million skilled workers by 2030. To achieve this goal, the government has committed 20% of the state budget to education, which is high by international standards, although limited government fiscal revenues mean that public spending on education is 3.5% of national GDP, which is relatively low in international comparison (Figure 3.5).

Going forward, participation in secondary and tertiary education should be increased to boost the basic skills of the Indonesian labour force. OECD simulations suggest that a one standard-deviation increase in years of schooling (around 3.4 years) would lift the hourly wage by 26.6% in Indonesia, almost twice the OECD average (14.4%). However, it will also be important to improve the efficiency of public spending on education which will include, among other things, enhancing teacher competencies and reducing teacher absenteeism (OECD, 2016b).

Figure 3.5. Education expenditure in Indonesia and other emerging-market economies, 2013 or latest available year

Percentage of GDP

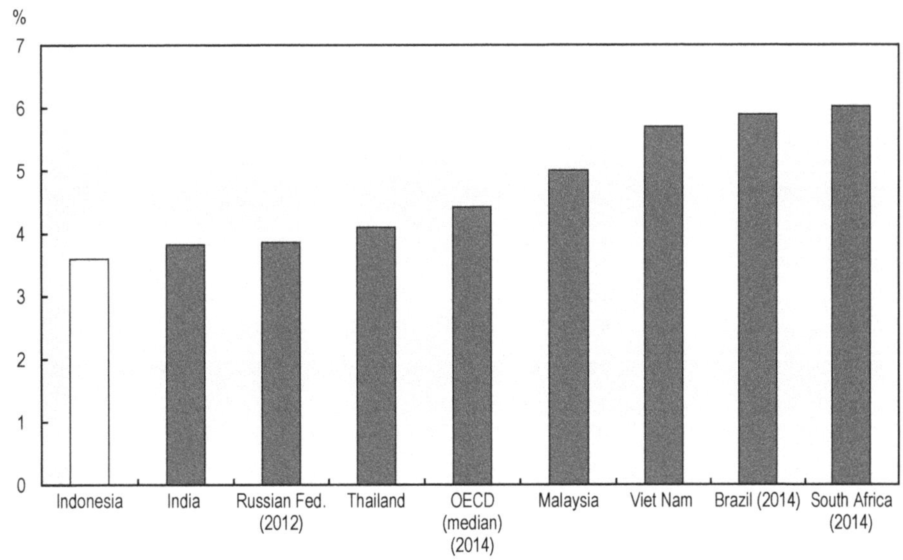

Note: Data for the Russian Federation refer to 2012; data for Indonesia, India, Thailand, Malaysia and Viet Nam refer to 2013; data for Brazil, South Africa and the OECD refer to 2014.
Source: World Bank World Development Indicators and OECD Education database.

StatLink https://doi.org/10.1787/888933824021

Vocational Education and Training (VET) in Indonesia

Similarly to other countries, training a student in the Indonesian vocational education and training (VET) system is more expensive than training a student in the general education system (IDR 6.8 million vs. IDR 5.3 million per year). Nonetheless, secondary VET graduates are the group facing the highest unemployment rate in Indonesia (almost 10% compared with the country average of 5.5%), and Indonesian employers consider as many as 20% of new hires with VET qualifications of poor or very poor quality (OECD/ADB, 2015). These figures suggest that issues of quality and cost-efficiency, which apply to the overall education system, are particularly apparent in VET.

One of the main challenges facing Indonesian VET is the lack of up-to-date equipment. Although a law from 1997 encourages collaboration between VET schools and private-sector companies, few of such collaborations exist, making it difficult for VET schools to address industry demands in a timely manner. Another issue concerns the skills level of VET teachers, with many of them coming from a purely academic background, having worked in the same school for many decades, and having never been subject to an assessment review of their performance (OECD/ADB, 2015).

In November 2016 the Ministry of Industry, Research, Technology and Higher Education, the Ministry of Education and Culture, the Ministry of State-Owned Enterprises and the Ministry of Manpower signed a Memorandum of Understanding to strengthen the participation of industry practitioners in the national VET system, including through the creation of internships and on-site training programmes for students and teachers. As a result, a pilot project involving a partnership between three private-sector firms and 20 VET schools has recently been launched (OBG, 2017). This model of collaboration between VET schools and the private sector should be expanded if it proves successful.

Product market regulations and the ease of doing business

Product market regulations, such as those governing business licenses and permits, have a direct impact on business start-up and business scale-up, as well as on the decision of entrepreneurs to operate in the formal or informal sector. The OECD Product Market Regulation (PMR) indicators assess regulatory complexity in three areas: i) state control of the economy; ii) barriers to entrepreneurship; iii) barriers to trade and investment. Indonesia ranks below the OECD average in each of these three categories, whereas compared to other major emerging-market economies such as Brazil, China and India its performance is mixed: Indonesia's barriers to entrepreneurship are the lowest of the four, whilst state control of the economy is the highest (Figure 3.6).

The World Bank Doing Business annual report is another important comparative source of information on the ease of doing business. Between 2015 and 2018, Indonesia gained 48 positions in the general "ease of doing business" world ranking, moving from the 120th position in 2015 to the 72nd position in 2018, with progress in the so-called "distance to frontier" (i.e. the distance to the best-performing country) in almost all sub-indicators comprising the overall index (Table 3.1). This improvement has been the result of some important recent targeted reforms.

For example, the 2016 "Economic Policy Package XII on the Ease of Doing Business" aimed at reducing the number of days needed to start a business from 48 to 10, the number of procedures from 13 to 7, and the cost linked to setting up a business from IDR 6.8-7.8 million to IDR 2.7 million (World Bank, 2017b). Additional recent reforms have included a reduction in the time needed to register property and acquire construction permits; less frequent tax compliance requirements; and the merger and digitalisation of two forms for business trading licenses and company registrations in Jakarta (World Bank, 2017b; OECD, 2016a).

Figure 3.6. Product market regulations in Indonesia and other emerging-market economies, 2013

From 0 (least restrictive) to 6 (most restrictive)

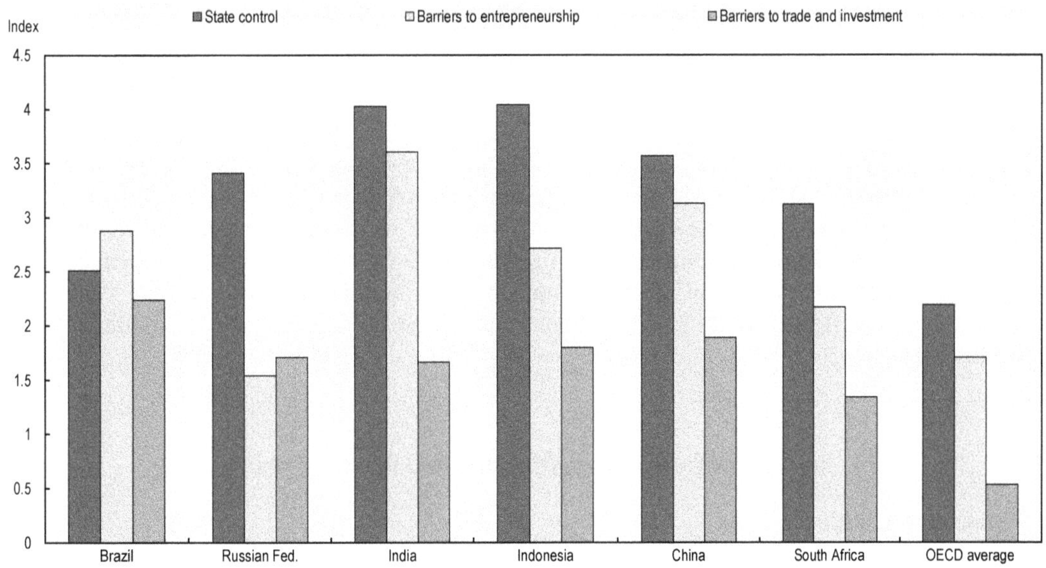

Note: "State control" refers to public ownership (e.g. scope and governance of state-owned enterprises, government involvement in network sectors, etc.) and public involvement in business operations (e.g. price controls); "barriers to entrepreneurship" include complexity of rules and procedures (e.g. the license and permit system), administrative burdens on start-ups (i.e. for both corporations and for sole proprietor firms) and regulatory protection of incumbents (e.g. legal barriers to entry and anti-trust exemptions); "barriers to trade and investment" encompass explicit barriers (e.g. tariffs) and non-explicit barriers (e.g. different treatment of foreign suppliers) to trade.
Source: OECD Product Market Regulation (PMR) database.

StatLink https://doi.org/10.1787/888933824040

Table 3.1. Indonesia's World Bank Doing Business performance, 2018

	Ranking	Distance to frontier (% points)
OVERALL	72	64.2
Getting electricity	38	83.9
Resolving insolvency	38	67.6
Protecting minority investors	43	63.3
Getting credit	55	65.0
Registering property	106	59.0
Dealing with construction permits	108	66.1
Trading across borders	112	66.7
Paying taxes	114	68.0
Starting a business	144	77.9
Enforcing contracts	145	47.2

Source: World Bank Doing Business Survey, http://www.doingbusiness.org/data/exploreeconomies/indonesia.

StatLink https://doi.org/10.1787/888933824059

Despite recent progress, more could be done to further improve the ease of doing business in Indonesia. For example, the national licensing system remains fairly complex and contributes to the very low position of Indonesia in the specific World Bank Doing Business indicator of "starting a business" (144th position worldwide). After the so-called Big Bang devolution of the early 2000s, many responsibilities related to business licensing were transferred to the subnational level. However, strong heterogeneity in institutional quality across Indonesia has hindered the development of an effective national system of business licenses and permits (OECD, 2012) (see chapter 6 for further details).

In mid-2018, the Indonesian government was in the process of developing an online single submission system to allow the centralisation of licensing procedures from all levels of government into one single website. This is a welcome development, which is likely to require some time to be fully implemented. In this area, the experience of another federal country (e.g. Canada) in managing its national business license system online across different levels of government can offer a policy model for Indonesia to follow (see Box 3.1).

Box 3.1. International inspiring practice: BizPaL, Canada

Description of the approach

BizPaL is a collaborative partnership between the federal, provincial and municipal governments of Canada, which includes the participation of over 34 federal government departments and agencies, 13 provinces and territories, and about 700 municipalities to provide information on the permits and licenses required to start and grow a business. Accessing the BizPaL website allows entrepreneurs to identify which permits and licenses they require and how to obtain them. From the website, they select the business activities they plan to undertake and BizPaL automatically generates a list of all required permits and licenses from all levels of government (federal, provincial, territorial and municipal), along with basic information and links to the specific government sites where the entrepreneur can learn more and, in some cases, apply online. The federal government manages the BizPaL project but each jurisdiction is responsible for maintaining its own data within the central database. Information is entered into this database using the BizPaL Administration Module, a secure web–based application. BizPaL receives CAD 3 million annually in federal funding.

Success factors

The success of BizPal rests on the partnership across different levels of government, outreach to other regional SME support organisations, and innovations in the use of information technology platforms to collate a variety of business-related government databases and disseminate information and services.

Obstacles and responses

It was more difficult than initially expected to bring municipalities into BizPal, especially those in smaller and more remote locations, as they lacked staff and capacity to participate. When the project was piloted in 2006, only 13 municipalities were part of the project, increasing to approximately 580 in 2008 (i.e. 16% of the total 3 647 municipalities of Canada). The BizPaL team realised that their target objectives for municipality participation were too ambitious and that much more intensive involvement with municipalities was needed to bring them on board. For example, provincial and territorial governments had to spend considerably more time uploading information on behalf of the local governments than they had originally thought.

Moreover, awareness of BizPaL among SME owners was low, even two years after the launch of the initiative. Thus, BizPaL undertook a national marketing campaign to increase awareness and interest among potential users. The specific objectives of the marketing campaign were to improve client awareness and usage of the BizPaL service and increase BizPaL recognition through cohesive and consistent marketing communication, activities and messaging.

Finally, there was uncertainty with respect to securing ongoing resources from federal and provincial governments, which was alleviated by the federal government decision to allocate an annual CAD 3 million to the project.

Relevance to Indonesia

Similarly to Canada, Indonesia is a federal country in which business licenses are managed by national, provincial and local governments. Better co-ordination between these different levels of government, supported by increased digitalisation of the whole licensing process, would help simplify Indonesia's business license system.

For a similar policy to be successful, however, complementary measures are needed, including faster and more widespread broadband connection across the country and capacity-building initiatives for the staff in local governments assigned to the project.

Sources for further information

OECD (2017b), SME and Entrepreneurship Policy in Canada, OECD Publishing, Paris, https://doi.org/10.1787/9789264273467-en.

Taxation affecting small businesses

Taxation is another important dimension of the national business environment which is closely related to product market regulations through tax compliance requirements. Of Indonesia's 260 million citizens only 33 million were registered tax payers in 2016, while only 2.9 million companies were known to the national tax authority (OECD, forthcoming). Both figures contribute to Indonesia's narrow tax base.

Since 2013, Indonesia has enforced a special tax regime for SMEs with the aim of encouraging small business formalisation.[1] Businesses in eligible sectors with an annual turnover below IDR 4.8 billion (around USD 350 000) can opt into the scheme and pay a rate of 0.5%, based on their monthly turnover. The rate was originally 1%, but it has recently been halved, with an additional cost to the government of between IDR 1-1.5 trillion in terms of foregone fiscal revenues. By mid-2018, this special tax regime had attracted 1.5 million small companies (OECD, forthcoming).

Above the IDR 4.8 billion threshold, statutory corporate income taxation applies. The corporate income tax rate for companies with revenues between IDR 4.8 billion and IDR 50 billion (USD 350 000 and USD 3.8 billion) is 12.5% on the first IDR 4.8 billion and 25% above this threshold, while for companies with turnovers above IDR 50 billion, corporate income tax is set at a flat rate of 25%. A lower corporate income tax rate of 20% applies to companies listed on the stock exchange with more than 40% of traded shares.

Personal income tax rates, which apply to the taxable personal income (i.e. after basic allowances and any possible dependent allowances) of small business owners who run sole-proprietor firms or unincorporated companies are, on the other hand, 5% up to IDR 50 million, 15% between IDR 50 million and IDR 250 million, 25% between IDR 250 million and IDR 500 million, and 30% over IDR 500 million (Indonesia Investment, 2017; PWC, 2016).

Indonesia's business income tax system has two main noteworthy features. First, it applies different rates depending on the annual revenues of the business. This is not uncommon to OECD countries and other G-20 economies, 14 of which have lower corporate income tax rates for small businesses (OECD, 2015). However, the average difference between the statutory corporate income tax rate and the preferential small business tax rate is four percentage points among the countries covered in this study, whereas in the case of Indonesia businesses are faced with a major tax threshold at IDR 4.8 billion, until which they can opt for a simplified turnover-based tax rate of 0.5%. A risk with major tax thresholds is that they can effectively discourage business growth, whether artificially (through tax evasion) or by companies deliberately restraining growth opportunities.

Second, although this special tax regime is meant to bring micro and small companies closer to the formal economy, the income threshold (annual IDR 4.8 billion) appears to be somewhat high, effectively exempting a large number of formal companies in Indonesia from contributing to the national tax base in line with their revenues. The income threshold could be lowered, while additional benefits could be offered such as access to book-keeping assistance and government support programmes (OECD, forthcoming), as done for example in Mexico through the *Régimen de Incorparación Fiscal* (RIF) (see Box 3.2).

More broadly, it will be important to strengthen tax collection capacity at the national and, if necessary, subnational level (see chapter 6). The latest OECD Economic Survey of Indonesia dedicates a special chapter to the issue of raising public revenues in a way that is favourable to growth and equity. Some of the suggested measures to improve tax collection will include: investing in tax administration, particularly staff, electronic services and databases; using technology to strengthen monitoring and detect non-compliance, including through the use of risk-based assessments for conducting tax audits; and building capacity at the subnational level through training (OECD, forthcoming).

Box 3.2. *Régimen de Incorporación Fiscal*, Mexico

In January 2014, Mexico replaced its earlier small-taxpayer regime (*Régimen de Pequeños Contribuyentes*, REPECOS) with the *Régimen de Incorporación Fiscal* (RIF). In order to reduce the size of the informal economy, the new regime offers substantially lower personal, social security and value-added and excise tax obligations over a period of ten years to small companies that decide to regularise their position. Tax rate reductions gradually phase out during the ten-year period. The RIF is specifically directed at small business owners whose income does not exceed MXN 2 million. To give a further incentive for business formalisation, the federal government also offers training, credit lines and an easy-to-use online book-keeping tool which facilitates tax compliance (called *Mis cuentas*, "My accounts").

Exemptions and reductions in taxes under the RIF in Mexico

	Year									
Reduction in tax liability	1	2	3	4	5	6	7	8	9	10
Income, VAT and excise tax	100%	90%	80%	70%	60%	50%	40%	30%	20%	10%
Social security contributions (up to max. income of three minimum wages)	50%	50%	40%	40%	30%	30%	20%	20%	10%	10%

StatLink http://dx.doi.org/10.1787/

To adhere to the programme beneficiaries must enrol in the Federal Taxpayer Registry, record revenues and expenses, invoice clients upon request and submit bi-monthly statements.

Source: OECD (2015), *Taxation of SMEs in OECD and G20 Countries*, OECD Tax Policy Studies, No. 23, OECD Publishing, Paris, http://dx.doi.org/10.1787/9789264243507-en.

Access to finance

Debt finance

In 2015, 59.8% of Indonesian firms had a current or savings account and 27.4% had a bank loan or a credit line. However, only 12.8% of business investment was financed by bank loans and 3.7% by supplier credit, with 66% being financed by internal resources (World Bank, 2015).

Business credit grew considerably in Indonesia over the period 2012-2016, at an annual rate of 62%, totalling IDR 4 505 trillion (about USD 335 billion) in 2016, i.e. 36% of national GDP. SME loans corresponded to about 18-20% of total business loans over the same time period.[2] Most SME loans are used to finance working capital (73%), suggesting that they are of short duration. Medium-sized enterprises (46%) are the main recipients of SME loans, followed by small enterprises (30%) and micro-enterprises (24%) (Figure 3.7).

Figure 3.7. Outstanding loans to micro, small and medium-sized enterprises in Indonesia, 2012-2016

IDR trillions

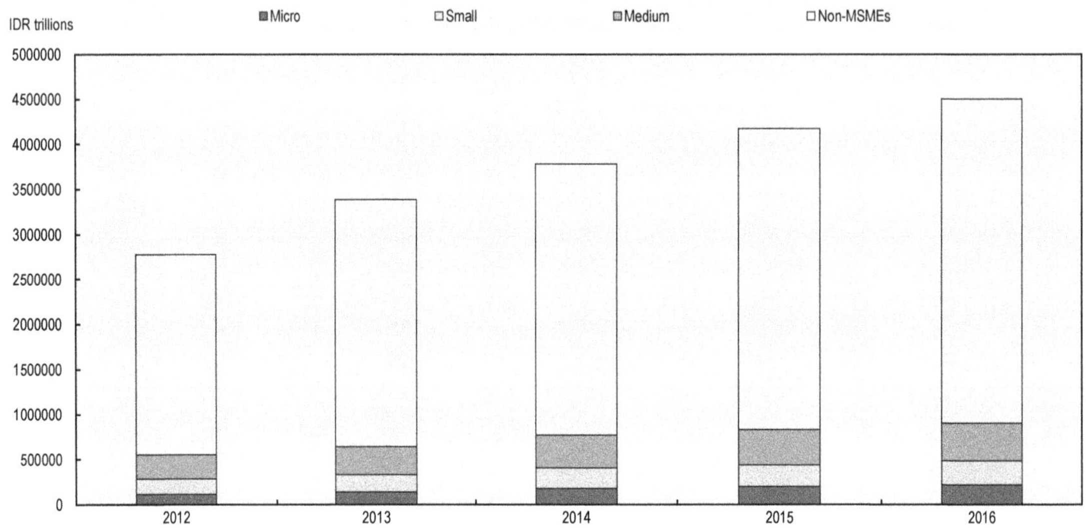

Note: Bank Indonesia's definition of SME loans follows the SME definition of Law 20/2008.
Source: Bank Indonesia Database, http://www.bi.go.id/id/umkm/kredit/data/Documents/Perkembangan%20Kredit%20UMKM%20dan%20MKM%20Des%202016_BD.pdf

StatLink https://doi.org/10.1787/888933824078

In 2016, half of total credit to SMEs was issued by state-owned banks, with an increase of 5% over the period 2012-2016. Commercial banks lost SME market shares, from 41.5% of total SME loans to 37%, over the same period. Regional development banks, which mostly target micro and small enterprises, still play a small role, only accounting for 7% of total SME loans (Figure 3.8).

State-owned and commercial banks operating in Indonesia must comply with set-aside requirements on the proportions of loans given to SMEs, the target for which has gradually increased from 5% in 2015, to 10% in 2016, 15% in 2017, and 20% in 2018. According to a 2017 report from the national Financial Services Authority (*Otoritas Jasa Keuanga*, OJK), around one-fifth of commercial banks in Indonesia (mostly joint ventures or foreign banks with local operations) had fallen short of this target, allocating less than 10% of their business loans to SMEs. On the other hand, state-owned banks, with an overall 26% share of SME loans in their business loan portfolios, were fully compliant with this legal requirement. Bank Indonesia is poised to impose administrative sanctions on non-compliant banks, which can take the form of a warning, a fine or a communication that further measures will be taken by the Financial Services Authority. Banks, for example, may be prevented from progressing to the above bank-tier until the target is achieved, which has implications for the range of financial services they can offer to the public.

Figure 3.8. Outstanding SME loans by type of credit institution in Indonesia, 2016

100% = IDR 900.4 trillion

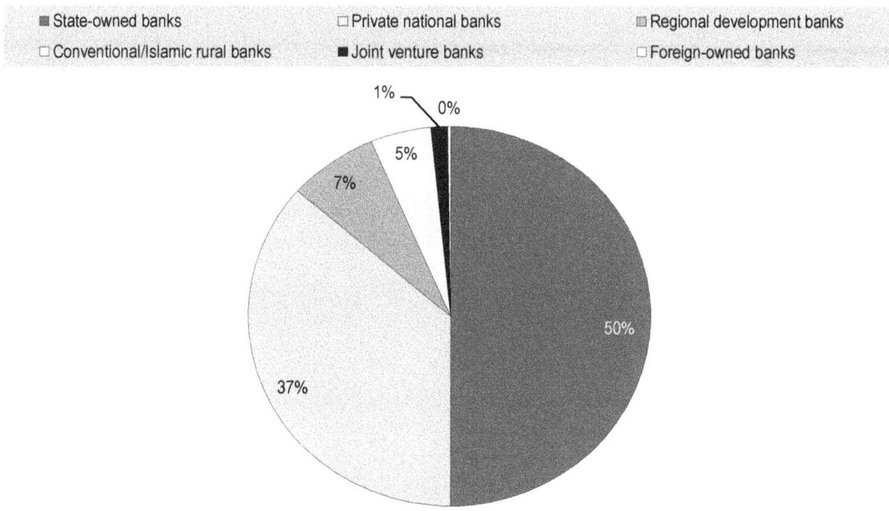

Source: Bank Indonesia Database, http://www.bi.go.id/id/umkm/kredit/data/Documents/Perkembangan%20Kredit%20UMKM%20dan%20MKM%20Des%202016_BD.pdf.

StatLink https://doi.org/10.1787/888933824097

In 2006, Bank Indonesia established the first public credit bureau (*Biro Informasi Kredit*, BIK) to collect personal debtor information history and make it available to financial institutions with the aim of reducing information asymmetries in SME credit markets. In 2013, Bank Indonesia also issued a "Regulation on Credit Information Management Bureaus", clearing the way for private credit bureaus to collect data on creditors. As of 2017, private credit bureaus covered 18% of the adult population in Indonesia. Box 3.3 provides international good-practice guidelines on the management of credit bureaus to help further expand the population coverage and strengthen the use of credit bureaus by financial institutions in Indonesia.

A collateral registry has also been recently established in Indonesia to favour asset-based lending to SMEs. In this field, Mexico offers an interesting example of a country which has established a collateral registry that collects information not only on fixed assets but also on moveable assets (Box 3.4), something which could be replicated in Indonesia.

Finally, the Financial Services Authority (OJK) has issued regulations to lower the risk weight for SME loans guaranteed by entities owned by regional governments (*Badan Usaha Milik Daerah*, BUMD) and to ask banks to focus on "payment capacity", which involves taking into account not only collateral requirements but also business revenues in the loan decision-making process.

Box 3.3. International guidelines on the effective management of credit bureaus

The aim of credit bureaus is to reduce information asymmetries between creditors and borrowers. Credit bureaus can support SME lending by helping lenders to assess the creditworthiness of borrowers which lack certified financial statements. For example, credit bureaus can collect information on the past behaviour of SMEs in contractual financial obligations such as trade credit, loans and other forms of finance, as well as on their payment history related to taxes and utilities.

According to the World Bank's General Principles for Credit Reporting (2011), there are five main success factors for the development of credit reporting systems:

- Credit reporting systems should have relevant, accurate, timely and sufficient data (including positive information) collected on a systematic basis from all reliable and available sources;
- Credit reporting systems should have rigorous standards of security and reliability;
- The governance arrangements of credit reporting service providers should ensure accountability and transparency concerning the risks associated with the business and fair access to this information by users;
- The regulatory framework for credit reporting should be clear, predictable, non-discriminatory, proportionate and considerate of consumer rights;
- The legal and regulatory framework should include effective judicial or extrajudicial dispute resolution mechanisms.

An important aspect that also needs to be taken into consideration is privacy and data protection since information gathered and stored in credit registries is often very sensitive. It should be a priority for the government to guarantee that regulation on the use of data is clear and strict, and that the judicial system can enforce it through administrative sanctions if necessary.

Source: World Bank (2011), *General Principles for Credit Reporting*, Washington DC.

Box 3.4. Unified Registry of Movable Collateral Assets, Mexico

In 2010, Mexico introduced a Unified Registry of Movable Collateral Assets to boost collateral registration. The goal of the registry is to allow borrowers to pledge additional assets beyond fixed assets to access debt finance. The registry makes information on collateral assets available online for all interested parties (notaries, lawyers, state officials, bank creditors), with no registration fee required. The digitalisation of the service provides an immediate and cheap alternative to the previous paper-based system.

In the first 18 months of the programme, nearly 67 000 collateral assets were registered, with an estimated increase of business loans by four times (more than USD

50 billion of additional financing), and USD 1.1 billion saved on fees, compared with the previous paper-based system.

Source: OECD (2013), *Mexico: Key Issues and Policies*, OECD Studies on SMEs and Entrepreneurship, OECD Publishing, Paris. https://doi.org/10.1787/9789264187030-en

On the whole, the government of Indonesia has enforced a vast array of measures to favour access to finance for SMEs. For example, compulsory SME lending set-asides should help expand credit to SMEs. The 20% SME loan target appears reasonable given the existing share of SME loans out of total business loans across OECD countries, although SME loan definitions vary by country making fully internationally comparable information unavailable (OECD, 2018a). However, considering the co-existence of other large SME financing programmes (e.g. the KUR Programme, see chapter 5), a similar policy needs to be closely monitored to ensure that it does not lead to an upsurge in non-performing loans. Similarly, while most state-owned banks have easily met the 20% target, commercial banks, notably foreign-owned banks, have experienced more difficulties due to the inability to find enough SMEs with the business permits, financial statements and collateral assets required by the operational rules of the bank to issue a loan. Thus, it will be important to monitor that a similar measure does not have the unintended consequence of reducing competition in the banking sector by pushing too many commercial banks out of the market.

The growing role of state-owned banks in SME lending should also be closely monitored. On the one hand, it clearly fills a market gap that some commercial banks are unwilling to serve. On the other hand, it can also lead to an increase in non-performing loans – state-owned banks face less market pressure from private shareholders and more political pressure to meet government targets – and to the possible crowding out of commercial banks from the SME market by introducing lending conditions (e.g. interest rates and loan repayment terms) that are not market-based.

Finally, the recent establishment of a collateral registry and credit bureaus are positive developments that should be further pursued and reinforced, including through stronger coverage of SMEs and use by financial institutions.

Equity finance

The Indonesian government actively supports the development of alternative sources of finance for SMEs. Indonesia's Financial Services Authority (OJK) has introduced lower requirements in terms of company assets and fundraising for SMEs interested in initial public offerings (IPOs), as well as a simplified financial accounting standard for smaller SMEs with assets up to IDR 50 billion. Furthermore, the OJK has issued regulations to facilitate peer-to-peer lending for small limited liability companies with capital up to IDR 1 billion. Loans must be denominated in Indonesian rupiah and cannot exceed IDR 2 billion for each borrower.

The Indonesia Stock Exchange (IDX) also actively supports the access of SMEs to capital markets through an SME Development Initiative comprising the Acceleration Board, i.e. a junior equity market with lower listing requirements than the main equity market, and an incubator programme intended to prepare growth-oriented start-ups for IPOs (both initiatives are further discussed in chapter 5 of the report).

From the investor's side, private equity funds that re-invest after-tax profits within the same year are exempt from the branch profit tax on these profits (on average 20%). In addition, income earned by venture capital companies from their investments in Indonesia is exempt from capital gains taxation, if the investment was directed at SMEs in one of the government priority sectors, defined as those with high value added and positive externalities (PWC, 2017).[3]

Altogether, this range of measures is well-intentioned to foster SME participation in equity markets, although very few Indonesian SMEs appear ready to enter the stock market, even when this involves junior equity listings where regulatory requirements are less strict. Increased government attention to the investment readiness of domestic growth-oriented SMEs would therefore be warranted.

Financial literacy and financial inclusion

Financial literacy and financial education have been used by the Indonesian government to enhance the financial inclusion of micro-enterprise owners. The government of Indonesia, through Regulation 82/2016, is currently implementing a National Strategy for Financial Inclusion. The strategy has been prepared by Bank Indonesia, the Ministry of Finance and the National Team for the Acceleration of Poverty Alleviation. It focuses on six pillars: financial education, public financing facilities, financial information mapping, supportive regulations, distribution networks, and intermediation facilities and consumer protection. The strategy particularly targets certain social groups, such as low-income people, women, and people living in rural/disadvantaged areas. The target is for 75% of the population to have access to formal financial institutions by 2019. The National Strategy for Financial Inclusion follows and complements the National Strategy on Financial Literacy, launched in 2013, which also had a chapter on SMEs.

The Financial Services Authority is also particularly active in this field. It has conducted financial education and entrepreneurship training programmes for SMEs through its network of regional Centres for Education, Consumer Services and Financial Access (PELAKU), with 14 of them active in the country in 2017. It has also established the Development Centre for Microfinance and Financial Inclusion (OJK-PROKSI) to give SMEs wider access to financial services, and it has developed an Inclusive Finance Framework (LAKU-PANDAI) which allows banks to offer financial services to customers through the use of mobile and internet banking to better serve remote areas. The latter programme has been rolled out by 18 banks and has reached 3.7 million customers so far through basic savings accounts, microcredit and micro-insurance services. Finally, the Ministry of Finance has recently launched a microcredit programme for firms that are too small to qualify for the KUR Programme.

The innovation system

Indonesia's spending on R&D is low by international standards, only 0.08% of GDP against the OECD average of 2.5%. By the same token, Indonesian companies tend to register few patents and trademarks and account for only 25% of domestic R&D spending, with the rest undertaken by government, higher education institutions and non-profit organisations.

Figure 3.9. R&D expenditure across OECD and selected emerging market economies, 2016

Percentage of GDP

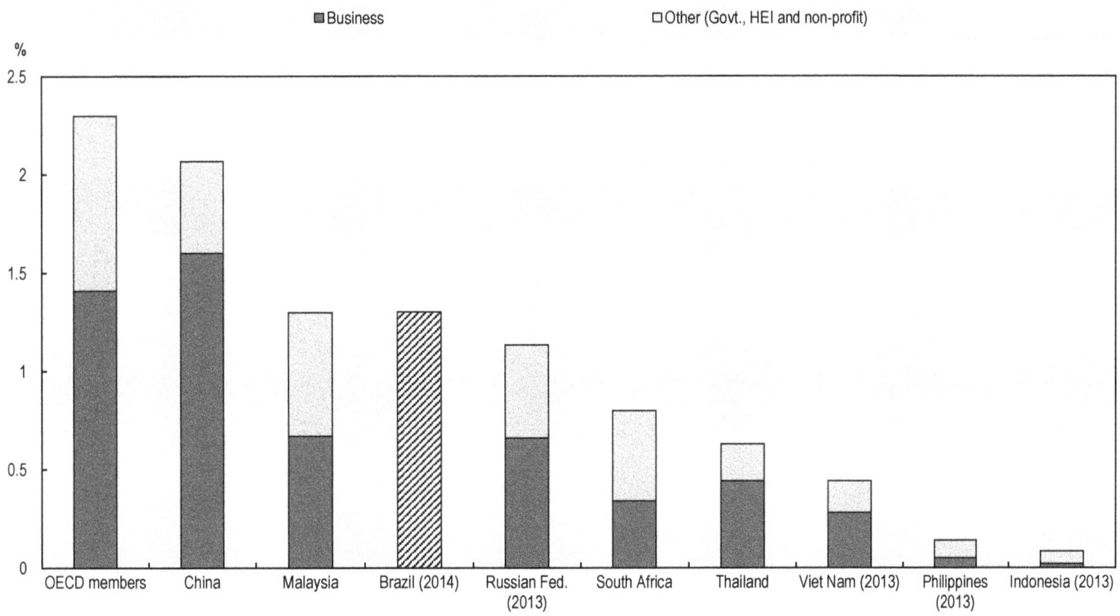

Note: "Other" includes R&D expenditures by government, higher education institutions and non-profit organisations. Data for Indonesia, Viet Nam, South Africa and the Philippines refer to 2013; data for Brazil refer to 2014 and are not differentiated by source of investment. Data for Indonesia, Viet Nam, Malaysia, Thailand and the Philippines are from the World Bank World Development Indicators; data for OECD members, China, Russia, Brazil and South Africa are from the OECD Main Science and Technology Indicator (MSTI) Database.
Source: OECD Main Science and Technology Indicator (MSTI) Database and World Bank World Development Indicators.

StatLink https://doi.org/10.1787/888933824116

The Indonesian government has recently introduced different policies to favour the development of the knowledge economy. The main institutional player is the Ministry of Research, Technology and Higher Education which has launched: i) the National Research Agenda 2015-2019, which primarily aims to encourage industry-university co-operation, for example by enabling researchers to obtain royalties from patents they develop while working for national universities (OECD, 2016c); ii) the Masterplan of National Research 2017-2045, which aims to boost the contribution of the national research system to economic growth; and iii) the National System of Science and Technology which offers regulations on technology transfer, technology audit and technology readiness (Kurniawan, 2016).

Indonesia's innovation policy mix is mostly geared towards technology consulting services, while fiscal incentives such as competitive grants, vouchers, and R&D tax breaks play a much lesser role (Figure 3.10). The Indonesian government could develop a new R&D tax credit to encourage more business R&D spending, although the design of this policy, as well as monitoring its implementation, would be important to ensure that the measure is not abused. For example, eligible costs should only include costs which are closely related to R&D (e.g. contracts with university and research labs, hiring of researchers and technicians, external consulting and training activities), while excluding investments in machinery and equipment whose link with R&D activity is harder to establish. By the same token, while cash refunds have been used in some OECD countries, in order not to penalise R&D investments in innovative start-ups without taxable income, they should be excluded in the context of Indonesia to rein in the cost of the policy. An example of an R&D tax credit specifically intended for SMEs is presented in Box 3.5.

Figure 3.10. Most relevant policy instruments for business R&D funding, 2016

Country self-assessment, index (9= highest; 0= lowest)

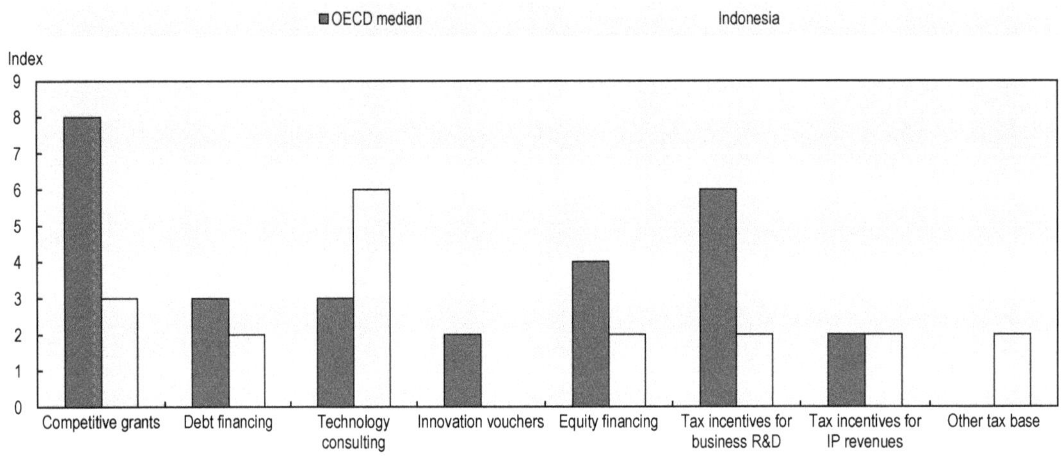

Note: Policy information comes from country responses to the EC/OECD International Survey on STI policies 2016 and 2014. Indonesia's responses are available at EC/OECD International Database on STI Policies, 2016 edition. http://qdd.oecd.org/DATA/STIPSurvey/IDN...STIO_2016

Source: OECD (2016c), *OECD Science, Technology and Innovation Outlook 2016*, OECD Publishing, Paris, http://dx.doi.org/10.1787/sti_in_outlook-2016-en

StatLink https://doi.org/10.1787/888933824135

Box 3.5. International inspiring practice: *Credit d'Impôt Innovation* (CII) for SMEs, France

Description of the approach

Since 2013 (*Loi de finance* 2013, art. 71) France has offered a tax credit for SMEs, the CII (*Credit d'Impôt Innovation*), which allows SMEs (less than 250 employees) to receive tax reductions on expenses related to prototypes or pilot trials of new products. Expenses subject to the tax credit are capped at EUR 400 000 per year and the tax credit rate is 20%, with any unused amount of credit allowed to be carried over for up to three years. Eligible costs include staff costs, intellectual property acquisition, and research contracts to third parties.

Success factors

By supporting prototype development, especially of new products with superior technical performance compared to those available on the market, the programme is particularly suited to encouraging research commercialisation. In addition, by covering only the development phase and not the production phase, the measure is intended to have less distortive effects on the market. Finally, by explicitly targeting, among other criteria, the eco-compatibility of the new products, the CII supports green innovations.

Obstacles and responses

A limitation of CII is that innovations in the services sector and non-technological innovations (e.g. innovations in marketing and business processes) are excluded from the tax credit. As innovation in services can often have an important impact on product innovation in manufacturing, this may limit the effect of the incentive. Another problem is the variety of programmes and incentives to support innovation in France, which makes it difficult for SMEs with limited staff and resources to seize the opportunities offered by the government.

Relevance to Indonesia

The CII offers a model of R&D tax credit specifically for SMEs, whereas R&D tax credits in Indonesia are rather undeveloped. An important element of the French policy is its explicit targeting of new-to-the-market innovations, rather than new-to-the-firm, which ensures stronger additionality and lower fiscal costs of the measure.

Sources for further information

Website of the programme:

https://www.entreprises.gouv.fr/politique-et-enjeux/credit-impot-innovation

Indonesian innovation policies have also taken, on occasion, an industry-focus approach. The Ministry of Research, Technology and Higher Education, for example, supports innovation in agri-food, shipbuilding, transport, machinery and textiles (OECD, 2016c). More recently, knowledge-based industries have also started to be prioritised, notably renewable energies through the creation of a government innovation centre and creative industries through the establishment of the Creative Economy Agency (*Badan Ekonomi Kreatif*, BEKRAF) (see chapter 5).

The Indonesian government has also ramped up spending on its broadband infrastructure. The national Broadband Plan is expected to provide fixed broadband access to all government offices, hotels, hospitals, schools and public spaces by 2019, at a speed of at least 2 Mbit/s. While this is a positive development, it will also be important to expand broadband access to private-sector facilities in order to better reach businesses, including SMEs. Complementary to the development of the broadband infrastructure, the government is also rolling out an E-Commerce Roadmap Strategy that involves several ministries and intends to accelerate the use of e-commerce by SMEs (see chapter 5).

Foreign Direct Investment

In emerging-market economies, foreign direct investment (FDI) is often a major source of capital investment, direct job creation and knowledge spillovers that can benefit local SMEs, especially larger SMEs operating in industries that are suppliers to the sector of the foreign investor (Lembcke and Wildernova, forthcoming).

A large internal market, solid growth prospects, a prudent fiscal framework, abundant natural resources and a relatively low labour cost are some of the main assets which Indonesia offers to foreign investors (Hornberger et al., 2011). Despite these clear assets, FDI inflows to Indonesia over the last ten years (relative to national GDP), albeit sustained, have not been as large as in some other BRICS (e.g. Brazil and China) and ASEAN countries (e.g. Malaysia, Thailand and Vietnam) (OECD, 2016a) (Figure 3.11).

Figure 3.11. FDI net inflows in Indonesia and selected emerging-market economies, 2000-2017

Percentage of GDP

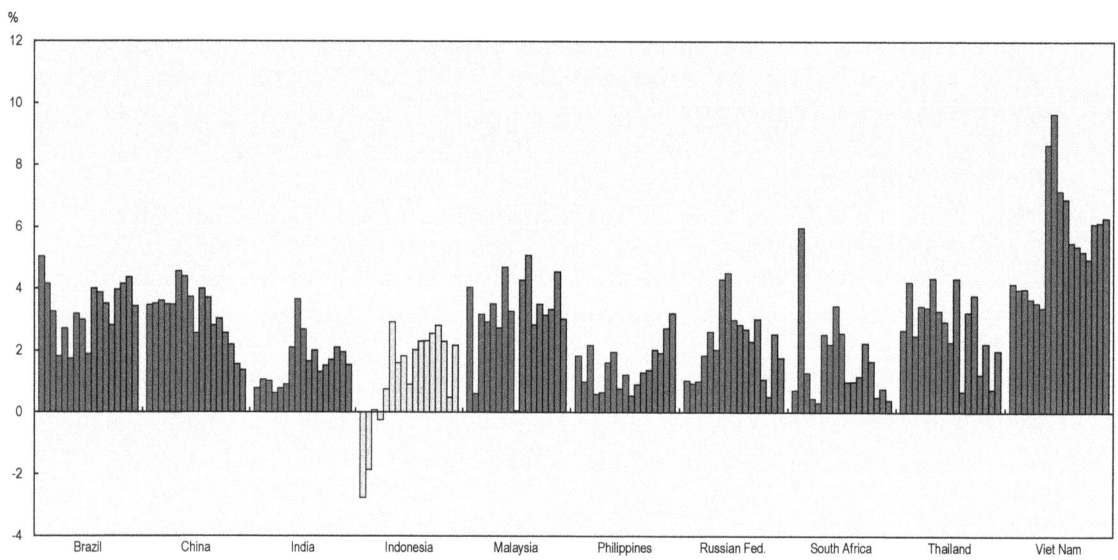

Source: International Monetary Fund, International Financial Statistics and Balance of Payments databases; World Bank, International Debt Statistics; and World Bank and OECD GDP estimates https://data.worldbank.org/indicator/BX.KLT.DINV.WD.GD.ZS?locations=BR-CN-IN-ID-MY-PH-RU-ZA-TH-VN

StatLink https://doi.org/10.1787/888933824154

Regulatory restrictions explain in part the untapped FDI potential of Indonesia. The OECD FDI Regulatory Restrictiveness Index collates the main regulations (e.g. foreign equity limits, screening and approval procedures, restrictions on key foreign personnel, and other operational measures) that may hinder the inflow of FDI at the national level. As shown in Figure 3.12, Indonesia has stricter FDI regulatory restrictions than both the OECD average and the ASEAN-9 average (which does not include Brunei Darussalam) (OECD, 2018b). In particular, among ASEAN economies, only the Philippines has stricter FDI restrictions than Indonesia.

Figure 3.12. FDI restrictiveness in Indonesia and other ASEAN countries, 2017

FDI Regulatory Restrictiveness Index (Open = 0; Closed = 1)

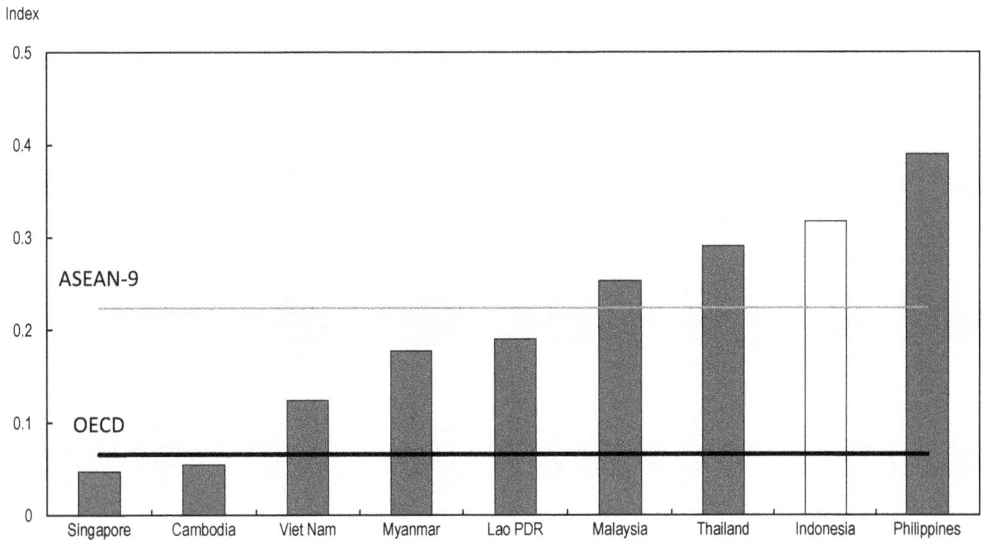

Notes: The OECD FDI Regulatory Restrictiveness Index covers only statutory measures discriminating against foreign investors (e.g. foreign equity limits, screening and approval procedures, restrictions on key foreign personnel, and other operational measures). Other important aspects of an investment climate (e.g. the implementation of regulations and state monopolies) are not considered. Data for Thailand and Singapore refer to 2016. ASEAN-9 is Cambodia, Indonesia, Lao PDR, Malaysia, Myanmar, Philippines, Singapore, Thailand and Viet Nam.
Source: OECD FDI Regulatory Restrictiveness Index database.

StatLink https://doi.org/10.1787/888933824173

Inward FDI also benefits from trade liberalisation in services. By way of example, logistics and financial services are key to the effective functioning of global supply chains. As a consequence, being able to tap freely into these global services from any location influences the investment choice of multinational companies.

The OECD Service Trade Restrictiveness Index (STRI) calculates service trade barriers in 22 sectors across 44 countries, representing over 80% of global service trade. In all 22 sectors considered, Indonesia exceeds the average restrictiveness of the 44 countries (35 OECD countries plus 9, including the 5 BRICS). The main underlying cause is "general regulations which apply to all sectors of the economy" rather than sector-based regulations, including: i) management positions in Indonesian corporations reserved to Indonesian nationals; ii) price preferences given to national companies in public procurement; iii) acquisition of land and real estate by foreigners restricted to the right of use for a limited number of years; and iv) restrictions to the movement of people. The most restrictive sectors in Indonesia are insurance, legal services and distribution, while the least restrictive are sound recording, rail freight and air transport (Figure 3.13).

Figure 3.13. Service Trade Restrictiveness by sector and policy area in Indonesia, 2017

Service Trade Restrictiveness Index (0=lowest; 1=highest)

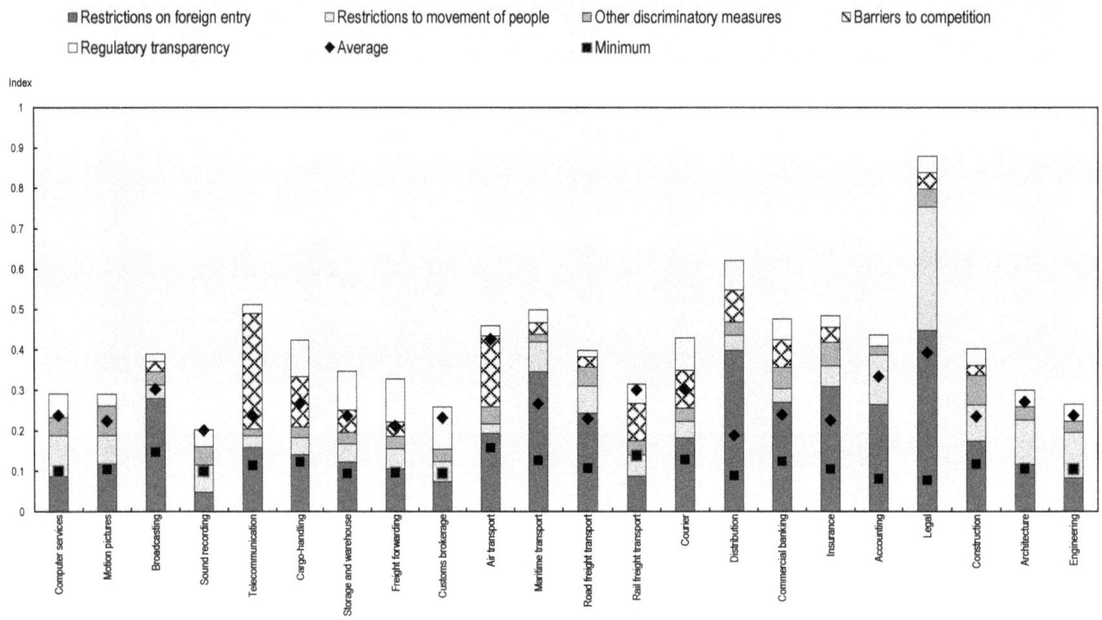

Note: The STRI indices take values between zero and one, one being the most restrictive. They are calculated using the STRI regulatory database which contains information on regulation for the 37 OECD member countries, Brazil, China, Costa Rica, India, Indonesia, Russian Federation and South Africa. "Average" is calculated over 44 countries (37 OECD countries plus 7, including the 5 BRICS); "minimum" is the lowest value by area of regulation among the 44 countries (the least restrictive).
Source: OECD Service Trade Restrictiveness Index (STRI) database.

StatLink https://doi.org/10.1787/888933824192

In May 2016, a Presidential Regulation revised the "Negative Investment List", the list of sectors with limitations to foreign ownership, removing 45 sectors from it (e.g. department stores, internet service providers, etc.). Nonetheless, the regulation still organises industries into six different investment categories:

- Reserved for or subject to partnerships with local MSMEs or co-operatives (Koperasi) through a mutual agreement;
- With limitation to foreign ownership;
- With location requirements;
- With special licensing requirements;
- Reserved 100% to domestic ownership;
- With higher allowed foreign ownership for companies from ASEAN countries.

Therefore, although Indonesia has fully or partially opened a number of new sectors to foreign investment in recent years, many restrictions still apply to a relatively large range of sectors. Furthermore, the existence of six different investment categories is likely to make the system difficult to navigate for some foreign investors, especially smaller ones which have been found to be more likely to engage in contractual relationships with local suppliers (Dimelis and Louri, 2004).

With the aim to stimulate inward FDI, the Indonesia Investment Co-ordinating Board (*Badan Koordinasi Penanaman Modal* – BKPM), has recently developed an "Investment One-Stop" online service to reduce the length of the foreign investment process, i.e. the time between application by foreign investors and response by the government, which in the past could take up to 24 months (OECD, 2016c). Furthermore, in collaboration with the Ministry of Finance, the BKPM can grant tax breaks (i.e. reduction in net income tax of up to 30% of the amount invested, accelerated depreciation and losses which can be carried forward for up to ten years) when the investment meets one of the following criteria: high investment value, export orientation, high absorption of manpower, or high local content.

Moving forward, FDI tax incentives could become more tailored to the development of local suppliers. For example, the government could introduce tax breaks for foreign investors who invest in the upgrading of local suppliers through training, mentoring or staff secondment programmes. Malaysia and Singapore have already used this policy in the ASEAN region with generally positive results (see Box 3.6) (OECD, 2018b).

Box 3.6. Fostering FDI-SME linkages through tax incentives: Malaysia and Singapore

Malaysia and Singapore offer two examples of ASEAN countries that support FDI-SME linkages through tax incentives. In Malaysia, under the Industrial Linkage Programme, investors can claim tax deductions for costs involved in providing support to local suppliers, including training, product development and testing, and factory auditing to ensure the quality of local suppliers. A Global Supplier Programme also offers financial and organisational support to multinational enterprises, if specialists from their foreign affiliates are seconded to local firms (for up to two years).

Singapore's Local Industry Upgrading Programme had a similar design, but it has now been replaced by the Pioneer Certificate Incentive and the Development and Expansion Incentive. These two tax incentives offer corporate tax exemption or a reduced concessionary tax rate on eligible income if the multinational enterprise sets up locally upstream and downstream activities previously conducted internally. The aim of the programme is to foster technology transfers and the scale-up of local businesses.

Source: OECD (2018b), *OECD Investment Policy Reviews: Southeast Asia*, OECD Publishing, Paris. http://www.oecd.org/daf/inv/investment-policy/Southeast-Asia-Investment-Policy-Review-2018.pdf

Conclusions and policy recommendations

Indonesia's business environment offers mixed conditions for the development of SMEs and entrepreneurship. Macroeconomic conditions are generally healthy and include a stable political system and a prudent fiscal policy framework, although Indonesia's tax base is low by international standards and affected by the large informal sector. Employment and education statistics point to skills gaps in the Indonesian labour market, which should be addressed through improved spending on education, including on vocational education and training.

Indonesia has made significant progress in the "ease of doing businesses". However, the business license system should be further streamlined through better co-ordination between the different levels of government involved in the issue of licenses and permits and through moving forward existing plans for the digitalisation of the overall system. Attention also needs to be paid to the design of the national tax system to enlarge the national tax base and to ensure that small business tax preferences do not have the unintended effect of discouraging business growth.

SME access to finance has been boosted by a number of regulatory reforms, not least the obligation for commercial banks to earmark 20% of their business loans for SMEs. When compared to OECD countries the 20% set-aside target appears realistic, although it should be monitored against the credit market conditions of Indonesia to ensure that it does not lead to a rise in non-performing loans and to reduced competition by forcing out of the market types of banks that are traditionally less inclined to working with SMEs. Much is also being done in Indonesia to diversify the sources of finance for SMEs, although results are still relatively modest due to the limited number of domestic SMEs ready to use these sources.

Indonesia also needs to spend more on its national innovation system if its productivity growth objectives are to be met (see chapter 2). Traditional innovation policy instruments such as R&D tax credits are not widely available in Indonesia, hindering the development of business R&D.

Finally, Indonesia has a strong potential to attract FDI, which can benefit domestic SMEs through the development of local supplier linkages. However, such potential is only partially exploited due to regulatory restrictions to FDI and trade in services.

Based on the analysis in this chapter, the following recommendations are put forward to strengthen the business environment for SMEs and entrepreneurship in Indonesia.

Recommendations on the business environment for SMEs and entrepreneurship

- Simplify regulatory protection in the labour market with the aim to reduce the size of the informal sector and to favour the scale-up of existing businesses. Possible pilot measures could include simpler procedures and circumstances for individual dismissals, the replacement of the high severance pay with a form of government-backed unemployment insurance and quarterly payments (instead of monthly payments) of social contributions for small firms (OECD, forthcoming).
- Improve literacy and numeracy skills in the labour force, a precondition for on-the-job training and skills development, by increasing participation rates in secondary and tertiary education and by strengthening efficiency in public spending on education (e.g. through an improvement in teacher competencies).
- Reform the existing VET system by strengthening dialogue and collaboration between private-sector companies and schools in VET provision and by increasing the proportion of teachers who also have an industry, rather than only academic, background.
- Move forward with current plans to integrate (across levels of government) and digitalise the national business license and permit system, drawing inspiration from consolidated international good practices in this field.
- Lower the income threshold (currently set at IDR 4.8 billion) to which the special 0.5% turnover-based business tax rate currently applies to better target micro-enterprises. Consider combining this tax measure with additional support in terms of access to book-keeping assistance and to government support programmes for enterprises that join this tax regime.
- Improve tax collection by investing in the tax administration system, particularly staff, electronic services and databases; using technology to strengthen monitoring and detect non-compliance, including through the use of risk-based assessments for conducting tax audits; and building capacity at the subnational level through training (OECD, forthcoming).
- Monitor the implementation of SME loan set-asides in commercial banks to ensure that they do not result in a rise in non-performing loans and/or in reduced competition in the banking sector.
- Apply international good-practice principles to the work of public and private credit bureaus and consider extending collateral registries to moveable assets (beyond fixed assets) to reduce information asymmetries in credit markets and boost SME lending.
- Strengthen junior equity markets through the scale-up of existing investment readiness programmes for medium-sized firms and growth-oriented SMEs.
- Strengthen R&D tax credits to encourage more R&D spending in SMEs while paying attention to the design and implementation of this policy to ensure that it is not abused, for example carefully considering which eligible costs to include.
- Continue to support the development of broadband infrastructure, making sure that it reaches not only government offices but also private-sector premises, including SMEs.
- Simplify the current FDI negative investment list by reducing the number of investment

categories and opening up more sectors to foreign direct investment.

- Open up more domestic services sectors to international trade with a view to attracting more FDI and improving Indonesia's performance in the OECD Service Trade Restrictiveness Index (STRI).
- Develop stronger FDI-SME relationships, including through tax incentives for multinational companies that invest in the upgrading of local suppliers through training, mentoring or staff secondment.

Notes

[1] Government Regulation No. 46 of 2013

[2] Bank Indonesia uses the SME definition of Law 20/2008 (see chapter 2). Thus, SME loans are loans to companies that have net assets below IDR 10 billion (not including land and buildings) or annual revenues below IDR 50 billion.

[3] The sectors are: upstream metal; oil refinery industry and/or infrastructure, including those under the Public Private Partnership (PPP) scheme; base organic chemicals sourced from oil and gas; machinery; telecommunication and information; sea transportation; processing industry for agriculture, forestry, and fishery products; economic infrastructure other than those under the PPP scheme.

References

Dimelis, S. and H. Louri (2004), "Foreign direct investment and technology spillovers: Which firms really benefit?", *Review of World Economics*, Vol. 140, No. 2, pp. 230-253, http://dx.doi.org/10.1007/BF02663647.

Hornberger, K., J. Battat and P. Kusek (2011), *Attractive FDI: How Much Does Investment Climate Matter?*, Viewpoint: Public Policy for the Private Sector, Note No. 327, World Bank, Washington DC.

ILO (International Labour Office) (2016), *Indonesia Labour Market Outlook*, Geneva.

Indonesia Investment (2017), *Tax System of Indonesia*, https://www.indonesia-investments.com/finance/tax-system/item277?

Kurniawan, E. (2016), *Science, Technology and Innovation Policies – A Progress from Indonesia*, US Mission to ASEAN, https://asean.usmission.gov/innovasean_20170124/

Lembcke, A. and L. Wildernova (forthcoming), "Does FDI benefit incumbent SMEs? FDI spillovers and competition effects at the local level", OECD Publishing.

OBG (Oxford Business Group) (2017), "Indonesia recruits industry leaders to strengthen vocational education", http://www.oxfordbusinessgroup.com/news/indonesia-recruits-industry-leaders-strengthen-vocational-education.

OECD (forthcoming), *OECD Economic Surveys: Indonesia 2018*, OECD Publishing, Paris.

OECD (2018a), *Financing SMEs and Entrepreneurs 2018: An OECD Scoreboard*, OECD Publishing, Paris, http://dx.doi.org/10.1787/fin_sme_ent-2018-en.

OECD (2018b), *OECD Investment Policy Reviews: Southeast Asia*, OECD Publishing, Paris, http://www.oecd.org/investment/oecd-investment-policy-review-southeast-asia.htm.

OECD (2017a), *Education at a Glance 2017: OECD Indicators*, OECD Publishing, Paris, http://dx.doi.org/10.1787/eag-2017-en.

OECD (2017b), *SME and Entrepreneurship Policy in Canada*, OECD Publishing, Paris, https://doi.org/10.1787/9789264273467-en.

OECD (2016a), *OECD Economic Surveys: Indonesia 2016*, OECD Publishing, Paris, http://dx.doi.org/10.1787/eco_surveys-idn-2016-en.

OECD (2016b), *Skills Matter: Further Results from the Survey of Adult Skills*, OECD Skills Studies, OECD Publishing, Paris, http://dx.doi.org/10.1787/9789264258051-en.

OECD (2016c), *OECD Science, Technology and Innovation Outlook 2016*, OECD Publishing, Paris, http://dx.doi.org/10.1787/sti_in_outlook-2016-en.

OECD (2015), *Taxation of SMEs in OECD and G20 Countries*, OECD Tax Policy Studies, No. 23, OECD Publishing, Paris, http://dx.doi.org/10.1787/9789264243507-en.

OECD (2013), *Mexico: Key Issues and Policies, OECD Studies on SMEs and Entrepreneurship,* OECD Publishing, Paris, https://doi.org/10.1787/9789264187030-en.

OECD (2012), *OECD Economic Surveys: Indonesia 2012*, OECD Publishing, Paris, http://dx.doi.org/10.1787/eco_surveys-idn-2012-en.

OECD/ADB (2015), *Education in Indonesia: Rising to the Challenge*, Reviews of National Policies for Education, OECD Publishing, Paris, https://doi.org/10.1787/9789264230750-en.

PWC (Price Waterhouse Cooper) (2017), *Indonesia Corporate Tax Credits and Incentives*, http://taxsummaries.pwc.com/ID/Indonesia-Corporate-Tax-credits-and-incentives.

Rothenberg, A., A. Gaduh, N. Burger, C. Chazali, I. Tjandraningsih, R. Radikun, C. Sutera and S. Weilant (2016), "Rethinking Indonesia's informal sector", *World Development*, Vol. 80, pp. 96-113, 10.1016/J.WORLDDEV.2015.11.005.

World Bank (2017a), *Indonesia Economic Quarterly March 2017: Staying the Course*, World Bank, Indonesia office, Jakarta, http://pubdocs.worldbank.org/en/278631490090358078/IEQ-MAR-2017-ENG.pdf.

World Bank (2017b), *Doing Business 2017*, World Bank, Washington DC, http://www.doingbusiness.org/~/media/WBG/DoingBusiness/Documents/Annual-Reports/English/DB17-Report.pdf.

World Bank (2015), *World Bank Enterprise Survey - Indonesia*, World Bank, Washington DC, http://microdata.worldbank.org/index.php/catalog/2665.

World Bank (2011), *General Principles for Credit Reporting*, World Bank, Washington DC.

4. The strategic framework and delivery system for SME and entrepreneurship policy in Indonesia

This chapter describes and assesses the legal and policy framework underpinning SME and entrepreneurship development in Indonesia, including existing mechanisms for policy formulation and policy implementation. The chapter shows that SME development is a policy priority in Indonesia, enshrined in Law 20/2008 (also known as the MSME Law) and in the National Medium-Term Development Plan that drives Indonesian development policies in each five-year legislation period. As a result, many ministries implement programmes for SMEs and entrepreneurs. This is generally good for the strengthening of domestic SMEs, but also raises co-ordination challenges and, on occasion, results in some programmes lacking sufficient scale. The chapter suggests that the draft of an SME Strategy and the establishment of an SME Inter-Ministerial Council could add clarity to the SME policy framework and strengthen policy co-ordination. Similarly, an SME policy portfolio analysis would help the government to understand whether SME policy spending is balanced and meets government priorities.

The SME and entrepreneurship policy framework

Indonesia's SME policy framework originates from Law 20/2008, also known as the Micro, Small and Medium Enterprise (MSME) Law, and applies to both central and local governments.[1] The aim of the law is to enhance the participation of Indonesian SMEs in economic growth, job creation, poverty reduction and regional development, with a view to making Indonesia an "equitable economic democracy". [2]

The main policy areas covered in Law 20/2008 are: SME financing (e.g. through loan guarantees and soft loans, financial literacy, factoring, venture capital development, etc.); facilities and infrastructure (e.g. industrial parks, science and technology parks, etc.); business information (e.g. use of databanks and business information networks); partnerships (among SMEs and between SMEs and large firms); business licensing (e.g. creation of one-stop services and exemption of micro and small enterprises from licensing); access to markets (e.g. public procurement and the reservation of certain sectors for micro and small enterprises); trade promotion (e.g. participation in fairs); and business development services.

Law 20/2008 also stipulates that the ministry responsible for SMEs within the government has the mandate to co-ordinate the empowerment of SMEs, while government Regulation 17/2013 on the implementation of the MSME Law states that this co-ordination is undertaken with technical ministers, non-ministerial government institutions, governors, regents, mayors, the business sector and civil society organisations.[3] Law 20/2008, therefore, makes it clear that SME policy is not the prerogative of only one ministry in Indonesia, and that it falls within the responsibility of both national and subnational governments.

The National Medium-Term Development Plan 2015-2019, which is prepared by the Ministry of National Development Planning/National Development Planning Agency (BAPPENAS) and is the main development plan document of Indonesia, also places a strong emphasis on SME development, setting important targets with respect to the contribution of SMEs to the national economy (BAPPENAS, 2014a) (see Table 4.1). These targets seem to be reasonable and in line with past growth rates in the SME sector over the period 2006-2013.[4]

Table 4.1. Economic development targets concerning SMEs and co-operatives in the National Medium-Term Development Plan, 2015-2019

Policy objective	Indicator	Target by 2020
Increase the economic contribution of SMEs	SME contribution to GDP	Average annual growth of 6.5%-7.5%
	SME employment	Average annual growth of 4%-5.5%
	SME (non-oil and gas) exports	Average annual growth of 5%-7%
Improve SME competitiveness	SME productivity growth	Average annual growth of 5%-7%
	Increase number of SMEs meeting quality standards	By 50 000
	Increase proportion of SMEs accessing formal financing	To 25% of total formal financing
Increase the number of new enterprises	Increase the number of new innovative entrepreneurs with support from national and regional governments	By 1 million
	Increase the number of small industry enterprises	By 20 000
	Increase the number of medium and large industry enterprises	By 9 000
Improve the institutional functioning and performance of co-operative businesses*	Increase participation of co-operative members in capital	From 52.5% (baseline) to 55%
	Increase the number of co-operatives (growth)	Annual increase of 7.5%-10%
	Increase the sales volume of co-operative businesses (growth)	Annual increase of 15.0%-18%

Source: BAPPENAS (2014a), "Regulation of The President of The Republic of Indonesia Number 2 Year 2015 about the National Middle Term Development Plan 2015–2019: Book I National Development Agenda", (*Peraturan Presiden Republik Indonesia Nomor 2 Tahun 2015 Tentang Rencana Pembangunan Jangka Menengah Nasional* 2015–2019: *Buku I Agenda Pembangunan Nasional*), pp. 133–134.

The National Medium-Term Development Plan 2015-2019 sets out five main priorities for SME development:

- *Improving the quality of human resources*, through workforce skills upgrading and vocational training, integrating entrepreneurship education into school and university curricula, and enhancing business coaching and mentoring to upgrade managerial skills.
- *Enhancing access to finance*, through developing special financial institutions for SMEs and co-operatives, promoting non-bank financial instruments, and improving the financial literacy of small business owners.
- *Increasing the value added of SME products and their international market penetration*, through product quality improvements, the development of trading houses, the improvement of market infrastructures, and support of online platforms.
- *Strengthening partnerships and networks to increase the scale of SMEs and co-operatives*, through support measures for co-operatives and clusters and the facilitation of business networks, including supply-chain linkages.
- *Improving rules and regulations for a better business environment for SMEs*, through simplified business licenses, the harmonisation of sectoral and regional permits and the development of a one-stop shop system where entrepreneurs can receive business-relevant information.

Additional policy priorities emerging from other government documents include: entrepreneurship development, SME digitalisation, enhanced access of SMEs to government contracts and sector development.

Entrepreneurship development: A Draft Law on National Entrepreneurship was prepared by the Ministry of Co-operatives and SMEs, in collaboration with other ministries and national stakeholders, in 2017.[5] The draft law includes chapters on: the preparation of a National Entrepreneurship Masterplan; the establishment of a National Entrepreneurship Task Force; support for social entrepreneurship, innovative entrepreneurship and entrepreneurship education; support for the registration of intellectual property rights; the creation of national entrepreneurship facilities providing business information; easier business licensing for new entrepreneurs; and a list of business sectors reserved for micro and small enterprises.

The 2017 Draft Law on National Entrepreneurship is complementary to the 2008 MSME Law and to the National Mid-Term Development Plan, with some of the items covering the same topics. The most interesting elements of this draft law are its reference to the preparation of a National Entrepreneurship Masterplan and to the creation of an Inter-Ministerial National Entrepreneurship Task Force, which could respectively add clarity to the national SME policy framework and strengthen cross-government policy co-ordination.

SME digitalisation: In the context of Indonesia, this mostly refers to increasing ICT adoption and the use of e-commerce in SMEs. The underlying rationale is that only 9% of the approximately 26 million non-agricultural Indonesian SMEs use e-ecommerce, and that this is a major barrier to their participation in the ASEAN market (Deloitte, 2015). The leading ministry is the Ministry of Communication and Informatics, which co-ordinates the national E-Commerce Roadmap, with support from 19 other ministries and government institutions. The main programmes in the Roadmap include the SME Go Online Programme, the One Million id. Domain Programme, and the 1 000 Digital Start-up Programme (see chapter 5 for more details).

Enhancing SME access to procurement opportunities: This is achieved by state-owned enterprises (SOEs) being increasingly required to integrate manufacturing SMEs into their supply chains, ministries progressively moving to an online tendering system, and foreign investors being subject to local content requirements.

Sector development: This is a cross-cutting feature of Indonesian SME policies that arise from many programmes for SMEs being run by sector-focused ministries such as the Ministry of Industry, the Ministry of Communication and Informatics and the Ministry of Tourism. Sector priorities are also enshrined in the National Medium-Term Development Plan, which outlines policy directions specific to accelerating growth in natural resources sectors (agro-industry, forest and timber products, fisheries, and mining products), manufacturing, tourism, and the creative economy.

Although there are several legal and policy documents in which SMEs feature prominently, Indonesia currently lacks an "SME Strategy" document pulling together the different programmes in a coherent manner. The fragmentation of SME and entrepreneurship policies across many different ministries and the lack of a comprehensive mapping of such policies make it difficult to regularly monitor and evaluate programmes and to hold ministries accountable for the achievement of high-level policy outcomes.

The draft of an SME Strategy document could help clarify policy objectives and policy targets, based on existing and new initiatives. The Strategy would also indicate which ministries and departments are responsible for the implementation of each policy measure and set out key performance indicators to monitor progress and evaluate the outcomes of the Strategy. The preparation of an SME Strategy document would have to be a cross-government effort, reflecting the horizontal nature of SME policy.

The Malaysian experience in developing an SME Masterplan could be a model for Indonesia to craft a more integrated and strategic approach to SME policy (see Box 4.1). Domestically, the experience of Indonesia's E-commerce Roadmap might also prove insightful. In this case, the Indonesian Ministry of Communication and Informatics has worked collectively with 19 other ministries and institutions to pull together elements from four different government ICT plans into an integrated strategy to accelerate the diffusion of e-commerce in Indonesia. A Steering Committee is responsible for co-ordinating and monitoring the implementation of the E-commerce Roadmap. The National Entrepreneurship Masterplan, which is foreseen by the Draft Law on National Entrepreneurship, could provide the basis for the preparation of the future SME Strategy, on the condition that its scope goes beyond business creation and start-ups to encompass existing SMEs as well.

Apart from the lack of a formal SME Strategy document, the current policy framework is in line with the priorities and specifications of the MSME Law, but with a strengthened emphasis on entrepreneurship development. Indeed, the Draft Law on National Entrepreneurship foresees stronger policy initiatives to support innovative and social entrepreneurship. At the same time, given the composition of the Indonesian SME sector, more emphasis could be placed on policy measures that support the scaling-up and formalisation of the myriad of domestic micro-enterprises, encourage the emergence of more high-growth firms, and strengthen more broadly the national innovation ecosystem.

Box 4.1. International inspiring practice: SME Masterplan, Malaysia

Description of the approach

The National SME Development Council (NSDC) is the Malaysian government body responsible for setting the strategic direction and long-term objectives of national SME policies. The first SME Development Blueprint (2006-2008) prepared by the NSDC brought together information from all ministries and agencies on their existing support measures. In 2007, the government established the Small and Medium Enterprise Corporation Malaysia (SME Corp. Malaysia), under the Ministry of International Trade and Industry, as the single government agency tasked with the formulation of SME policies and the co-ordination of the implementation of programmes across all related ministries and agencies. SME Corp. also performs the role of Secretariat to the NSDC, ensuring that the NSDC's decisions are effectively implemented.

The SME Masterplan (2012-2020) was first launched to enhance the contribution of SMEs to achieving Malaysia's Vision 2020. The Masterplan's vision is to "create globally competitive SMEs that enhance wealth creation and contribute to the social well-being of the nation" (NSDC 2012, p.35). The overarching targets of the Masterplan (adjusted in 2015) are to increase SME contribution to GDP from 32% in 2010 to 41% in 2020, employment share from 59% to 65%, and export share from 19% to 23%.

Four strategic goals of the SME Masterplan	Six focus areas to support the strategic goals
• Support a constant stream of new entrants into the market (target of 6% annual increase in the registration of new companies). • Raise labour productivity in SMEs (target of 93% increase by 2020). • Expand the number of high-growth and innovative firms (by 10% per year). • Step up the formalisation of SMEs to promote growth and fair competition (the target is to reduce the size of the informal sector from 31% of gross national income to 15% in 2020).	• Innovation and technology adoption among SMEs. • Human capital and entrepreneurship development among SMEs. • Access of creditworthy SMEs to financing for working capital and investment. • Market access for goods and services produced by SMEs. • Legal and regulatory environment conducive to the formation and growth of SMEs. • Effective infrastructure for the development of SMEs (e.g. construction/upgrading of industrial premises, utilities, incubators, broadband).

The SME Masterplan is translated on an annual basis into the Annual SME Integrated Plan of Action (SMEIPA), which collects information on the policy measures from each of the ministries and agencies in charge of SME programmes. Through the SMEIPA, Malaysian ministries and agencies co-ordinate SME programmes and review their roles and responsibilities pertaining to SME development. Furthermore, the SME Corp.'s website includes a matrix displaying all government programmes by focus area, indicating the sponsoring ministry, the implementing ministry/agency, the objectives, and the sectors and stage of business being targeted (e.g. start-up, growth, exporting). The publication of this information online and in the SMEIPA makes it more easily accessible within the government, as well as by small business owners and private-sector bodies.

SME Corp. also provides updates on the implementation of the SME Masterplan, including how programmes are advancing in relation to quantitative targets and milestones. This enables SME Corp. to co-ordinate the monitoring and evaluation of the SME development programmes implemented by the different ministries and agencies.

Success factors

A national government-wide SME policy has been made possible in Malaysia by the creation of the NSDC and of SME Corp. as the central co-ordinating agency, which has ensured the effective implementation and monitoring of SME policies across various ministries and agencies. The launch of the SME Masterplan and the annual publication of SMEIPA have also enabled the government to enhance collaboration and reduce duplication, to foster greater synergies across ministries and agencies, and to optimise funding allocations. In this context, setting a common SME definition used by all ministries and agencies was also important.

Obstacles and responses

The major obstacle in adopting a cross-government approach to SME policy relates to the formation of a high-level inter-ministerial council with responsibility for crafting and governing the implementation of the national masterplan. This was dealt with in Malaysia by a directive of the Prime Minister requiring the council to be formed and outlining its membership, roles, responsibilities and accountabilities. Moreover, reporting on policy measures requires a commitment from ministries and agencies to co-operate, which is facilitated in Malaysia through the preparation and issuance of the annual SMEIPA publication.

Relevance to Indonesia

The Indonesian government does not currently produce a comprehensive and integrated SME Strategy document. Each ministry/agency proposes and implements its own policy measures, but there is no central platform for the co-ordination of SME policies across ministries and agencies, which can lead to overlaps, inconsistencies and gaps in policy design and implementation. Indonesia could draw inspiration from Malaysia's SME Masterplan to draft a document that comprises all government policy measures affecting and/or supporting SMEs.

Sources for further information

National SME Development Council (NSDC) (2012), *SME Master Plan 2012–2020: Catalysing Growth and Income*, Kuala Lumpur, Malaysia. Online at: http://www.smecorp.gov.my/index.php/en/resources/2015-12-21-11-07-06/sme-masterplan/.
Small and Medium Enterprise Corporation (SME Corp.) (2016), *SME Annual Report 2015/16: Breaking Barriers*, SME Corporation Malaysia, Kuala Lumpur.

Policy co-ordination across ministries and agencies

Improving policy co-ordination is one of the main priorities in Indonesia's SME policy. Although there is a dedicated national ministry for SMEs (i.e. the Ministry of Co-operatives and SMEs), it is not the only ministry responsible for SME policy, nor is it responsible for co-ordinating the work of the other ministries that implement SME programmes based on the guidelines of the National Medium-Term Development Plan.[6]

The purpose of the National Medium-Term Development Plan is to lay out strategic directions and specific measures in economic development policy for a five-year period, reflecting development priorities set out at the Presidential level. Based on the objectives of the Medium-Term Development Plan, each ministry is required to develop a "Strategic Plan" to fulfil its mandate relative to such objectives. Each ministerial "Strategic Plan" includes information on policy objectives, programmes, performance targets, and government funding. Since SME development is a priority of the Medium-Term Development Plan, a large number of ministries include an SME policy component in their individual Strategic Plans.

Additionally, four national Co-ordinating Ministries play an important role in setting national policy directions and co-ordinating the work and budget of technical ministers: the Co-ordinating Ministry for Economic Affairs; the Co-ordinating Ministry for Human Development and Culture; the Co-ordinating Ministry for Political, Legal and Security Affairs; and the Co-ordinating Ministry for Maritime Affairs and Natural Resources.

The Co-ordinating Ministry mostly responsible for SME policy is the Co-ordinating Ministry for Economic Affairs, which also oversees the work of the Ministry of Co-operatives and SMEs. The Co-ordinating Ministry for Economic Affairs prepares "SME policy packages" for each of the relevant technical ministries and agencies, taking into consideration the policy directions of the National Medium-Term Development Plan and budget allocations decided by BAPENNAS and the Ministry of Finance. However, some ministries involved in SME policy fall under the responsibility of a different co-ordinating ministry. For example, the Ministry of Youth and Sports and the Ministry of Research, Technology and Higher Education fall under the remit of the Co-ordinating

Ministry for Human Development and Culture; the Ministry of Tourism and the Creative Economy Agency fall under the responsibility of the Co-ordinating Ministry for Maritime Affairs and Natural Resources; and the Ministry of Communication and Informatics reports to the Co-ordinating Ministry for Political, Legal and Security Affairs. Table 4.2 offers an overview of the main government institutions and programmes in support of new and small businesses in Indonesia.

Table 4.2. An overview of main SME and entrepreneurship programmes in Indonesia

Category	Programmes
Entrepreneurship development and start-up support	**Ministry of Youth and Sports** – offers Youth Entrepreneurship Development Programme; supports more than 60 Youth Entrepreneurship Centres. **Ministry of Co-operatives and SMEs** – operates 51 Integrated Business Services Centres (PLUT-KUMKM Centres); Entrepreneur Incubators Programme; Start-up Incubator Programme; Co-operatives Training Programme. **Ministry of Home Affairs/Ministry of Co-operatives and SMEs** – Free Business License Programme (Presidential Regulation 98/2014 on Licensing for Small and Micro-enterprises). **Ministry of Communication and Informatics** – National 1 000 Digital Start-up Programme; support for start-up ecosystems in ten major cities. **Ministry of Industry** – offers New Industry Entrepreneur Training Programme; Incubator Business Centres; Bali Creative Industry Centre and Incubator (for fashion and crafts sectors). **Creative Economy Agency (BEKRAF)** – delivers entrepreneurship training for SMEs in creative industries. **Ministry of Manpower** – offers Entrepreneurship Development Programme and Start-up Business Advisory Programme. **Ministry of Social Affairs** – provides entrepreneurship training for people with disabilities. **Ministry of Women's Empowerment and Child Protection** – offers enterprise development programmes for women. **Ministry of Agriculture** – delivers Young Agricultural Generation to increase the entrepreneurial skills of young farmers. **Ministry of Education** – delivers Community Entrepreneurship Programme to encourage entrepreneurial spirit and provides entrepreneurship education through educational institutions and training centres. **Financial Services Authority (OJK)** – delivers financial education and entrepreneurship training for SMEs and working-age youth. **Bank Indonesia** – delivers the Entrepreneur Development Programme.
Business management skills	**Ministry of Co-operatives and SMEs** – operates 51 Integrated Business Services Centres (PLUT KUMKM Centres); partners with the Association of Business Development Services of Indonesia (ABDSI) to provide consultants for the PLUT-KUMKM Centres. **Ministry of Industry** – operates more than 40 SMI Technical Services Units (i.e. SMIs are industry-based SMEs); supports 7 400 SMI *sentras* through technical advice (*sentras* are self-help groups of companies in the same or related sectors); delivers management training for industry SMIs. **Ministry of Youth and Sports** – delivers Business Development Programme for Young Entrepreneurs. **Ministry of Agriculture** – delivers SME/Entrepreneurship Support Programme for Farmers. **Ministry of Trade** – delivers Business Meeting (*Temu Usaha*) Coaching Programme to connect SMIs with modern retailers. **Ministry of Manpower** – operates 22 Productivity Centres (productivity training and consulting for SMEs). **Ministry of State-Owned Enterprises** – operates 145 Creative Houses (launched at end of 2016) in 145 districts with target of 514 Creative Houses nationwide. **Bank Indonesia** – delivers SME clinics using coaches/mentors to help SMEs develop their businesses.
Market development support and access	**Ministry of Industry** – provides assistance with product certification and SME participation in exhibitions. **Ministry of Co-operatives and SMEs** – manages the Small and Medium Enterprises and Co-operatives Indonesia Company (SMESCO), an agency to promote SMEs' products; SME Gallery in Jakarta; SME product exhibitions. **Ministry of Co-operatives and SMEs** – operates the Marketing Service Agency for Co-operatives and SMEs (i.e. trading house for products of co-operatives and SMEs); partners with other entities on marketing and design training; promotes the use of e-commerce.

	Ministry of Trade – provides coaching and other forms of internationalisation support for groups of SMEs; operates Export Communication Forum for SMEs, SME Export Training Centre, and Online Trade Facilitation Programme.
	Ministry of Women's Empowerment and Child Protection – organises trade expos for women entrepreneurs.
	Creative Economy Agency (BEKRAF) – provides technical guidance on marketing of SMEs' creative goods and services.
	Ministry of State-Owned Enterprises – operates 145 Creative Houses to help SMEs with online marketing of products, training and coaching. It also manages the Business Aggregator Programme whereby SOEs act as trading houses for smaller companies.
	Telekom Indonesia – supports Digital SME Village Programme to foster online market access for SMEs (in co-operation with PLUT-KUMKM Centres).
	Eximbank – offers a range of export-related financial services. It also delivers the Coaching Programme for New Exporters, i.e. a capacity-building programme for SMEs looking to export.
Innovation and technology upgrading	**Ministry of Research, Technology and Higher Education** – delivers the Techno-Entrepreneurship Programme (in co-operation with 20 universities). It also operates the Business Innovation Centre providing assistance to innovative companies; Technology Business Incubation Centre; Technology Business Incubation Programme; and the Technology-Based Start-up Company Programme.
	Agency for Assessment and Application of Technology – provides technological advice and guidance. It operates the Centre for Development, Education and Training; the Centre for Technological Services; and the Centre for Information Management (launched in 2017) (but not focused specifically on SMEs).
	Ministry of Communication and Informatics – delivers SME Go Online Programme; One Million id. Domain Programme; 1 000 Digital Start-up Programme.
	Indonesia Stock Exchange (IDX) – operates IDX Incubator.
Access to finance	**Bank Indonesia** – requires banks to allocate 20% of total business loans to SMEs; delivers policy for SME access to finance (research, training, information, facilities, co-ordination, regulation).
	Ministry of Finance – supervises the People's Business Credit/*Kredit Usaha Rakyat* (KUR) Programme, in collaboration with Bank Indonesia and national credit guarantee institutes.
	Ministry of Co-operatives and SMEs – supports savings and local co-operatives and is responsible for the Revolving Fund Management Agency (LPDB). It also delivers the Beginner Entrepreneur Programme.
	Ministry of Industry – offers financing through Start-up Capital Assistance Programme and the Restructuring Machinery and Equipment Programme.
	Ministry of Research, Technology and Higher Education – offers seed funding component of the Technology Business Incubator Programme (IDR 50 million per tenant).
	Ministry of Youth and Sports – responsible for Youth Entrepreneurship Capital Institutions.
	Financial Services Authority (OJK) – delivers financial education initiatives for SMEs; operates Centre for Education, Consumer Services and Financial Access for SMEs (PELAKU Centres) located in 35 OJK regional branches.
	Indonesia Eximbank – extends financing to SMEs for export activities; delivers KUR financing for export-oriented SMEs (KURBE Programme).

Note: Some of the programmes fall within more than one category.
Source: OECD elaboration.

The involvement of such a large number of ministries in SME policy illustrates the importance of SMEs within Indonesian economic development policies, but also comes with the risk of policy overlaps and duplications, thus raising a co-ordination challenge within the government.

Reflecting this fragmentation, on occasion, SME programmes in Indonesia lack sufficient scale, reaching only a limited number of recipients nationwide. This points to the importance of policy consolidation through the merge of programmes sharing similar objectives and activities, but which are currently implemented by different ministries. Two cases in point are business incubators and business development services, with many ministries actively engaged in these two areas (see chapters 5 and 7 for further details).

The Ministry of Co-operatives and SMEs seeks to promote policy co-ordination by holding at least one meeting a year with all ministries and agencies delivering SME programmes, as well as four regional meetings a year with provincial governments. Moreover, Memorandums of Understandings (MOUs) are also commonly used to co-ordinate the implementation of cross-cutting SME policy initiatives (see Box 4.2). Moving forward, co-ordination in SME policy would be enhanced by the establishment of an Inter-Ministerial SME and Entrepreneurship Policy Council, following, for example, the model of Spain's State Council on SMEs and Entrepreneurship (Box 4.3).

Box 4.2. The Ministry of Co-operatives and SMEs' MOUs and co-operation agreements to co-ordinate SME policy delivery

Memorandums of Understanding (MOU) are commonly used by the Ministry of Co-operatives and SMEs to co-ordinate the implementation of SME policies and programmes with other government entities. Some of the main MOUs in place are the following:

- MOU with the Ministry of Home Affairs and the Ministry of Trade on the implementation of the Micro and Small Business License (IUMK) Programme.
- MOU with the Ministry of Home Affairs and the National Land Agency on the certification of land rights for micro and small enterprises to enable them to obtain certificates of ownership to use as collaterals.
- MOU with the Ministry of Law and Human Rights to streamline, in terms of cost and time, the application process by co-operatives and SMEs for intellectual property rights (IPR).
- MOU with the Ministry of Women's Empowerment and Child Protection, whereby the Ministry of Co-operatives and SMEs supports the participation of women in co-operatives and facilitates their access to finance and markets.
- Co-operation Agreement with *Bank Rakyat Indonesia* (BRI), which specialises in microcredit, to assist the Integrated Business Services Centres for Co-operatives and SMEs (PLUT-KUMKM Centres) in facilitating access to bank credit.
- MOU with Telkom Indonesia to develop the Digital SME Village Programme within each of the operating PLUT-KUMKM Centres.
- Co-ordination with the Ministry of Religious Affairs, Ministry of Manpower, the Indonesian Association of Islamic Microfinance Institutions and other entities to develop Sharia financing literacy and growth of savings and loans co-operatives focused on Sharia financing principles.

Box 4.3. Inter-Ministerial State Council on SMEs and Entrepreneurship, Spain

Spain's State Council on SMEs and Entrepreneurship is attached to the Ministry of Economy, Industry and Competitiveness and is the government body in charge of planning and co-ordinating all policies and actors affecting the creation, growth and competitiveness of SMEs in Spain.

The Council was created and is regulated by Royal Decree 962/2013. It is responsible for: informing the multi-annual SME support plan; developing recommendations and proposals on priorities, policy actions, regulatory changes and implementation arrangements necessary to improve the competitiveness of Spanish SMEs; co-ordinating the policies undertaken by different government authorities and harmonising eligibility criteria and quality standards in SME support measures; monitoring the application of the EU Small Business Act (SBA); promoting entrepreneurship in education, the media and society at large; and reporting on regulatory projects and regulatory improvements.

The Council is chaired by the Head of the Ministry of Economy, Industry and Competitiveness and consists of 52 members: 13 members representing ministerial departments (e.g. Ministry of Justice, Ministry of Finance and Public Administration, Ministry of Education, Ministry of Agriculture, Ministry of Foreign Affairs and Co-operation, Ministry of Employment and Social Security), 8 representatives of state agencies (e.g. State Society for the Management of Innovation and Tourism Technologies, Centre for Industrial Technology Development, Spanish Patent and Trademark Office, Spain Exports and Investments, Official Credit Institute), one representative from each autonomous region, selected representatives of local governments, representatives of business and labour organisations, and the Council of Chambers of Commerce and Industry.

The plenary body of all Council members meets at least once a year as a consultative and advisory body on all matters affecting SMEs, as outlined above. It also promotes dialogue among public administrations and stakeholders in order to provide greater rationality and efficiency to SME policies and to formulate relevant proposals for action by the public authorities and intermediary agents. The work of the Council is supported by a Standing Committee, which is chaired by the General Directorate of Industry and SMEs and comprises representatives from the Ministry of Economy, Industry and Competitiveness and the Ministry of Energy, Tourism and Digital Agenda. This committee is responsible for co-ordinating and enforcing the work approved by the plenary body. The plenary body is also empowered to establish working groups to carry out specific tasks relative to the work of the Council that require special technical analysis or expertise, as deemed appropriate.

Source: Website of the Council: http://www.ipyme.org/esES/PoliticasMedidasPYME/ConsejoGeneralPYME/Paginas/ConsejoEstatalPYME.aspx/.

The Draft Law on National Entrepreneurship includes provisions for the establishment of a National Entrepreneurship Task Force, which is expected to decide on cross-sectoral policies affecting entrepreneurship. The draft law proposes that the Task Force be headed by the Co-ordinating Ministry for Economic Affairs, with the remaining members to be stipulated by a Presidential decree. The National Entrepreneurship Task Force will be responsible, among others, for drafting the National Entrepreneurship Masterplan, based on inputs from ministries and other parties.

The creation of a National Entrepreneurship Task Force is a positive development which is expected to strengthen policy co-ordination in Indonesia, although it is recommended that the policy focus of the Task Force be extended to measures supporting existing SMEs and not only new entrepreneurs, as the former account for a much larger share of government programmes and funding. One of the first assignments of the Task Force could be the draft of a national SME Strategy document.

The work of this enhanced National Entrepreneurship Task Force could be supported by the creation of an "SME and Entrepreneurship Policy Working Group" comprising the existing SME focal points from other relevant ministries/agencies (e.g. director generals and/or directors of SME programmes). The role of the Policy Working Group would be to organise regular meetings (e.g. between twice and four times a year) to discuss issues affecting SME development, to share information on existing policy measures, and to identify opportunities for co-operation. The establishment of a small technical unit, either at the Co-ordinating Ministry for Economic Affairs or at the Ministry of Co-operatives and SMEs, could serve as the secretariat of the Task Force and the Policy Working Group, preparing the work of both on a regular basis.

Dialogue with the private sector

The government of Indonesia consults with private-sector stakeholders mostly on an ad-hoc basis. The Indonesia Chamber of Commerce and Industry (*Kamar Dagang dan Industri*, KADIN), which is the largest national business association, holds regular meetings with government officials and is invited to comment on draft laws affecting the business sector. The Indonesia Co-operative Council also has a close relationship with the Ministry of Co-operatives and SMEs; for example, the Council was extensively consulted during the process of redrafting the Co-operatives Act. The Indonesia Business Women Association (IWAPI), which represents around 40 000 women entrepreneurs and has more than 250 branches in 32 Indonesian provinces, has a close relationship with both the Ministry of Women's Empowerment and Child Protection and the Ministry of Co-operatives and SMEs, mostly on initiatives to support access to markets for women entrepreneurs. BAPPENAS, too, holds sessions with these associations and other private-sector stakeholders when it develops the National Medium-Term Development Plan.

These consultation practices are noteworthy, although the Indonesian government could also benefit from more formal and regular mechanisms for public-private sector dialogue to incorporate the views of entrepreneurs and small business owners more consistently in the policy-making process. For example, many OECD governments have established SME advisory committees to allow for a more structured public-private dialogue with SME associations. The membership of these committees is generally broad and includes chambers of commerce and industry, small business associations, business support organisations, SME financing institutions, business leaders, and independent experts (OECD and UNIDO, 2004).

The SME policy portfolio

An SME policy portfolio consists of an analysis of the distribution of government spending by main policy area (e.g. access to finance, business development services, export development and internationalisation, etc.) and by main targeted population (e.g. potential entrepreneurs, new start-ups, micro-enterprises, high-growth firms, innovative

SMEs, etc.). This approach involves mapping all SME policy measures across ministries and agencies, categorising each programme by policy area and targeted stage of enterprise development, and attaching budgets to each policy measure. An SME policy portfolio analysis is helpful in understanding whether government spending for SMEs is balanced and reflects government priorities. Together with the monitoring and evaluation of programmes, it can help channel government resources into the measures with the greatest social and economic benefits. A methodology to build an SME policy portfolio is outlined in Box 4.4.

Box 4.4. A portfolio approach to SME and entrepreneurship policy and its evaluation

The basic framework for the policy portfolio approach entails an analysis of all entrepreneurship and SME policies and measures by policy category and by stage of entrepreneurship and SME development. Focusing on the enterprise life cycle allows the development of an integrated set of supports to take "would-be" entrepreneurs from the pre-nascent stage to start-up, expansion and internationalisation, with business support systematically addressing market failures in key areas of each life cycle stage. These might include education and training, advice and counselling, and finance, as common examples. This type of categorisation is important because nascent entrepreneurs are, for example, more likely to need training and advisory/mentoring support, while an established SME is more likely to warrant strategic government interventions to promote productivity, for example through technology upgrading or internationalisation support. Thus, tailored policy responses are required to address the specific needs of each life cycle target. Combined with budget detail, the policy portfolio is also a useful tool for managing the distribution of spending across projects and programmes in line with the government's policy priorities for SME development.

The resulting framework (a matrix of cells reflecting the types of policy measures by entrepreneur/enterprise development stage) can be adapted to the policy context of any particular country.

The first step would be to prepare a description of all relevant policy measures and programmes, with each policy/programme assigned to a main policy focus and a stage, or stages, of enterprise development which the policy measure appears to target. Budget figures would then fill the cells, based on the list of projects and budgets from all programmes (see table below).

Thus, the total for cell 1A would represent the total budget for all programmes and projects which provide education or training to pre-nascent entrepreneurs. The subsequent analysis would help identify where there are relative gaps in programme activity, and where a reallocation of resources could improve the balance of the whole policy portfolio. Nonetheless, a portfolio analysis should recognise that different interventions have different objectives and that, according to government priorities, certain objectives may be worth greater spending than others.

Proposed portfolio framework for SME and entrepreneurship policy intervention

Enterprise segments (A-G) (enterprise development stages)		Policy and programme categories (focus areas) 1 Education training, human capital development	2 Information knowledge	3 Finance	4 Market access/ development	5 Technology innovation	Total by business stage
A	Pre-nascent	1A	2A	3A	4A	5A	
B	Nascent	1B	2B	3B	4B	5B	
C	Start-up	1C	2C	3C	4C	5C	
D	Operation	1D	2D	3D	4D	5D	
E	Growth	1E	2E	3E	4E	5E	
F	International	1F	2F	3F	4F	5F	
G	Adjust exit	1G	2G	3G	4G	5G	

If coupled with an impact evaluation of government programmes, the policy portfolio analysis can help assess not only the distribution of government spending, but also its effectiveness, i.e. whether government spending is more effective in certain policy areas than others. Indeed, the policy portfolio categorisation can facilitate programme evaluation by allowing more precise identification of the target segments (such as start-ups), making the allocation and management of the entire budget portfolio more transparent, and clarifying which market failures policy funding is intended to address.

By way of example, a policy portfolio analysis was undertaken in the framework of the OECD Review of SME policy in Thailand, revealing gaps in the funding of projects related to the pre-nascent, start-up and enterprise growth stages, as two-thirds of the budget expenditure (excluding financial assistance programmes) was directed to existing SMEs. The analysis also revealed that the bulk of the SME Development Agency's total project budget (again excluding finance measures) was spent on education and training, with considerable gaps in the internationalisation stage and in support of technology and innovation. In the Thai context, gaps in addressing the needs of start-ups and the growth-phase of existing SMEs were identified as requiring further attention by the government.

Source: Adapted from OECD (2011), *Thailand: Key Issues and Policies*, OECD Studies on SMEs and Entrepreneurship, http://dx.doi.org/10.1787/9789264121775-en

There are two main factors that hinder a full SME policy portfolio analysis in Indonesia. First, the SME policy budget, which is developed by BAPPENAS and the Ministry of Finance, is distributed across a large number of ministries and agencies, each of which has an "SME Policy Package" prepared by the relevant Co-ordinating Ministry (mostly the Co-ordinating Ministry for Economic Affairs). Second, an effective co-ordinating mechanism to calculate total spending allocation by programme activity is currently missing.

On the whole, however, there are signs that government spending on SMEs has declined for some programmes and increased for others in recent years. For example, spending by the Ministry of Co-operatives and SMEs was IDR 971 billion in 2017, down from IDR 1.49 trillion in 2015 (Ministry of Co-operatives and SMEs, 2017; 2016). By the same token, the Ministry of Industry's budget for the "Small and Medium Industry Growth and Development Programme" was IDR 258 billion in 2017 (i.e. 8.14% of the Ministry's total budget), down from IDR 530 billion in 2016 (i.e. about 13.5% of the Ministry's total budget) (Ministry of Industry, 2017; 2016). On the other hand, the budget of the KUR Programme (i.e. *Kredit Usaha Rakyat*, or People's Business Credit Programme) has been ramped up since a reform in 2015 which added an interest rate subsidy on top of the original loan guarantee of the programme (see chapter 5 for more details).

A preliminary illustration of how the policy portfolio analysis could be approached in Indonesia uses the example of the budget of the Ministry of Co-operatives and SMEs (Table 4.3 and Table 4.4).

Table 4.3. Allocation of the Ministry of Co-operatives and SME budget by activity/ programme, 2016 and 2017

Percentage of total actual expenditure (2016) and percentage of budget (2017)

	2016	2017
1. Management Support Programme and implementation of other technical tasks	18.6%	23.6%
2. Programme for Improving Facilities and Infrastructure	9.4%	9.2%
3. Programme for Increasing Competitiveness of SMEs and Co-operatives	50.1%	53.4%
4. Co-operatives Institutional Strengthening Programme	8.5%	5.6%
5. Micro-Based Business Sustainable Livelihood Enhancement Programme	13.3%	8.2%
Total	100.0%	100.0%

Source: OECD calculations based on budget and expenditure figures outlined in Annual Report 2016 (*Kementerian Koperasi dan Usaha kecil dan Menengah*, 2016) and Quarter II Results 2017 (*Kementerian Koperasi dan Usaha Kecil dan Menengah*, 2017) of the Ministry of Co-operatives and SMEs.

In 2016 and 2017, the Ministry of Co-operatives and SMEs implemented five major programme activities. Of the total budget allocated to the Ministry, slightly less than one-quarter was used in 2017 to cover the administrative costs related to programme management, with the rest spent on programme activities. The largest programme of the Ministry of Co-operatives and SMEs was aimed at increasing the competitiveness of co-operatives and SMEs and absorbed about half of the total budget (53.4%).

A further disaggregation of the 2017 budget of the Ministry of Co-operatives and SMEs reveals that 33.3% of programme funding was allocated to financing measures, 18.8% to support access to markets, 17.3% to human resource development, 16.5% to business development services (BDS) facilities, and 3.7% to improvements in the regulatory environment for co-operatives and SMEs (Table 4.4). Altogether, programme spending by the Ministry of Co-operatives and SMEs appears to be balanced. Similarly to other countries, access to finance, which is a key enabler of investment and cash-flow management, is the main programme area, followed equally by promotion of access to markets, human resource development and BDS.[7]

A full policy portfolio analysis should include the SME and entrepreneurship policy measures of all ministries and agencies. While this is a complex exercise, findings from this analysis would help the government to analyse whether the distribution of resources reflects existing policy priorities and the most pressing development needs of Indonesian SMEs. For example, the analysis may reveal a disproportionate allocation of the total SME support funding to the KUR Programme and underspending on certain other priorities that would create a greater impact on growth-oriented entrepreneurship and SMEs. On the policy side, one of the important questions for the central government is which SMEs to support, i.e. which SMEs will have the most impact, as well as the extent to which SME development in lagging regions should be targeted. Answers to these questions would be facilitated by the policy portfolio analysis.

Table 4.4. Ministry of Co-operatives and SME programmes by type of support, 2017 budget

Type of policy support / Programme	Financing/ access to financing (IDR)	Marketing/ access to markets (IDR)	Human resources capacity development (IDR)	Product development/ production issues (IDR)	BDS (IDR)	Regulatory environment (IDR)	Other (IDR)
Management Support Programme and Implementation						2 985 520 000	
Improving Facilities and Infrastructure					89 079 292 000		
Increasing Competitiveness of SMEs and Co-operatives	197 365 152 000	72 839 182 000	115 000 000 000	2 312 343 000	18 458 313 000		4 263 305 000
Co-operatives Institutional Strengthening	18 342 887 000					22 238 931 000	22 576 029 000
Micro-Based Business Sustainable Livelihood Enhancement	11 819 485 000	54 960 647 000		5 440 940 000	4 546 718 000		
Total (IDR)	**227 527 524 000**	**127 799 829 000**	**117 397 320 000**	**7 753 283 000**	**112 084 323 000**	**25 224 451 000**	**26 839 334 000**
Total (%)	**33.3%**	**18.8%**	**17.3%**	**1.1%**	**16.5%**	**3.7%**	**4.0%**

Note: The totals in Indonesian rupiah are based on the total Ministry of Co-operatives and SMEs budget of IDR 926 052 494 000. Sub-programmes under the Finance heading include management and distribution of the Revolving Fund Management Agency, the Capital Support for Beginner Entrepreneurs, etc. Marketing/access to markets includes promotion and marketing services of the Marketing Services Agency and quality standardisation and product certifications. Human resources capacity development includes the Entrepreneurship Development Programme, the SME Training Centre, etc. Product development/production issues include strengthening of business and production systems in micro-enterprises, production of environment-friendly products, etc. BDS includes programmes to increase the range and quality of the Integrated Business Services Centres and capacity building of business coaches and mentors. Regulatory Environment includes preparation of legislation, rules, and regulations in support of co-operatives and SMEs. Other includes research and policy analysis and general promotional measures to strengthen the co-operative movement.

Source: OECD calculations based on figures from the Quarter II 2017 Results of the Ministry of Co-operatives and SMEs (*Kementerian Koperasi dan Usaha Kecil dan Menengah*, 2017), http://www.depkop.go.id/berita-informasi/data-informasi/laporan-triwulanan/.

Policy delivery arrangements

Policy delivery arrangements refer to how government programmes are effectively implemented on the ground. This section examines the delivery arrangements for SME policy measures in Indonesia, i.e. the organisations involved in delivering policy measures and the different policy implementation arrangements. Detailed descriptions and assessments of SME and entrepreneurship support programmes are presented in chapter 5 and chapter 7 (business development services).

Delivery of SME financing programmes

Governments can deliver SME financing programmes directly through centrally-managed agencies and funds, or use an incentive system to encourage private-sector financial institutions to channel more credit into SMEs. Indonesia uses both approaches in different programmes.

In the case of the large *Kredit Usaha Rakyat* (KUR) Programme, financing to eligible micro and small enterprises is delivered through partner banks (mostly state-owned banks) with a government-backed guarantee, facilitated by state-owned guarantee agencies, and an interest rate subsidy. Funding for the KUR Programme comes from the Ministry of Finance and supervisory functions are within the remit of the Finance and Development Supervisory Agency. The Ministry of Co-operatives and SMEs promotes the programme to potential users and delivers advisory services to KUR clients through the Integrated Business Services Centres for Co-operatives and SMEs (i.e. PLUT-KUMKM Centres). Bank Indonesia monitors the implementation of the programme at partner banks (see chapter 5 for more details).

In other instances, ministries manage finance programmes through an internal agency, with funding still distributed by financial institutions. For example, the Revolving Fund Management Agency at the Ministry of Co-operatives and SMEs disburses its funding through more than 600 microfinance institutions and savings and loan co-operatives (see chapter 5 for more details).

Ministries also directly execute some of their own financing programmes. Examples include the Beginner Entrepreneur Programme at the Ministry of Co-operatives and SMEs; the Capital Assistance for New Entrepreneurs in Industry Programme at the Ministry of Industry; and the Technology Business Incubator Programme at the Ministry of Research, Technology and Higher Education, which offers seed funding to tenant entrepreneurs.

Delivery of business development services

Governments can provide business development services (BDS) directly through government-operated centres staffed with government employees, indirectly through public or private-sector intermediaries, or through a mixed approach in which the government delivers some of the services, usually the initial or the simplest information and advisory services, while drawing on private-sector expertise to provide more sophisticated technical advice.

Three main reasons for governments to partner with third-party organisations in delivering BDS are: the high fixed costs of establishing a widespread regional presence through government-operated centres, whereas partner organisations may already have a consolidated regional presence through their branch offices; leveraging the expertise of private-sector organisations, especially where technical advice is concerned; and fostering the development of a local market for BDS by incentivising demand for such services.

In cases where the government works in partnership with third-party organisations to deliver BDS, the relationship tends to be governed by formal agreements that lay out the nature of the services, delivery standards, performance expectations and reporting requirements. Furthermore, it is common for governments to provide capacity building for staff in intermediary organisations to ensure consistency in the quality of the services being offered.

The government of Indonesia uses a mixed approach in delivering BDS nationwide. It has a network of government-operated centres that are managed by different ministries and that, to varying degrees, draw on the expertise of private-sector organisations, including the Association of Business Development Services Indonesia (ABDSI). In particular:

- The Ministry of Co-operatives and SMEs has recently launched the "Integrated Business Services Centres for Co-operatives and SMEs" (PLUT-KUMKM Centres) to improve the co-ordination and standardisation of BDS across Indonesia. The Ministry collaborates with ABDSI to recruit qualified consultants and advisors from its members for the PLUT-KUMKM Centres. This ensures access to a pool of existing expertise and minimises the negative effects from the possible crowding-out of the private-sector consultancy industry (see chapter 7 for further details).
- The Ministry of Industry operates more than 40 Small Medium Industry (SMI) Technical Services Units to facilitate product development, intellectual property acquisition, design and product marketing in industry-based SMEs through a network of 500 technology extension workers (see chapter 5). In addition, it also manages SMI *Sentras*, which are groups of at least five industry-based SMEs which share similar raw material needs, production processes or end products and which come together to receive technical assistance. The work of the former programme is somewhat similar to that of the PLUT-KUMKM Centres, although it is confined to industry-based SMEs.
- The Ministry of State-Owned Enterprises (SOEs) runs "Creative Houses" to support product development, access to finance and skills development in SMEs through partnerships with large SOEs. The Creative Houses have more recently developed collaborative arrangements with the PLUT-KUMKM Centres to further enhance the integration of BDS delivery in Indonesia.

Delivery of business incubators

Presidential Regulation 27/2013 governs business incubation activity in Indonesia, allowing the central government, universities and the private sector to operate incubators and setting the parameters of business incubators in terms of space, facilities and services. According to the Association of Indonesian Business Incubators (AiBI), there are about 100 active business incubators in Indonesia, i.e. one incubator per 2.61 million people, much less than in the United States (one incubator per 290 000 people) or the United Kingdom (one incubator per 402 000 people).[8] The AiBI additionally reports that three-quarters of the business incubators are university-based, 14 are operated by ministries, state-owned enterprises or regional governments, and the rest belong to the private sector. Government funding for incubators generally includes a portion to cover the management costs of the host organisation, with the rest assigned on a per-tenant basis.

Similarly to what has been observed for BDS, the Ministry of Co-operatives and SMEs has developed a partnership with AiBI to develop an accreditation programme for incubators and a certification programme for incubator managers with the aim of ensuring consistency in the quality of the services offering. Moreover, with the intention of building a comprehensive national system of business incubators, the Ministry of Co-operatives and SMEs and the Co-ordinating Ministry for Economic Affairs have produced a Roadmap for Incubator Development 2014-2029 and issued Regulation 24/2015 on the norms and standards for the activity of business incubators.[9] Regulation 24/2015 states, *inter alia*, that each province/special region will have at least five incubators, and each regency or municipality will have at least one (see chapter 5 for more details).

Delivery of other technology and innovation policy measures

Two Indonesian ministries strongly involved in technology and innovation policy are the Ministry of Research, Technology and Higher Education and the Ministry of Communication and Informatics.

The Ministry of Research, Technology and Higher Education delivers its programmes mostly through the university system. For example, both the Techno-Entrepreneurship Programme and the Technology-Based Start-up Company Programme are based on competitive funding for which universities can apply (see chapter 5).

The Ministry of Communication and Informatics, on the other hand, often works with private-sector companies, such as KIBAR (a technology start-up ecosystem builder) and Telkom Indonesia, to encourage SME digitalisation and the creation of new digital start-ups.

The way forward: an online web portal dedicated to SME programmes

The large number of SME support programmes available in Indonesia and their distribution across many ministries, government agencies and subnational entities make the compelling case for a web portal to collect information on such programmes. In Indonesia, many SMEs are, indeed, unaware of support institutions and programmes and, even when they are aware, find it difficult to obtain information about how to participate (Burger et al., 2015).

A web portal (and mobile phone application) could include information on existing regulations and support programmes from different ministries and levels of government, with information on how to apply, including web links to apply directly from the portal. In addition, it could include simple guidelines on how to start, manage and grow a business through videos, tutorials and case studies. Because of the many institutional actors involved in SME policy, the creation of such a portal should be a collaborative endeavour involving national and subnational governments.

The Draft Law on National Entrepreneurship provides for an entrepreneurship information system that should include data and information on regulations, administrative procedures, initiatives and programmes of both national and local governments. This initiative is a step in the right direction and should include information on programmes not only aimed at new entrepreneurs, but also at existing SMEs.

Web portals of this nature already exist in Southeast Asia, such as Singapore's SME Portal (https://www.smeportal.sg/) and Malaysia's SME Info (http://www.smeinfo.com.my/). The Canadian experience of building a multi-channel information system for entrepreneurs and SMEs through the Canada Business Network is presented in more detail in Box 4.5, as both Canada and Indonesia are federal countries with national and subnational governments actively involved in SME policy. This system consists of a comprehensive web portal (www.canadabusiness.ca) collecting information on federal, provincial and territorial government programmes and services, a call centre, and a network of one-stop shops for walk-in assistance.

Box 4.5. International inspiring practice: The Canada Business Network and web portal

Description of the approach

In 2000, the Canadian federal government, under the "Government Online Programme", funded the development of the online "Business Gateway Initiative", a federal internet portal for business information and services, led by Industry Canada (now called the Department of Innovation, Science and Economic Development, ISED), to create a national website bringing together a number of different federal, provincial and territorial websites. In 2004, the Business Gateway Initiative was combined with the Canada Business Centres (CBC) Programme, the national network of physical business information offices which had been in place since 1992, to form the Canada Business Network (CBN), thus creating a so-called "click, call, and visit" business service nationwide.

Beyond the general "how-to" information that is applicable to anyone seeking guidance and information on planning, starting, growing and closing a business, the CBN portal links visitors to the appropriate sites for information on government programmes and services, both at the federal and provincial levels, as well as to the sites of local community and non-profit organisations, many of which are partners with the government in providing business-related services. The visitors of the web portal can also search for programmes and services specifically tailored to young entrepreneurs, students, women, disabled people, indigenous people, and immigrants. Online services such as interactive business planners and workshop materials are also available. In 2005, the Business Gateway web portal was enhanced through an online service for accessing information on business permit and licensing requirements at the federal, provincial and municipal levels (i.e. the BizPaL service, see Box 3.1 for more details).

The development of the Business Gateway portal received CAD 20 million of federal funding from Fiscal Year 2000-2001 to Fiscal Year 2005-2006. The Canada Business Network receives an average of CAD 15 million a year for ongoing operations, which includes some cost-sharing arrangements with the provincial governments.

The Canada Business National Secretariat (housed in ISED) is responsible for developing policies, standards and practices to promote a consistent national network operation. Activities of the network are co-ordinated nationally through the Canada Business Managing Partner Committee, which is instrumental in developing consensus on major operational decisions and defining new services, products, and standards.

Success factors

In Fiscal Year 2012-2013, the national web portal recorded 2.2 million visits, with another 1.7 million visits to regional sites maintained by the CBCs, compared to 153 000 officer-assisted client interactions in the CBC physical centres. Over time, the website has been the major point of contact for business-related information, including on SME support programmes and services, supplemented with use of the call centres. In fact, some regions have closed their CBC physical centres because the walk-in traffic did not warrant their continuation. Internet users value the single-window design of the web portal to access advice and information and links to government programmes, which they would otherwise find difficult to navigate given the large number of government entities they would have to interface with.

More specifically, the success of the CBN and its web portal is based on the partnership between federal and provincial/territorial governments (co-location, shared services, co-funding), outreach to other regional SME support organisations, training and ongoing professional development of CBC staff, and innovation in the use of information technology platforms to consolidate a variety of business-related government databases.

Obstacles and responses

One of the initial challenges for the federal government was to convince some of the provincial governments to partner with them on the CBC initiative, especially with respect to cost-sharing arrangements. In cases of reticence, the federal government moved ahead and eventually all provincial and territorial governments realised the benefits of co-operation and became partners, agreeing to cost-sharing arrangements for the CBCs and collaboration on the web portal.

Initially created before the emergence of the Internet, the CBN has strived to transform its business model to one that produces information and services that can be easily consumed on the Internet. Efforts have been made to apply user-designed practices for this purpose, including better access to the website from mobile devices, and increased use of video conferencing, webinars and YouTube. According to recent evaluations, the awareness of the CBN and the canadabusiness.ca website could be stronger. ISED and partners are focusing more on online advertising campaigns, including social media, besides promotion at trade shows and events, to raise the awareness of services.

Relevance to Indonesia

In Indonesia, a partnership between central and regional governments could build on the PLUT-KUMKM Centres model to create a national network of business support centres that provide a unified and co-ordinated point of entry for information and services to SMEs and entrepreneurs.

At the same time, it would be beneficial to create an SME web portal displaying the range of financial and non-financial assistance programmes and supporting organisations throughout the country. A web portal (and mobile phone application) would create more transparency regarding government support programmes and the organisations delivering the support, thus helping entrepreneurs seeking information on the available programmes and services. Critical to designing the web portal will be cross-government collaboration, as well as mapping all the financial and non-financial support programmes and services. Funding arrangements will also be required from the national budget.

Sources for further information

Small Business Policy Branch, ISED Canada, Ottawa, Canada and the Canada Business website at: https://canadabusiness.ca/.

AEB (Audit and Evaluation Branch) (2014), *Evaluation of the Canada Business Network*, Final Report, May, Presented to the Departmental Evaluation Committee on 20 May 2014, ISED Canada, Ottawa. https://www.ic.gc.ca/eic/site/ae-ve.nsf/vwapj/CBN_Evaluation_Report_eng.pdf/$file/CBN_Evaluation_Report_eng.pdf/

Conclusions and policy recommendations

The Indonesian SME policy framework reflects the policy directions stipulated in the 2008 MSME Law and in the current National Medium-Term Development Plan (2015-2019). Many ministries are involved in the design and implementation of SME policies in Indonesia which, on occasion, leads to fragmentation in SME support measures.

Co-ordination would be reinforced by the adoption of an SME Strategy document that outlines main priorities, objectives, targets and support measures, as well as by the creation of a high-level Inter-Ministerial SME council in charge of overall policy co-ordination. Proposals for a similar structure are laid out in the Draft Law on National Entrepreneurship, which provides for a National Entrepreneurship Task Force and an Entrepreneurship Masterplan whose mandate should, however, be extended to cover existing SMEs. Enhanced co-ordination would also help the government to undertake a full policy portfolio analysis to clarify whether spending on SMEs reflects the main government priorities and responds to the main challenges facing new and small businesses in Indonesia. A very simple analysis of budget figures, for example, suggests that a large share of government funding is spent on the KUR Programme supporting access to finance for micro and small enterprises, while programmes aimed to encourage productivity growth at the firm level (e.g. R&D and innovation measures) receive less attention.

The Indonesian government often partners with third-party organisations to implement some of its main programmes, especially with regard to programmes upgrading managerial skills, such as BDS and business incubators. Similarly, SME finance is typically disbursed via partner banks and other financial and non-financial institutions. Partnerships with third-party organisations allow the government to leverage existing technical expertise from the private sector and to create a local demand for such expertise. Moving forward, strengthening the presence of facilities such as one-stop centres and incubators will improve access to information, advice and training for entrepreneurs, although the government should continue its efforts to consolidate and simplify the delivery of these services across the country. Moreover, the launch of a web portal and mobile phone application with information on national and subnational regulations and SME support programmes would help entrepreneurs to find relevant information on the web.

Based on this analysis, the following recommendations are put forward to strengthen the strategic framework and delivery arrangements of SME policy in Indonesia.

Recommendations on the strategic framework and delivery system for SME and entrepreneurship policy

- Prepare an SME Strategy document that outlines the main SME policy objectives, targets and support measures and that defines roles and responsibilities of implementing ministries and agencies.
- Establish an Inter-Ministerial State Council on SME Policy to strengthen cross-government co-ordination on SME policy. The newly created National Entrepreneurship Task Force could play this role if its mandate were extended to encompass existing SMEs and not only new entrepreneurs and start-ups.
- Adopt an SME policy portfolio approach to better assess whether spending on SMEs adequately reflects government priorities and the perceived needs of SMEs.
- Explore opportunities for integrating and merging programmes offering similar services with the aim to rationalise the national SME policy offer.
- Create a national web portal and mobile phone application to collate and display business regulations and SME assistance programmes in an accessible way for small business owners and entrepreneurs.

Notes

[1] National recognition of the importance of SMEs to the Indonesian economy gained earlier prominence in 1995 with Law 9/1995 regarding small enterprises. This was subsequently replaced by Law 20/2008.

[2] "Law of the Republic of Indonesia Number 20/2008 Regarding Micro, Small, and Medium Enterprises", promulgated in Jakarta on 4 July 2008, State Gazette of the Republic of Indonesia Year 2008, Number 93, Minister of Law and Human Rights, Republic of Indonesia, Jakarta. http://eng.kppu.go.id/newkppu/wp-content/uploads/2016/11/LAW-OF-THE-REPUBLIC-OF-INDONESIA-20-OF-2008.pdf

[3] "Government Regulation Number 17/2013 on the Implementation of the Law of the Republic of Indonesia Number 20/2008 on Micro, Small, and Medium Enterprises", promulgated on 1 March, State Gazette of The Republic of Indonesia Number 40/2013, Republic of Indonesia, Jakarta. http://bppm.kaboki.go.id/index.php/investasi/regulasi?download=7:pp-no-17-2013/

[4] Over the period 2006-2013, employment in SMEs has grown at an annual average rate of 4%, GDP generated by SMEs at an annual 6%, and SME exports at an annual 8%.

[5] Draft Law on National Entrepreneurship, House of Representatives (*Rancangan Undang-Undang Tentang Kewirausahaan Nasional, Dewan Perwakilan Rakyat*), Republic of Indonesia. http://dpr.go.id/doksileg/proses2/RJ2-20160226-015135-1145.pdf/

[6] The National Medium-Term Development Plan, prepared by BAPPENAS, states that increasing the competitiveness of SMEs and co-operatives requires the synergy and co-operation of many core institutions, involving the Ministry of Industry, the Ministry of Trade, the Ministry of Communication and Informatics, the Ministry of Manpower, the Ministry of Youth and Sports, the Ministry of Tourism, the Ministry of Agriculture, the Ministry of Marine Affairs and Fisheries, the Ministry of Environment and Forestry and the Ministry of Villages, Disadvantaged Regions and

Transmigration (BAPPENAS, 2014b, p. 3-129). In addition, the National Medium-Term Development Plan points to other ministries that have a role in enabling easier access to technology, partnerships, and the application of product quality standards, such as the Ministry of Research, Technology and Higher Education, the Ministry of Law and Human Rights, and the Agency for the Assessment and Application of Technology.

[7] Policy programmes are implemented by the various divisions and agencies of the Ministry of Co-operatives and SMEs according to their areas of responsibility (e.g. Finance Division, Production and Marketing Division, Human Resource Development Division, Institutional Affairs Division, etc.), which cross-cut the policy programmes. The categorisation of policy support by programme area is an estimate for illustrative purposes.

[8] Density figures are approximations based on populations of the United States (323.1 million), the United Kingdom (65.6 million) and Indonesia (261.1 million) and the estimated number of incubators of 1 115 for the United States (National Business Incubator Association reports), 163 for the United Kingdom (not including accelerators as per Bone et al., 2017), and 100 for Indonesia (AiBI data).

[9] A copy of Regulation 24/2015 can be viewed at: http://smecda.com/wp-content/uploads/2015/11/PERMEN-permen-kukm-nomor-24-tahun-2015-tentang-nspk-inkubator.pdf/

References

AEB (Audit and Evaluation Branch) (2014), *Evaluation of the Canada Business Network*, Final Report, presented to the Departmental Evaluation Committee, ISED Canada, Ottawa, https://www.ic.gc.ca/eic/site/ae-ve.nsf/vwapj/CBN_Evaluation_Report_eng.pdf/$file/CBN_Evaluation_Report_eng.pdf/

BAPPENAS (Indonesian Ministry of National Development Planning /National Development Planning Agency) (2014a), *Regulation of The President of The Republic of Indonesia Number 2 Year 2015 about the National Middle Term Development Plan 2015–2019 – Book I: National Development Agenda*", Republic of Indonesia, Jakarta.

BAPPENAS (Indonesian Ministry of National Development Planning /National Development Planning Agency) (2014b), *Attachment Regulation of the President of the Republic of Indonesia Number 2 Year 2015 about the National Medium-Term Development Plan 2015-2019 – Book II: Development Agenda Field*, Republic of Indonesia, Jakarta.

Bone, J., O. Allen, and C. Haley (2017), "Business incubators and accelerators: The national picture", *BEIS Research Paper N.7*, Department for Business, Energy and Industrial Strategy, London, UK.

Burger, N., C. Chazali, A. Gaduh, A. Rothenberg, I. Tjandraningsih and S. Weilant (2015), *Reforming Policies for Small and Medium Enterprises in Indonesia*, RAND Corporation and Tim Nasional Percepatan Penanggulangan Kemiskinan (TNP2K), Jakarta, Indonesia.

Deloitte (2015), *SMEs Powering Indonesia's success: The Connected Archipelago's Growth Engine*, Deloitte Access Economics, Sydney, Australia.

Ministry of Co-operatives and SMEs (2017), *Quarter II Results 2017*, Republic of Indonesia, Jakarta, http://www.depkop.go.id/berita-informasi/data-informasi/laporan-triwulanan.

Ministry of Co-operatives and SMEs (2016), *Building Strong, Creative and Highly Competitive Co-operatives and SMEs: Annual Report 2016*, Republic of Indonesia, Jakarta.

NSDC (National SME Development Council) (2012), *SME Master Plan 2012-2020: Catalysing Growth and Incom*e, Kuala Lumpur, Malaysia. http://www.smecorp.gov.my/index.php/en/resources/2015-12-21-11-07-06/sme-masterplan/.

OECD (2011), *Thailand: Key Issues and Policies*, OECD Studies on SMEs and Entrepreneurship, OECD Publishing, Paris, http://dx.doi.org/10.1787/9789264121775-en.

OECD and UNIDO (United Nations Industrial Development Organisation) (2004), *Effective Policies for Small Business: A Guide for the Policy Review Process and Strategic Plans for Micro, Small and Medium Enterprise Development*, OECD, Paris.

SME Corp. (Small and Medium Enterprise Corporation) (2016), *SME Annual Report 2015/16: Breaking Barriers*, SME Corporation Malaysia, Kuala Lumpur.

5. National programmes for SMEs and entrepreneurship in Indonesia

This chapter describes and assesses national programmes in support of SMEs and entrepreneurship in Indonesia, covering the following thematic policy areas: access to finance, innovation, internationalisation, workforce training, entrepreneurship education, social entrepreneurship, target groups and public procurement. Indonesia's flagship programme for SMEs is the People's Business Credit Programme (Kredit Usaha Rakyat, KUR), a large-scale microcredit instrument that combines a loan guarantee with an interest rate subsidy. Incubators and e-commerce have also been prioritised through the development of two government roadmap strategies, while support to SME internationalisation remains relatively limited in scope and scale, in part because of the limited involvement of Indonesian SMEs in export activity. Both entrepreneurship and management training (outside the education system) and entrepreneurship education (within the education system) are relatively common, while existing initiatives targeting specific population groups such as youth and women are relatively small in scale.

Financing programmes

The Kredit Usaha Rakyat (KUR) Programme

Indonesia's main access to finance programme for SMEs is the *Kredit Usaha Rakyat* (KUR, i.e. People's Business Credit), which has been in place since 2007. The overarching objectives of the KUR Programme are to support the development of the SME sector, to reduce poverty and to reinforce social inclusion by boosting SME lending and improving the relationships between financial institutions and SMEs. KUR is effectively a large-scale microcredit programme providing cheaper credit than otherwise available at market conditions to micro and small enterprises.

The government supervises the KUR Programme through its Finance and Development Supervisory Agency (*Badan Pengawasan Keuangan dan Pembangunan*, BPKP), while Bank Indonesia oversees the banks that participate in the programme. Given its targeting of poverty alleviation, KUR also falls under the responsibility of the National Task Force for the Acceleration of Poverty Reduction (*Tim Nasional Percepatan Penanggualangan Kemiskinan*, TNP2K), which has the mandate to co-ordinate poverty alleviation policies in Indonesia.

Between 2007 and 2014, KUR was a standard government guarantee scheme offering bank loan guarantees to small businesses. The government injected capital into the two state-owned credit guarantee companies (CGCs), i.e. JAMKRINDO and ASKRINDO, and additionally covered the cost of the guarantee fee that participating banks had to pay into the two CGCs. The two CGCs covered between 70% and 80% of the losses incurred by commercial banks on their KUR-backed loans.

By 2014, KUR was already a large programme, backing loans worth IDR 49.5 trillion, i.e. about 14% of total outstanding SME loans (World Bank, 2017). The rate of KUR non-performing loans (NPLs) was only 3.3%, which is low by international standards. While there is no comprehensive information on the default rates of national credit guarantee programmes, Indonesia's KUR default rate was lower than that of similar programmes in Spain (6.1% before the global recession and 12.7% in its immediate aftermath) or Italy, where 50% of local mutual guarantee societies were registering net losses in the wake of the 2008 global recession (OECD, 2012).

The KUR Programme was significantly overhauled in 2015, when the loan guarantee was matched by an interest rate subsidy to allow banks to lend to SMEs at a capped interest rate. The interest rate subsidy also covers the guarantee fees which banks pay into to the two CGCs. In doing so, the main objective of KUR has moved from favouring access to finance for SMEs to promoting cheaper finance for SMEs.

In the revamped version of KUR, there are two main types of loans: micro loans (up to IDR 25 million) and retail loans (between IDR 25 million and IDR 500 million). The interest rate was capped at 12% for both types of loan in 2015 and 9% from 2016 onwards. The interest rate subsidy corresponds to 10% of the loan amount in the case of micro loans and 4.5% in the case of retail loans. Contrary to the previous version of the scheme where the guarantee coverage ratio was set by the government, this is now directly agreed by banks and CGCs, which should in principle lead to better market-based outcomes. As many as 34 banks are enrolled in the programme, although state-owned *Bank Rakyat Indonesia* (BRI, i.e. People's Bank of Indonesia) plays a major role in the scheme, and almost all economic sectors are eligible to apply. Table 5.1 provides a snapshot of the major features of KUR before and after the 2015 reform.

Table 5.1. Main features of old and new KUR Programme

Aspect	KUR 2007-2014	KUR 2015 onwards
Loan size	Micro: up to IDR 20 million Retail: between IDR 20 million and IDR 500 million Linkage*: up to IDR 2 billion	Micro: up to IDR 25 million Retail: between IDR 25 million and IDR 500 million
Maximum effective interest rate p.a.	Micro: 22% Retail: 14%	Micro and Retail: 12% (2015); 9% (2016 onwards)
Maximum tenor	Investment capital: 5 years Working capital: 3 years	Investment capital: 5 years Working capital: 4 years
Partial risk guarantee (Wholesale credit guarantee)	Pari-passu 70% (in general) and 80% (for priority sectors: agriculture, fishery and small industries) on the outstanding amount and accrued interest for banks with NPL below 5%.	Negotiated and agreed between banks and CGCs
CGCs fees	Stipulated by the government and paid to CGCs 2007-2009: 1.50% 2010-2014: 3.25% of guaranteed part of the loan	Negotiated and agreed between banks and CGCs, reportedly facilitated by KUR Committee, upfront 1.5% of loan amount
Interest rate subsidy	None	Micro: 10% of loan amount paid as subsidy Retail: 4.5% of loan amount paid as subsidy Interest rate subsidy calculated based on monthly outstanding amount and paid directly to the bank. Includes credit guarantee fee

Note: *Linkage loans are loans to rural banks and other microfinance institutions that implemented KUR micro loans. In the 2015 version, KUR investment loans can be up to seven years if the loan is prolonged, the nominal amount is increased or restructured.

Source: World Bank (2017), *Indonesia Economic Quarterly March 2017: Staying the Course*, World Bank, Indonesia Office, Jakarta.

Topping up the credit guarantee with an interest rate subsidy has had major budgetary implications for the KUR Programme. A report by the World Bank estimates that, once direct and indirect subsidies are calculated, the subsidy component of the KUR Programme amounted to IDR 12.3 trillion (USD 885.6 million) in 2016, ten times more than under the previous version of the programme and 14.8% of the KUR outstanding loan balance (World Bank, 2017). For 2017, the government allocated an additional IDR 9.5 trillion (about USD 684 million) to pay for the KUR interest rate subsidy.

As a result, the KUR Programme has taken a new prominence in the landscape of Indonesian SME policies. In 2016, the total loan amount disbursed through KUR was IDR 94.4 trillion, i.e. 22% of total outstanding micro and retail loans (IDR 423 million), with the 2017 target set even higher at IDR 110 trillion (World Bank, 2017). In addition, in 2016, of the total KUR loans of IDR 94.4 trillion, IDR 65.6 trillion (69%) was disbursed through micro loans, IDR 28.7 trillion via retail loans (30%), and IDR 177 billion (less than 1%) via migrant worker loans.

Table 5.2 points to a strong variation in the distribution of KUR loans among provinces: in 2016 Bali had the highest KUR loan value per person (IDR 941 000) and North Kalimantan had the lowest (IDR 99 000). The coefficient of variation across all provinces, a statistical measure of variance from the mean, is 37%. When Bali and North Kalimantan are not taken into consideration because they have opposed extreme values the coefficient of variation drops to 29%.

Table 5.2. Allocation of KUR loans by province, 2016

Million rupiahs (Total budget)

Province	Total Budget	Micro	Retail	Migrant Worker	Population	IDR/person
Central Java	16 927 926	12 609 506	4 256 736	61 684	32 382 657	522 747
East Java	14 580 166	10 248 000	4 301 202	30 964	37 476 757	389 046
West Java	11 958 824	8 887 475	3 037 134	34 216	43 053 732	277 765
South Sulawesi	5 118 398	3 868 119	1 249 936	342	8 034 776	637 031
North Sumatera	4 355 200	2 733 072	1 618 406	3 722	12 982 204	335 475
Bali	3 662 489	2 422 856	1 239 417	216	3 890 757	941 331
DKI Jakarta	3 595 885	1 734 667	1 843 945	17 274	9 607 787	374 268
Lampung	2 772 964	2 180 513	582 310	10 141	7 608 405	364 461
West Sumatera	2,385,905	1 699 794	685 777	334	5 133 989	464 727
DI Yogyakarta	2 323 578	1 543 793	779 573	212	3 457 491	672 042
Riau	2 141 982	1 402 828	738 965	188	5 538 367	386 753
West Nusa Tenggara	2 127 924	1 553 562	571 625	2 737	4 500 212	472 850
Banten	2 030 833	1 189 973	833 312	7 548	10 632 166	191 008
South Sumatera	1 943 729	1 163 377	774 278	6 074	7 450 394	260 889
South Kalimantan	1 764 441	1 256 895	507 476	70	3 626 616	486 525
East Kalimantan	1 696 418	1 171 636	524 641	141	3 026 060	560 603
Nangroe Aceh Darussalam	1 561 970	1 093 947	467 983	40	4 494 410	347 536
Jambi	1 445 172	768 651	676 486	35	3 092 265	467 351
East Nusa Tenggara	1 340 155	925 422	414 623	110	4 683 827	286 124
Southeast Sulawesi	1 207 911	810 722	397 148	41	2 232 586	541 037
Central Kalimantan	1 159 617	789 958	369 619	40	2 212 089	524 218
West Kalimantan	1 138 735	651 268	487 367	100	4 395 983	259 040
Central Sulawesi	1 089 539	745 537	343 920	82	2 635 009	413 486
Papua	1 025 548	574 874	450 623	50	2 833 381	361 952
North Sulawesi	893 456	615 249	278 163	43	2 270 596	393 490
Bengkulu	877 049	708 652	168 288	109	1 715 518	511 244
Kepulauan Bangka Belitung	644 688	318 808	325 880	-	1 223 296	527 009
Gorontalo	524 424	452 409	71 945	70	1 040 164	504 174
West Sulawesi	512 792	373 501	139 248	43	1 158 651	442 577
Maluku	451 126	338 121	112 991	14	1 533 506	294 179
West Papua	439 147	291 041	148 106	-	760 422	577 504
Kepulauan Riau	412 421	295 855	116 501	65	1 679 163	245 611
North Maluku	236 905	154 350	82 545	10	1 038 087	228 213
North Kalimantan	61 708	5 832	55 876	-	622 350	99 153
TOTAL	94 409 025	65 580 263	28 652 045	176 715		

Source: Ministry of Co-operatives and SMEs and Ministry of Home Affairs. Population is from the 2010 census.

StatLink https://doi.org/10.1787/888933824211

The new KUR Programme has some important features. First, together with other policies, such as the 20% SME loan target which banks operating in Indonesia must comply with (see chapter 3), KUR is succeeding in meeting its objective of increasing credit flows to micro and small enterprises. While micro and small business loans amounted to IDR 353.5 trillion in 2014 (14% of which backed by KUR), they totalled up to IDR 423 trillion in 2016 (22% of which backed by KUR), an increase of 16.5% over only two years. By fostering stronger credit flows to small businesses, KUR is favouring social inclusion through economic activity. Second, in situations where credit markets function imperfectly, interest rate subsidies can bring capital allocation closer to second-best efficiency to the extent that they can help divert capital from less productive to more productive activities (Morduch, 1999).[1] Third, it is often argued that interest rate subsidies can become a regressive form of policy support because the larger the size of the loan, the larger the government subsidy. In the case of KUR, this risk is mitigated by the presence of different interest rates and different loan ceilings applied to micro and retail loans.

However, the KUR Programme is also faced with some challenges. The tenfold increase in its costs casts doubts on its long-term sustainability and large opportunity cost, to the extent that some of the resources committed to this single programme mostly favouring social inclusion could be spent on other policy initiatives that support business innovation, global market integration and, more broadly, productivity growth. A smaller version of KUR could become more tailored, targeting certain groups that the government would consider worthier of support than others, for example first-time borrowers, firms in lagging regions, or firms in sectors where there are greater constraints in access to finance. Policy targeting, however, is likely to require better mapping of the features and performance of SMEs across Indonesia.

A World Bank analysis of KUR raises three additional concerns. First, KUR may crowd out commercial micro-lenders, whose market rates hover between 20% and 26%. Second, in economic literature, sustainable access to finance has often been considered more important for small businesses than cheap finance through lower interest rates. Third, the current KUR interest rates are not financially self-sustainable, to the extent that they only cover a fraction of the costs incurred by lending institutions in the microfinance market (World Bank, 2017). Research from Indonesia additionally suggests that there might be cases of misuse in the new KUR Programme, with as much as 10% of total credit being disbursed to borrowers holding invalid data, and that the rate of KUR-backed NPLs is on the rise, albeit still below 10% (Mardanugraha and Yappi, 2017).

The Revolving Fund Management Agency (LPDB)

The Revolving Fund Management Agency (*Lembaga Pengelola Dana Bergulir*, LPDB) was established in 2006 at the Ministry of Co-operatives and SMEs to support the financing of co-operatives and SMEs. The LPDB Agency offers three types of credit: credit to co-operatives (both savings and credit co-operatives and industry co-operatives), direct loans to SMEs and credit to financial intermediaries. The LPDB loans to savings and credit co-operatives have a maturity of 3-5 years and a sliding annual interest rate of 7%. Savings and credit co-operatives are subsequently allowed to lend LPDB resources to micro and small businesses at a capped interest rate of 18%. Direct loans to SMEs have, on the other hand, longer maturities (5-10 years) and a lower fixed interest rate of 4.5%. The minimum amount that co-operatives and SMEs can borrow is respectively IDR 150 million and IDR 250 million.

The LPDB Agency has a central office in Jakarta and five local branch offices. The central office deals with the evaluation and approval of the loans, whereas the branch offices monitor the performance of loans at the local level. This is slightly counterintuitive, since small business loans are more likely to be approved and loan prices are more likely to reflect the actual risk when lenders and borrowers are located close to each other (Agarwal and Hauswald, 2010; Degryse and Ongena, 2005; Petersen and Rajan, 2002). Geographical distance makes it difficult for lenders to collect soft information on borrowers (e.g. on the current performance of the business and its future growth prospect), thus negatively impacting on the allocative efficiency of loans.

Unsurprisingly, as of 2017, over 65% of the LPDP loans had been disbursed to firms on the central island of Java (which includes Jakarta), whereas in the case of KUR Java had only absorbed 50% of the overall loans.

Table 5.3. Annual distribution of LDPB funds

Number of businesses and Million rupiahs

	2012		2013		2014		2015		2016	
Type of business	Number of businesses	Approved credit	Number of businesses	Approved credit	Number of businesses	Approved credit	Number of businesses	Approved credit	Number of businesses	Approved credit
Co-operative	583	984 654	742	1 374 997	314	855 686	150	271 103	100	245 225
SMEs										
Direct	5	17 400	26	43 005	252	109 430	33	54 789	29	64 265
Indirect	30	358 750	26	263 500	166	976 300	103	1 554 890	18	695 964
Total	618	1 360 804	794	1 681 502	732	1 941 416	286	1 880 782	147	1 005 454

Note: Credit in million rupiahs. For SMEs, direct indicates a loan directly from LPDB and indirect indicates a loan via a bank or non-bank financial institution.
Source: LPDP Agency.

StatLink https://doi.org/10.1787/888933824230

Moving forward, a decentralised loan approval process could help address the two issues of whether loans are effectively given to the most creditworthy firms and whether they are priced correctly. Nonetheless, the national government would still have to closely monitor the approval and disbursal process to ensure that this is not captured by local vested interests.

The Beginner Entrepreneur Programme

The Beginner Entrepreneur Programme (BEP) (*Program Bantuan Dana Bagi Pengembangan Wirausaha Pemula*) of the Ministry of Co-operatives and SMEs, offers small-sized soft loans (up to IDR 25 million) to new entrepreneurs who are less than 45 years old and who hold an entrepreneurship training certificate from the Ministry of Co-operatives and SMEs dated within two years. Successful applicants report on the use of the funds within three months of the disbursement, and then twice a year for the following two years. This programme complements other (larger) youth entrepreneurship programmes, such as the Young Entrepreneur Programme (*Wirausaha Muda Pemula*, WMP) and the Youth Entrepreneurship Centres (*Sentra Kewirausahaan Pemuda*, SKP), which are operated by the Ministry of Youth and Sports and target entrepreneurs under the age of 30 (see section on programmes for specific target groups).

In its first two years of existence, the BEP was implemented through the intermediation of co-operatives, while since 2013 its loans have been disbursed directly to the entrepreneurs. The BEP has seen strong fluctuations between 2011 and 2017 with respect to the overall budget allocation, maximum loan size and number of recipients (see Table 5.4). However, the programme has never been particularly large, reaching a maximum of 3 560 entrepreneurs across the whole of Indonesia in 2015. In 2017, for example, the BEP targeted 1 200 new entrepreneurs divided into three groups: underdeveloped and border areas (200), special economic zones (300), and entrepreneurs from low-income groups (700).

Table 5.4. Beginner Entrepreneur Programme's budget and loans, 2011-2017

Million rupiahs

Year	Budget allocation	Loan maximum	Target number of recipients	Final number of recipients
2011	7 000	25	280 (co-operatives)	280
2012	6 400	25	256 (co-operatives)	277
2013	54 000	25	2 160	3 860
2014	51 500	25	2 060	4 326
2015	89 000	25	3 560	8 362
2016	8 000	20	400	N/A
2017	15 600	13	1 200	602

Note: Budget allocation and loan maximum in million rupiahs. Target numbers were set for co-operatives who then distributed the allocated capital to their members during 2011-2012 and for individual recipients during 2013-2017.
Source: Ministry of Co-operatives and SMEs.

StatLink https://doi.org/10.1787/888933824249

Similarly to other Indonesian SME finance programmes, the main objective of PBE is social inclusion rather than business growth, with 75% of participants in 2017 coming from low-income groups or underdeveloped regions. The programme, however, lacks the scale to make a significant impact on its final objective, with an annual average of less than 2 000 entrepreneurs reached nationwide between 2013 and 2017. Budget allocations have also fluctuated significantly during the lifespan of the programme, whereas larger and more regular budget allocations could help lift the profile and visibility of this policy initiative. The way the programme is implemented could also be streamlined, for example reducing the number of times entrepreneurs need to report annually on the use of programme resources. Finally, consideration could be given to better integrating, if not merging, the activities of the PBE with those of other youth entrepreneurship programmes at the Ministry of Youth and Sport.

On the whole, Indonesian enterprise debt-finance programmes are quite traditional, consisting of grants, credit guarantees and interest rate subsidies. In the future, Indonesia could also experiment with small-scale new approaches such as so-called commercial credit circuits (CCCs) where participating businesses exchange services and goods for credits to be spent within the network. The spread of CCCs is still relatively limited, but participating companies have access to complementary payment and credit mechanisms that can help overcome credit constraints. This instrument also has other positive externalities such as enhancing local business linkages and supporting the formalisation of economic transactions. An example of a similar initiative is Sardex, a business-to-business CCC launched in 2010 in the Italian region of Sardinia (see Box 5.1).

Box 5.1. Commercial credit circuits: The example of Sardex, Italy

Within the business-to-business Commercial Credit Circuit *Sardex*, businesses can exchange goods and services without using an official currency. When a firm provides a service or a product it receives a credit, calculated with a rating-based system, and such credit can be spent on goods and services from other companies in the system. At the end of every year, companies pay the debit that they did not cover in EUR, based on the fixed conversion rate of one *Sardex* to one euro. To sum up, companies guarantee each other's credit, without a central authority and through multilateral trust relationships. Credits traded on *Sardex* exceeded EUR 65 million in 2016, and the innovative company behind it reported an annual turnover of EUR 2.8 million in the same year.

Capital market programmes

The Indonesian equity market is still at an early stage of development. Indonesia's market capitalisation was 48.8% of national GDP in 2016, compared with 106.5% in Thailand, 153% in Malaysia and 269% in Singapore (Rowter, 2016). State-owned enterprises (SOEs) account for 26% of the Indonesian stock market capitalisation.

The Indonesia Stock Exchange (IDX) currently has a main board and a development board. The main board's listing requirements include at least three years of operations and audited financial statements and net tangible assets of at least IDR 100 billion. Listing requirements for the development board are less strict: one year of operations, one year of audited financial statements and net tangible assets of at least IDR 5 billion. While the formal listing requirements for the development board are similar to other small and mid-cap markets in Southeast Asia (e.g. Malaysia's ACE and Thailand's MAI), Indonesia's development board has not been able to attract many SMEs, i.e. only seven between 2003 and 2015, making liquidity and trading on this stock exchange very thin.

More recently, it has been proposed that IDX establishes a third board, the acceleration board, to offer an opportunity for more SMEs to attract equity finance. Listing requirements on the acceleration board would be lower than for the development board; for example, an annual fixed listing fee would replace listing fees proportional to market capitalisation. The proposed acceleration board is a step in the right direction to develop alternative sources of finance for SMEs although, given the limited success of the development board, a reasonable alternative would be to simplify the listing requirements of this second board rather than creating a third board.

On the whole, thin trading and high market concentration suggests that the Indonesian capital market is not yet fully developed, pointing to the importance of strengthening the equity market infrastructure through research, brokering, ratings and the creation of specialised SME banks (OECD, 2015). Furthermore, the government should consider scaling up existing investment readiness programmes, such as the IDX Incubator Programme, where companies learn management skills, reporting requirements and corporate governance standards to become ready for an initial public offering (IPO).

Venture Capital initiatives

In 2017, there were 61 licensed venture capital (VC) firms in Indonesia, broadly divided into four groups: conglomerate/family-backed, foreign/regional, local/joint ventures, and corporate-backed (OJK, 2017). Aggregate investments by Indonesian VC firms are still modest. Out of USD 90 billion of VC investments in Asia in 2016, only USD 6.8 billion (7.5%) were made in Southeast Asia, with Indonesia accounting for 19% of this last figure (USD 1.29 billion) (Google/AT Kearney, 2017). The two sectors receiving most VC investment are e-commerce (58% of the total between 2012 and 2017) and transport (38%). A more recent trend has also been the growing influence of investments from China in the Indonesian VC market (Google/AT Kearney, 2017).

Indonesia does not have a large programme to nurture the development of the domestic VC industry, whereas governments have often played a proactive role in the early development of this industry. For example, in the 1990s the Israeli government established the YOZMA Fund, based on the principle of co-investment by the government and the private sector. The fund was successful in kick-starting the Israeli VC industry and was later privatised (see Box 5.2). The Indonesian government could follow a similar approach, playing a more active role in the promotion of the national VC industry.

Finally, as noted earlier, there is no well-functioning stock-exchange that provides a suitable exit for VC investors in high-growth firms. The proposed acceleration board, or a reform of the existing development board, could help attract more SMEs onto the stock market and encourage more private-equity investors to invest in unlisted SMEs.

Box 5.2. International inspiring practice: YOZMA Venture Capital Funds, Israel

Description of the approach

Israel's venture capital (VC) industry started in the early 1980s with the creation of Athena Venture Partners. A few other VC companies were established in the following years, but it was not until 1993 that the industry took off thanks to the YOZMA government initiative. YOZMA's main principle was to attract venture capital and the related investment skills from abroad by matching private investments with government funding. Foreign investors primarily came from the United States. A second YOZMA initiative was launched in 1995 with support from well-established American, European and Israeli VC funds. In 2000, the private sector accounted for most VC investments, and the government decided to drastically reduce its presence in this industry.

The YOZMA Fund's investments were primarily in life science, biotechnology and ICT and were typically in the range of USD 1-6 million. The YOZMA Fund developed a close relationship with national leading academic institutions and incubators, which led to some of the most successful start-ups in the programme. A YOZMA CEO club was also created to involve senior executives and founders in the initiative's activities.

The YOZMA Programme has played a key role in kick-starting Israel's VC industry. VC-backed companies rose from 100 to 8 000 between 1991 and 2000, and by 1999 Israel ranked second worldwide in terms of private-equity investments as a share of GDP.

Success factors

The Israeli VC industry has been successfully built on the combination of public and private funding. However, over time, when private investment started to gather steam, the government progressively moved out of the industry. As a result, over the course of the 1990s, the government position in the industry passed from 50% of total investments to nearly zero.

The success of the YOZMA Programme also depended on its ability to attract foreign capital and know-how. The presence of an initial government investment and the option to buy out the government share after five years offered sufficient incentive for leading international VC firms to invest in Israeli start-ups.

Finally, the presence of equity guarantees for foreign investors, the nurturing of linkages between domestic start-ups and foreign business angels, and the preparation of Israeli VC-backed firms for IPOs in foreign stock exchanges were additional contributing factors to the success of the initiative.

Obstacles and responses

The main difficulty for the YOZMA Fund was to find investors ready to invest in a relatively small and isolated market such as Israel. Israeli residents could not meet the financing needs of the country's growing high-tech industry on their own, so the government looked abroad, mostly to the United States, to attract qualified investors. As mentioned above, the option to buy out government shares five years after the original investment together with the prospect of launching IPOs of successful start-ups on foreign stock exchanges, notably NASDAQ, proved pivotal to drawing foreign investors into the nascent Israeli VC market.

Relevance to Indonesia

The Indonesian VC industry is still underdeveloped. An approach similar to that of the YOZMA Fund could allow the government to grow its domestic VC industry, for example by attracting back Indonesian capital investments from Singapore.

Sources for further information

Note: The statistical data for Israel are supplied by and under the responsibility of the relevant Israeli authorities. The use of such data by the OECD is without prejudice to the status of the Golan Heights, East Jerusalem and Israeli settlements in the West Bank under the terms of international law.

Baygan, G. (2003), "Venture Capital Policies in Israel", *OECD Science, Technology and Industry Working Papers*, 2003/03, OECD Publishing, Paris.

(OECD, 2016a), *SME and Entrepreneurship Policy in Israel 2016,* OECD Studies on SMEs and Entrepreneurship, OECD Publishing, Paris, https://doi.org/10.1787/9789264262324-en.

Innovation programmes

Business incubation activity

Based on information from the Association of Indonesian Business Incubators (AiBI), there were about 100 active business incubators in Indonesia in 2017. About three-quarters were in universities; 14 were directly operated by government ministries, state-owned enterprises, or regional governments; and ten were private-sector initiatives. Ten incubators focused on ICT, eight on agriculture and food, and two on creative industries. The others adopted a mixed approach where different industries were represented at the same time.

As noted in Chapter 4, the density of incubators in Indonesia is low, i.e. one incubator per 2.61 million people, compared with one per 290 000 people in the United States and one per 402 000 people in the United Kingdom. Indonesia also does not rate very favourably compared to other ASEAN countries, with only one technology-based incubator per 4.17 million people, compared with one per 42 333 people in Singapore, one per 250 545 people in Malaysia and one per 774 157 people in Thailand.[2]

Business incubation activity in Indonesia has not, therefore, yet reached its full development potential. Most incubators are small in scale (with 3-5 tenant enterprises) and do not offer a full range of services in the form of consulting, technical support, mentoring/coaching, and linkages to sources of finance for tenant enterprises. Outcomes are also less than optimal, with only 10-20% of incubated enterprises estimated to graduate and move on to become sustainable companies. AiBI estimates that only about 1 300 companies have graduated from Indonesian incubators in total.

On the whole, Indonesian incubators suffer from limitations in operational facilities, lack of seed capital, and an insufficient number of experts to advise and mentor entrepreneurs. Other issues, as reported by the Working Group on Business Incubator Development formed in 2015 following a Decree of the Co-ordinating Minister for Economic Affairs (184/2015), include the lack of homogenous national standard procedures governing the establishment and operations of incubators and the lack of an integrated online national database collecting information on the performance of incubator tenants.

The national business incubation policy: The Roadmap for Incubator Development 2014–2029

The main national policy to remedy these problems has been the "Roadmap for Incubator Development 2014–2029", which was prepared by the Co-ordinating Ministry for Economic Affairs and the Ministry of Co-operatives and SMEs in collaboration with a large number of other ministries. Through this Roadmap, the Co-ordinating Ministry for Economic Affairs assigns responsibility for incubator development to as many as 17 different ministries and agencies, including the Ministry of Research, Technology and Higher Education, the Ministry of Communication and Informatics, the Creative Economy Agency and the Ministry of Manpower and Transmigration.

The Roadmap responds to Presidential Regulation 27/2013 on the Development of Business Incubators, which mandates every sector (including universities and the private sector) to increase the number of business incubators in order to support technology transfer and improve innovation in SMEs. This regulation additionally provides that every province and special region shall have at least five incubators and each regency/municipality shall have at least one. Business incubators are also a policy mechanism advocated by the ASEAN Strategic Action Plan for SME Development, especially technology incubators.

The overarching aim of the Roadmap is to improve the quantity and quality of business incubators in Indonesia by mapping and benchmarking existing incubators; establishing criteria for the activity of the incubators and for building the capacity of their managers, staff and tenant enterprises; and clarifying funding arrangements and policy co-ordination mechanisms. The Roadmap for Business Incubator Development, for example, stipulates the services to be provided by incubators, which include: i) training, seminars and workshops on entrepreneurship and business planning during a pre-incubation phase; ii) training on business management, one-to-one counselling, and business development assistance during the incubation phase; iii) networking opportunities with business partners outside the incubator during the incubation and post-incubation phases.

The Roadmap for Incubator Development sets ambitious plans for increasing the number of business incubators in Indonesia, from a base of about 75 in 2014 to 732 by the end of 2029 (Table 5.5). These growth projections are based on the assumption that the concurrent government strategy to develop 100 Science and Technology parks unfolds as planned (see next subsection). The experience of Brazil's national business incubation system can offer useful insights for Indonesia on how to succeed in increasing the number and improving the standards of business incubators nationwide (Box 5.3).

Table 5.5. Cumulative targets for expansion of business incubators

	2015–2019	2020–2024	2025–2029
Number of incubators (cumulative and new)	391 (316 new)	586 (195 new)	732 (146 new)
Number of tenants (e.g. start-ups) (cumulative)	43 792	65 520	81 800
Number of graduated SMEs (cumulative from the incubators)	4 379	9 828	16 366
Jobs created by graduated SMEs	65 585	196 560	337 320
Estimated turnover of graduated SMEs (cumulative)	IDR 16.41 trillion	IDR 61.425 trillion	IDR 122.746 trillion

Source: Report of the Working Group on the Business Incubator Development Roadmap.

Box 5.3. International inspiring practice: National business incubation system, Brazil

Description of the approach

Brazil had 369 business incubators in 2016 (40% of which were technology-based), i.e. one incubator per 560 000 inhabitants compared with one incubator per 2.61 million inhabitants in Indonesia. The development of a relatively dense incubator system has been enabled in Brazil by federal government funding from the National Programme for Supporting Business Incubators and Technology Parks. The programme is implemented by the Brazilian Innovation Agency (ANPROTEC) in collaboration with a wide coalition of government partners. The work is guided by an Advisory Council co-ordinated by the Ministry of Science, Technology, Innovation, and Communication.

The programme offers competitive grants worth up to 80% of the project cost (in the range of BRL 4-8 million) to public administrations, universities and non-profit bodies responding to calls for proposals. While the services offered include physical space and hard infrastructure, there is greater emphasis on soft services, including counselling, advice, financial and legal consulting, networking, and access to finance. Selection criteria vary by incubator, but product and/or service innovativeness is always one of the main requirements for start-ups to join the programme. The average incubation period is three years, but tenant companies can continue to receive advisory and follow-on support for up to one year after leaving the incubator.

Success factors

Several factors are associated with the success of the Brazilian incubator system:

- Government support. Incubators are funded by the government's national incubator programme and a multitude of other federal, state and local government organisations.
- Private-sector involvement. Private-sector business associations are often active partners in the consortia that establish the incubators. In some cases, business associations assist incubators by offering mentoring and in-kind support to the incubated enterprises. In other cases, large corporations have invested in incubators.
- University involvement. Universities play a pivotal role. They typically support incubators by providing buildings, staff and the use of laboratories. Technical universities and technological research institutes also constitute the knowledge base for many incubators, supplying technical skills and innovations and offering access to professional networks.
- Innovative models. The business incubation landscape in Brazil is now varied and complex with a plethora of incubation models, some of which have evolved in response to specific local needs. For example, the social model of incubation has developed in response to the need for job creation in poor areas.

Obstacles and responses

One challenge was the initial lack of visibility of business incubator services among potential entrepreneurs and newly-established enterprises. The government responded by increasing efforts to provide more information on such services and to improve the co-ordination of support services available for SMEs and entrepreneurs at national and local levels.

An additional obstacle was the lack of a national monitoring and evaluation system to assess the performance of incubators. A Tracking System for Business Incubators and Technological Parks (SAPI) was developed in response, which includes indicators on the performance of graduated companies, the financial sustainability of incubators, and the volume and quality of services provided.

Finally, ANPROTEC soon realised that the skills of the incubator managers and staff members needed to be strengthened and made more homogenous across the country. This led to an initiative to reinforce the training and professional development of incubator managers and staff, i.e. the Reference Centre for Support of New Ventures (CERNE), which is detailed in the following case study (see Box 5.4).

Relevance to Indonesia

The experience of Brazil points out the importance of the involvement of the private sector and university for the successful implementation of a national business incubation strategy. It also shows that successful incubators will mostly support technology-based entrepreneurship, but that variants focussing on social entrepreneurship can also perform well. Finally, a systematic evaluation of business incubation activity is pivotal to identifying problems and improving the performance of business incubators.

Sources for further information

Technology Development and Innovation Secretariat, Ministry of Science, Technology, Innovation, and Communications, Brasilia (www.mctic.gov.br)
National Association of Entities Promoting Innovative Enterprises (ANPROTEC), Brasilia (http://anprotec.org.br/)
Tracking System for Business Incubators and Technological Parks (SAPI), www.portalinovacao.mct.gov.br/sapi

The budget required to implement the Roadmap for the first five years (2015–2019) was set at IDR 8.9 trillion, 33% of which for the establishment and growth of business incubators; 15% for capacity building of managers and coaching staff; 49% for seed funding, product development and advanced growth of the incubating start-ups; and the remaining 3% for the co-ordination of the overall strategy. However, as of end 2017, the financing of the Roadmap had not yet been approved by BAPPENAS.

As part of the Roadmap, the Ministry of Co-operatives and SMEs has also worked with AiBI to develop operating standards for business incubators and a certification programme for business incubator managers, both of which are expected to be launched by end-2018. The experience of Brazil in this area – developing competency standards for business incubators and their managers – can again offer some useful insights for Indonesia as the national government seeks to develop a national incubator certification programme (see Box 5.4).

Box 5.4. Competency improvement programme for business incubators in Brazil

A key mechanism of the Brazilian government to reinforce the training and professional development of incubator managers and staff was the creation, by the Brazilian Micro and Small Business Support Service (SEBRAE) and the National Association of Entities Promoting Innovative Enterprises (ANPROTEC), of the Reference Centre for Support of New Ventures (CERNE). CERNE is a platform intended to enhance the ability of incubators to generate successful innovative ventures and thereby reduce the level of variability in the performance of incubators.

CERNE offers training for incubator managers and consultants on generating innovative companies, managing and organising an incubator, and building and managing professional networks. SEBRAE invested about USD 28 million in the support of the CERNE project.

The CERNE training allows incubators to be certified at four levels of maturity:

- CERNE 1 – concerns the processes and practices related to the creation of an incubator and the selection of incubating enterprises.
- CERNE 2 – focuses on how to effectively manage an incubator organisation, including strategic management, service provision and the monitoring of results and impacts.
- CERNE 3 – deals with building a strategic network of partners to expand the incubator's operations and strengthening its role in the local entrepreneurial ecosystem.
- CERNE 4 – concentrates on building the capability of the incubator to support the further growth and internationalisation of the incubated enterprises.

Source: Garcia et al. (2015), "Reference Center for Business Incubation: A proposal for a New Model of Operation"; CERNE website at: http://anprotec.org.br/cerne/menu/english/

Moving forward, as suggested by AiBI, it would be useful to categorise business incubators by their level of development and capacity. For example, AiBI currently estimates that over 60% of the incubators are at a very early stage of development, while only 10% are mature. Such categorisation would allow targeted capacity building to strengthen the performance of early-stage incubators, for example through appropriate training for their managers and mentors, assistance with the implementation of operational standards, and the expansion of the services offering.

The creation of a monitoring and evaluation framework to follow the activity of the incubators and the performance of tenant enterprises would also help maximise the impact of existing and future business incubators. An evaluation of business incubation activity should consider inputs (e.g. financing, management resources, project proposals), processes (e.g. provision of incubator space and other services), and outputs (e.g. performance of tenant enterprises in terms of survival rate, growth and profits) (European Commission, 2002; OECD, 2010).

Finally, incubators need to be better integrated into the wider national and local entrepreneurial ecosystem. Possible ways to do this are through a credit programme aimed at start-ups that graduate from national incubators or next-step support in the form of an accelerator and/or access to sources of equity investment.

Selected examples of business incubator programmes

As noted earlier, 17 different ministries and government entities are involved in the support of business incubators in Indonesia. This section outlines some of the most relevant incubator programmes.

The Ministry of Research, Technology and Higher Education's Technology and Business Incubator Programme

The Ministry of Research, Technology and Higher Education operates a Technology and Business Incubator Programme (*Inkubasi Bisnis Teknologi*, IBT) that offers funding, training and mentoring assistance to technology-based ventures. Incubators propose potential tenants to the Ministry, which carries out a first screening of the proposals. Shortlisted candidates are subsequently invited to Jakarta, together with the sponsor incubator, to defend their business idea before a panel of industry and government representatives. Selected candidates are finally invited to join the programme which lasts one year. Thanks to the careful selection process, IBT is one of the most prestigious incubator programmes in Indonesia.

The basic participation requirement is that the start-up belongs to a technology-based sector. Potential industries include ICT, food, defence, transportation, health medicine, raw materials, and maritime. Start-ups must have been operational for no more than three years and their products must have passed the development stage and be ready for commercialisation. In 2017, there were about 37 incubators enrolled in the programme, each with about 3-5 tenant companies. For each accepted start-up, 75% of the funding goes to the tenant company and the remaining 25% to the incubator to cover its operational costs.

The Ministry of Research, Technology and Higher Education's University Incubator Programme

The Ministry of Research, Technology and Higher Education also operates a programme which specifically encourages university-based start-ups (*Perusahaan Pemula Berbasis Teknologi – Perguran Tinggi*, PPBT-PT). The selection process, operational rules, funding arrangements and time spent in the incubator are similar to those of the IBT Programme. However, in the case of PPBT-PT, applicant start-ups should be run by students, alumni or lecturers who intend to commercialise the outcome of the research they have conducted at the university hosting the incubator. In 2017, 32 incubators and about 115 tenant companies were enrolled in the PPBT-PT Programme.

University-linked incubators exist in many OECD countries. However, empirical evidence suggests that restricting university-based incubators to students, alumni and lecturers from the same university has often proven an unnecessary restraint that has undermined the performance of these incubators (Åstebro and Bazzazian, 2011). Thus, it has been suggested that university-based incubators should instead be open to applicants from outside the university and be run in partnership with other professional business support organisations for the local entrepreneurial ecosystem.

The Indonesia Stock Exchange's Incubator Programme

The Indonesia Stock Exchange (IDX) has recently established an incubator programme (March 2017) in collaboration with selected state-owned enterprises, such as *Bank Mandiri* which leases the office space and *Telekomunikasi Indonesia* which provides the internet infrastructure. Twenty-five companies were accepted in the first round of the programme, mostly from digital and technology-related fields. One of the main selection criteria is that the company has already reached the stage of prototype development. Business ideas with a strong social impact, such as new approaches to microfinance, are also sought after. One of the goals of the programme is that at least one of the supported companies reaches the IPO stage on the national stock exchange. The programme provides office space, mentorship, training in accounting and corporate law, as well as opportunities to meet with investors. It runs over six months, after which participants are introduced to potential investors. If the current programme in Jakarta proves successful, IDX aims to launch similar incubators in other major cities such as Bandung, Medan, and Surabaya.

One unique aspect of the IDX incubator is its organisational proximity to the stock exchange. As a consequence, IDX could consider moving this programme towards an accelerator format that targets established growth-oriented SMEs, for these are typically closer to the IPO stage than newly-created companies.

Science and technology parks

The Indonesian government announced in 2015 the creation of 100 national science and technology parks by 2019, an objective which is included in the National Medium-Term Development Plan, 2015-2019. Out of the 100 science and technology parks, 4 will be national science and technology parks, 19 will be science parks and 77 will be technology parks. Five ministries and agencies have been assigned the responsibility of working towards this target: the Ministry of Agriculture, the Ministry of Ocean and Fisheries, the Agency for the Assessment and Application of Technology (*Badan Pengkajian Penerapan Teknologi*, BPPT), the Indonesian Institute of Sciences (*Lembaga Ilmu Pengetahuan Indonesia*, LIPI), and the National Nuclear Energy Agency (*Badan Tenaga Nuklir Nasional*, BATAN).

The establishment of 100 science and technology parks over a short period of time is ambitious, but also comes with some challenges. First, the parks need to be set up correctly and qualified managers need to be recruited, calling for the development of operational standards for the parks and certification programmes for managers and staff similar to those being rolled out for incubators and business development services (BDS) organisations (see chapter 7). Second, there are some regional conditions that have to be met for science and technology parks to succeed, such as a good base of innovative firms and knowledge-based workers, relatively strong local and domestic markets, and the possibility for hosted companies to tap into domestic or global supply chains through the presence of large companies (European Commission, 2013). As a result, the location of the park is key for its success and needs to be driven by economic rather than political considerations. Third, leadership also affects a science/technology park's chances of success, notably the ability of the park's manager to set out a clear development strategy and to nourish strong relationships with the public sector and the local community. Finally, tax incentives (e.g. free use of land) can bolster the growth of science and technology parks especially at an early stage of development.

Business digitalisation programmes

The involvement of Indonesian SMEs in digitalisation is still relatively limited. According to a report by Deloitte (2015), only around 18% of Indonesian SMEs are currently engaged in e-commerce through the use of a website or social media, while only 9% adopt more sophisticated e-commerce strategies. The same study argues that greater use of digital technologies (including social media, broadband, and e-commerce) could help SMEs increase their revenues by up to 80%, become 17 times more likely to introduce innovations, and become one-and-a-half times more likely to create jobs. Considering that Indonesia had 105 million internet users in 2017, projected to increase to 140 million by 2022, digitalisation strategies can help domestic SMEs to scale up and become more productive.

Indonesia's main business digitalisation policy is the E-Commerce Roadmap. This strategy is led by the Ministry of Communication and Informatics and is implemented in collaboration with 19 other ministries and government institutions. The Roadmap includes financial and non-financial support for e-commerce adoption and digital start-ups, as well as tax incentives and simplification of tax requirements for technology-based companies. The Roadmap also intends to strengthen consumer protection through improved cyber-security and information campaigns on the opportunities and risks linked to e-commerce.

As part of the E-Commerce Roadmap, the Ministry of Communication and Informatics implements three main programmes: the SME Go Online Programme, the One Million id. Domain Programme, and the 1 000 Digital Start-up Programme. The SME Go Online Programme is tailored to small companies with no or very limited experience of selling online. The objective is to help 1 million small companies to take their business online via one of the established online platforms available in the country (e.g. www.blanja.com). In doing so, the Indonesian government also supports the development of so-called "marketplaces", i.e. online platforms typically managed by large national or multinational companies where small businesses can offer their products and services against the payment of a fee (usually a percentage of the revenues raised through the marketplace).

The One Million id. Domain Programme, where id. refers to Indonesia's internet country code, can be considered a follow-up intervention to the SME Go Online Programme: the next step once small businesses have learned the basics of doing business online. In this case, the goal is to provide, by 2019, 1 million SMEs with a domain, website content and a fully-functioning website that can support online sales. Government support lasts for one year, after which participants are expected to cover the costs of keeping their presence online.

Finally, the 1 000 Digital Start-up Programme is implemented in collaboration with KIBAR, a technology start-up ecosystem builder. The objective is to generate 1 000 high-quality digital start-ups for a total valuation of USD 10 billion by 2020. Funding covers the cost of pre-incubation workshops, boot-camps and hackathons, three months in the incubator (which works more like an accelerator), and post-start-up follow-up. The whole programme takes one year to complete and, as of 2017, was active in ten cities.

On the whole, the three main SME digitalisation programmes of the Ministry of Communication and Informatics appear to complement each other. The first two help SMEs expand their markets by building an online presence, while the third encourages digital start-ups. An important challenge with the existing programmes, however, is not only to meet the ambitious targets that they have set, but also to make such achievements sustainable after the phase-out of government support. For example, the new one million id. domains, even if they are effectively created, will need to remain active and generate business revenues if the corresponding programme is to have an impact on the economy.

More generally, while most digitalisation policies in Indonesia have focused on the adoption of e-commerce, the integration of ICT at the firm level has also been an important dimension of business digitalisation policies in many OECD and non-OECD countries. The experience of Mexico (see Box 5.5) in supporting the adoption of digital technologies in small firms in low value-added sectors (e.g. retail trade and low-tech manufacturing) could offer insights for the development of a similar programme in Indonesia.

Box 5.5. International inspiring practice: "Tablet" Programme to upgrade digital and managerial skills in micro-enterprises, Mexico

Description of the approach

Mexico's so-called "Tablet" Programme was launched in 2015 and mostly targets micro-enterprises employing less than ten employees in traditional sectors of the economy such as retail trade (e.g. convenience stores and restaurants) and low value-added manufacturing (e.g. blacksmith's forges). Most participant companies (around 60%) operate in the retail trade industry. The programme is innovative in the way it combines basic training in key management principles with the provision of new ICT solutions.

The programme offers six hours of basic management training on six thematic areas considered very relevant to the survival and growth of small businesses: inventory management, accounting, customer relationships, micro-market analysis, repayment capability, and the use of management software. Moreover, participants receive a tablet which includes the management software, another software programme that enables customers to pay utility bills and phone charges, and a swipe-card extension to the tablet that allows customers to pay by credit/debit card.

Success factors

The programme has been innovative in the way it has combined digitalisation support and managerial skills upgrading in small traditional enterprises. The main goal is to help these companies to increase their market shares by accepting payments by credit card and the payment of utility bills in their shops. Another goal is to bring these enterprises, which are very often operating in the informal economy, within the purview of the government.

Another feature of Mexico's Tablet Programme has been its ability to reach a relatively large number of participants, about 70 000 over two years, thanks to a sizeable budget (MXN 660 billion, i.e. about USD 34 million) and low per-enterprise implementation costs.

Obstacles and responses

The main challenges facing the Tablet Programme have been high intermediation costs and possible displacement effects. The programme is managed through a government call for tender for which only regional governments (state-level governments in the case of Mexico), national business associations and chambers of commerce can apply. However, the activities of the programme are delivered by training organisations further contracted by the chambers, business associations and regional governments. The existence of two layers of intermediation between the Ministry and the final beneficiaries of the policy (i.e. the small businesses), implies high overhead costs that reduce the amount of spending on programme activities.

With respect to displacement effects, these are more likely to materialise in mature sectors of the economy, such as retail trade and low value-added manufacturing, where public support for companies offering services/products similar to others can lead to the exit of the non-supported companies. In the case of the Mexican programme, however, the competitors of the main recipients were chain stores, making the risk of displacement effects less compelling.

Relevance to Indonesia

An overwhelming majority of businesses in Indonesia are micro-enterprises, many of which operate in low value-added sectors of the economy. A key challenge for these companies is to grow and possibly graduate to the small-firm size. A programme that aims to improve productivity in the companies through a change in process efficiency and technology is, therefore, particularly relevant for the current development stage of the Indonesian economy.

Sources for further information

OECD (2016b), "Increasing Productivity in Small Traditional Enterprises: Programmes for Upgrading Management Skills and Practices", unpublished report.

Promoting the creative economy

The creative economy ranks high on the political agenda of Indonesia, as shown by the creation of the Creative Economy Agency (*Badan Ekonomi Kreatif*, BEKRAF) in 2015 and the recent inclusion of the cities of Bandung and Pekalongan in the UNESCO Creative Cities Network in the field of design and arts. The Indonesian government expects the creative economy to contribute 12% of national GDP, 10% of national export, and 13% of national employment by 2019.[3]

The overarching objective of BEKRAF is to nourish a national ecosystem for the creative economy by focusing on six strategic areas (research, education, and development; access to capital; infrastructure; marketing; facilitation and regulation of IPR; and inter-institutional and regional relations) and working on 16 different sectors (applications and game development; architecture; interior design; visual communication design; product design; fashion; film, animation, and video; photography; crafts; culinary arts; music; publishing; advertising; performing arts; fine arts; and television and radio). BEKRAF executes its own set of programmes, which however do not provide funding, and liaises with government and financial institutions which can support the growth of the creative economy through funding.

The establishment of BEKRAF should expand the scope and improve the performance of Indonesia's cultural and creative industries, although it has been suggested that its start was slow because of limited funding.[4] Moving forward, BEKRAF could receive a stronger mandate to better co-ordinate government support to the creative economy, including by helping other government institutions to channel more resources into the support of this sector.

Internationalisation programmes

Indonesia encourages business internationalisation through a range of both traditional and innovative programmes (e.g. the Business Aggregator Programme). The most active government institutions in this field are Indonesia Eximbank, the Ministry of Trade, the Indonesia Investment Co-ordinating Board (i.e. *Badan Koordinasi Penanaman Modal*, BKPM) and the Co-ordinating Ministry for Economic Affairs.

Export financing and export training

Indonesia Eximbank is the national export financing agency responsible for export credit, export guarantees and export insurance services. In addition to export financing services, it also manages training programmes for export-oriented companies. Indonesia Eximbank is a relatively new institution, having only been established in September 2009 under the responsibility of the Ministry of Finance. As of 2017, it had eight offices and approximately 480 employees across the country.

Indonesia Eximbank's main programme is the Export Oriented People's Business Credit Programme (i.e. *Kredit Usaha Rakyat Beriorientasi Ekspor*, KURBE), a spin-off of the KUR Programme. KURBE offers working-capital financing (for up to three years) and investment financing (for up to five years) at a subsidised interest rate of 9%. The loan ceilings change depending on the size of the company and the purpose of the credit: IDR 5 billion for micro-enterprises; IDR 15 billion for small enterprises (IDR 25 billion for investment loans); IDR 25 billion for medium-sized enterprises (IDR 50 billion for investment loans). KURBE's main target is suppliers of large national employers, making the programme mostly intended for sizeable companies. Indeed, in 2016, of the IDR 88.53 trillion disbursed by KURBE, only 12% was used by SMEs, although on a year-on-year basis KURBE's SME financing increased by 45% between 2015 and 2016.[5]

Indonesia Eximbank also administers the Coaching Programme for New Exporters, a training programme where potential exporters can learn about export regulations, customs procedures, packaging, foreign language skills and online marketing. In 2017, this programme was delivered to ten sets of companies.

The Ministry of Trade, through the Directorate General for National Export Development, organises its support to business internationalisation activity under four pillars: i) market information (e.g. market intelligence and market briefs); ii) product development (e.g. compliance with standards, design development and packaging); iii) export information (e.g. trade fairs and trade mission); iv) export training (both short-term courses of a week and long-term courses of up to three months). Some of the Ministry of Trade's training programmes are tailored to local industry needs, which are identified through policy dialogue with local governments and local business associations.

The Ministry of Trade also has trade representatives (i.e. trade attachés) in 34 embassies which help Indonesian companies market their products and find local partners in the countries in which they operate. Indonesian firms looking to utilise this support first need to register at the Ministry of Trade and undergo a quality control of their products, after which the Ministry decides whether to grant its support. In addition, recognising the potential of the recent creation of the ASEAN Economic Community (AEC) for the

Indonesian business sector, the Ministry of Trade established an AEC Centre in Jakarta in September 2015. The centre offers advocacy and business counselling to prepare Indonesian companies for increased market integration at the ASEAN regional level.

The programmes of Indonesia Eximbank and the Ministry of Trade offer traditional financing and training solutions to exporting companies and companies seeking to enter international markets. Some of these programmes are also well tied-in with local industry needs, tailoring national support to local sectors with the strongest export potential. However, Indonesia's export support measures are somewhat small in scale and are mostly aimed at large businesses, which is in part the consequence of the low involvement of domestic SMEs in exports (see chapter 2). Additional budgetary resources could help these programmes, especially training measures, reach more SMEs. Furthermore, KURBE's target could be expanded beyond existing suppliers of large companies to include SMEs which are currently Tier-II suppliers or which, based on pre-existing product quality requirements, would be considered ready to become Tier-I suppliers.

The SOE-led Business Aggregator Programme

An innovative approach to SME internationalisation has recently been trialled by the Co-ordinating Ministry for Economic Affairs through the Business Aggregator Programme. The underlying rationale is that small enterprises find it difficult to understand the regulations and handle the documentation required to be able to export. State-owned enterprises (SOEs) can step in to help SMEs by acting as "trading houses" offering a range of support services for SMEs ready to export. In addition to boosting the exports of small producers, especially to other ASEAN countries, an objective of this initiative is to nourish business linkages between rural SMEs and urban SOEs and thereby favour regional and rural development.

The Business Aggregator Programme is an innovative measure whose success is likely to depend on the extent to which the SOEs will be able to play the leading role that the programme assigns to them. Furthermore, while the programme makes it easier for SMEs to export by passing the related "regulatory burden" on to large SOEs, it prevents SMEs from getting first-hand exposure in the export process.

One complementary strategy could, therefore, consist in a new policy initiative to help SMEs obtain direct exposure to export, for example through the financial support of export-oriented consortia or co-operatives. This policy would also have a significant multiplier effect by reaching a larger number of SMEs than would be possible through targeting individual companies. Box 5.6 provides an example of a similar policy from Italy.

Box 5.6. International inspiring practice: Export consortia, Italy

Description of the approach

The Italian government has a long tradition of supporting export consortia. Export consortia are voluntary alliances of SMEs, which come together to improve their export performance through the development of common activities. Each consortium needs to have at least eight SMEs (five in southern Italy). A consortium grant is worth on average EUR 2-3 million per year and funds are primarily used to finance visits abroad, workshops and advertising. Grants are disbursed annually, based on the expenses incurred in the previous year. A maximum of 40% of promotional expenses (60% for consortia based in Southern Italy) can be funded through the grants.

In 2014, the policy had funded over 1 600 companies grouped in 110 consortia. The Italian Federation of Export Consortia (Feder-export) has been set up to represent the consortia. It provides tax and legal advice, organises conferences and market surveys, arranges trade delegations, and negotiates credit lines with banks to finance the export activities of the consortia.

Success factors

Export consortia provide SMEs with the opportunity to develop the scale needed to internationalise. Moreover, the policy also achieves a leverage effect by channelling resources to a group of SMEs, rather than individual firms; in doing so, financial benefits are spread across a larger number of beneficiaries, while implementation costs are reduced by the fact that the government only interfaces with the leaders of the consortia. Finally, the creation of consortia naturally favours collaboration and knowledge exchange which can go beyond the initial objective of increased export activity.

Obstacles and responses

One drawback in this programme is that turnover in the government-supported consortia has been limited, making some consortia overly reliant on government support for their export activity. Moreover, it is important to set limits to the share of funding allocated for promotional activities (e.g. participation in international trade fairs), as done in Italy, to ensure that government resources are also used for other purposes, such as improving the quality of products and services of the consortium's members.

Relevance to Indonesia

Indonesian SMEs do not sufficiently partake in export activity. Supporting the export of SMEs through consortia, or co-operatives which have a stronger tradition in Indonesia, would enable policy makers to reach out to a larger number of SMEs than through policies targeting individual enterprises. Moreover, through this policy, SMEs would gain direct exposure to exporting and increase their chances of becoming long-term exporters.

Sources for further information

OECD (2014), *Italy: Key Issues and Policies,* OECD Studies on SMEs and Entrepreneurship, OECD Publishing, Paris, https://doi.org/10.1787/9789264213951-en.

Supporting SME participation in global value chains

In addition to exporting directly to foreign markets, SMEs can indirectly participate in international markets by supplying exporters. Besides the KURBE Programme, the Indonesian government fosters SME participation in global value chains through local content requirements in certain industries (machinery, motor vehicles, food, beverage, etc.). The Indonesia Investment Co-ordinating Board (i.e. *Badan Koordinasi Penanaman Modal*, BKPM) oversees the sectors subject to local content requirements, as well as the sectors fully or partly closed to foreign investment (see chapter 3).

BKPM has also recently taken a more proactive approach in building business linkages between local SMEs and multinational enterprises (MNEs) through the development of a website that hosts information on location and product specialisation of potential suppliers and through the organisation of matchmaking events between local SMEs and MNEs. Stronger MNE-SME linkages could also be favoured through tax incentives similar to those outlined in chapter 3, with Malaysia and Singapore offering good examples (see Box 3.6).

Workforce training programmes

Workforce training refers in this chapter to the training of current SME employees, inside or outside the workplace. The participation of Indonesian workers in certified training is low and proportional to their educational attainments. In 2015, only 0.9% of workers with qualifications up to junior high-school had participated in training courses, rising to 9% for senior high-school graduates, and to 26% for workers with tertiary education. Thus, re-skilling and up-skilling activities are low especially for those who need it most. Furthermore, only about 5% of Indonesian firms offer formal training to their workers, a figure which is affected by the large proportion of informal enterprises in the Indonesian economy.

Both government and accredited private training institutions deliver workforce training programmes. The main government institution in this field is the Ministry of Manpower and Transmigration, which operates 22 SME Productivity Centres that deliver technical training to upgrade the productivity of SME workforces. In addition, in collaboration with the national government, the UN International Labour Organisation (ILO), offers its globally-tested training programme SCORE (Sustaining Competitive and Responsible Enterprises), which aims to upgrade the productivity of SME workforces while improving their working conditions (health and safety at work, labour rights, etc.).

Entrepreneurship and management training programmes

Entrepreneurship and management training aims to instil entrepreneurial attitudes (risk-taking, leadership, etc.) and improves managerial skills in existing and would-be entrepreneurs. It differs from entrepreneurship education (see next section) by taking place outside the national education system and assuming many different formats and durations. More than 100 entrepreneurship training programmes are conducted annually in Indonesia by various ministries and agencies. Some of the most notable examples are the following:

- The Ministry of Co-operatives and SMEs supports entrepreneurship training for youth, women, fishing and farming communities, disadvantaged communities and communities living in border regions. One of the most relevant programmes is the

National Entrepreneurship Movement, which supports 1 000 young nascent entrepreneurs every year through a range of skills development activities, including learning from successful entrepreneurs.

- The Ministry of Research, Technology and Higher Education provides entrepreneurship training to tenant firms as part of its incubation programmes (see section on business incubation activity).
- The Ministry of Industry's Entrepreneurship Programme offers incubation, training and mentoring to increase start-up activity in manufacturing sectors.
- The Ministry of Social Affair's entrepreneurship training is mostly aimed at low-income people and other vulnerable groups.
- The Creative Economy Agency (BEKRAF) targets would-be entrepreneurs in cultural and creative industries which include 16 different sectors and activities.
- The Ministry of Youth and Sports organises entrepreneurship training for youth aged between 16 and 30 (see section on programmes for specific target groups).
- The Ministry of Manpower and Transmigration offers entrepreneurship training to unemployed people who cannot find jobs in the formal economy, people with disabilities, migrant workers, and women (see section on programmes for specific target groups).

Some of these training programmes are in collaboration with universities, chambers of commerce and industry or entrepreneur associations, which helps training to remain hands-on and of practical nature.

The Ministry of Co-operatives and SMEs also takes a different approach to entrepreneurship training by encouraging internships and apprenticeships for students and graduates in SMEs through the Youth Entrepreneurship Apprenticeship Programme (see Box 5.7).

Box 5.7. The Youth Entrepreneurship Apprenticeship Programme of the Ministry of Co-operatives and SMEs

The Youth Entrepreneurship Apprenticeship Programme (MKU) promotes exchanges between students and SMEs for the purpose of mutual learning. Students work for about three months in SMEs, acquiring direct knowledge and managerial skills from industry. The internship experience focuses on improving the managerial, communication and networking skills of the students, as well as on stimulating their motivation to become self-employed or business partners in their place of apprenticeship.

In 2017, the Ministry of Co-operatives and SMEs had a target of placing 500 interns in 100 SMEs. While the programme operates on a modest scale, it gives higher education institutions an opportunity to co-operate more closely with industry and to better adapt their learning offer to the skills demanded in the labour market.

Source: Liunir, Z. et al. (2017), "Enterprises internships to increase managerial ability of business students" (*Magang Kewirausahaan Sebagai Upaya Peningkatan Manajerial*), http://jurnal.upi.edu/file/Liunir.pdf.

International organisations are also active in entrepreneurship training. For example, the International Labour Organisation (ILO) offers its Start Your Business (SYB)

Programme, which includes "train the trainer" sessions to build up the capacities of local training organisations implementing the programme at the national level. The Association of Business Development Services of Indonesia (ABDSI) has established the Indonesian SME-institute.id website, which tailors training materials from the online ASEAN SME Academy to the Indonesian market. These international initiatives are helpful in increasing the supply of quality training programmes for entrepreneurs and should be widely promoted and supported.

This is especially the case because, with the exception of these international initiatives, there are no national standards for entrepreneurship training in Indonesia. This means that each programme uses its own approach, curriculum, and modules. Furthermore, although thousands of Indonesians participate in these trainings on an annual basis, there is no central database collecting and reporting data on total number of participants and programme effectiveness, including outcomes in terms of new enterprises. The government should strive to collect such information to better assess outcomes and identify national good-practices.

This effort will also support the current work of the Ministry of Manpower and the Ministry of Education and Culture to develop a standardised competency-based curriculum for entrepreneurship training.[6] The intention is to require entrepreneurs to hold this certificate in order to access government financing programmes. The merits of asking entrepreneurs to have a certificate of competency in order to access government funding are questionable; for example, this could favour larger or new companies over smaller and existing ones, whose owners are less likely to have the time to undertake a full training course. Nonetheless, a positive outcome of a national curriculum would be the draft of national guidelines for government-supported entrepreneurship training programmes. Mexico provides an example of an official government-backed entrepreneurship training scheme, where the government has been delivering a standard 150-hour training programme to thousands of its citizens every year (see Box 5.8).

Box 5.8. Broad-based access to entrepreneurship training opportunities in Mexico

In 2007, the Mexican Ministry of Economy launched the New Entrepreneur National Programme, the general objective of which was to contribute to the creation of jobs, new entrepreneurs and new enterprises by building a stronger entrepreneurship culture, fostering an "entrepreneurial mind-set", and imparting entrepreneurial and business planning skills to potential entrepreneurs.

The programme had four major components:

- Entrepreneurship promotion roadshows;
- Entrepreneurship training workshops;
- The national system of business incubation;
- The Seed Capital Programme.

Particularly relevant to Indonesia are the first two components.

The roadshows were part of a national promotional and information dissemination effort to create widespread awareness about entrepreneurship and encourage people to consider starting a business. Mobile units travelled from city to city throughout the year holding two-day events that provided information on the steps to take to start a business and the government support available. These events were often organised in co-operation with universities and local business associations.

During the course of these roadshow events, Mexicans interested in taking the next step could apply to participate in the entrepreneurship training workshop (Young Entrepreneurs Model), a 150-hour programme on how to start a business resulting in the preparation of a business plan. The design, piloting and testing of the workshop and its modules took three years to develop under the auspices of the Ministry of Economy and began to be implemented in 2010. The training workshop, consisting of a combination of online and classroom sessions, was delivered through a network of 153 "franchises" (normally held by private consulting and training firms) previously approved by the Ministry of Economy. Over 70 000 people were trained in these workshops between 2010 and 2013. This entrepreneurship training model has been used by at least 67 Mexican universities and technology institutes.

In addition to building a stronger entrepreneurship culture, fostering an entrepreneurial mind-set and providing business know-how to trainees, one of the objectives of the roadshows and workshops was to build demand for the national system of business incubators.

Source: OECD (2013), *Mexico: Key Issues and Policies*, OECD Studies on SMEs and Entrepreneurship, OECD Publishing, Paris, https://doi.org/10.1787/9789264187030-en.

Entrepreneurship education

Entrepreneurship education includes all the pedagogical activities aimed at promoting entrepreneurial skills (e.g. creativity, risk-taking, leadership) and an entrepreneurial mind-set among young people. The objective is to instil, through the national education system, a positive view in the younger generations about the effects and possibilities related to entrepreneurial activity. To achieve this goal multiple tools are typically used: classroom lectures, business games, the creation of real or virtual student business start-ups, business idea competitions, guest-speaker lectures, etc.

In 2017, the Ministry of Education and Culture issued Regulation 17/2017 on Assistance in the Implementation of Entrepreneurship Skills Education Programmes, which applies to both early childhood education and community education. Through this regulation the Ministry of Education and Culture is expected to provide funding to schools, universities and other educational organisations and community learning centres to organise entrepreneurship education programmes. The priority targets are school drop-outs or graduated students who are not currently undertaking any school or training activity (16-21 years of age). The regulation has, therefore, a mostly social vocation to help young people who are neither in employment nor in education. Between 2017 and 2018, the Ministry of Education and Culture allocated IDR 228 billion and reached 85 500 people. Institutions are required to deliver standardised courses of at least 150 hours, with 50 hours dedicated to entrepreneurship theory and 100 hours dedicated to practice.

Entrepreneurship education in primary and secondary schools

At the primary and secondary levels of education, the inclusion of entrepreneurship as a topic in school curricula was first mentioned in the Presidential Instruction 4/1995 and, subsequently, in Law 203/2003. However, a competency-based curriculum of entrepreneurship education has only been in place since 2010, and entrepreneurship teaching at this level remains mostly limited to secondary schools with a focus on social sciences.

Entrepreneurship education in higher education

The Ministry of Research, Technology and Higher Education and the Ministry of Education and Culture are both active in supporting entrepreneurship education in higher education institutions. As of 2017, almost all Indonesian universities offered seminars and training courses on entrepreneurship, with some of them also offering majors in entrepreneurship (Hermanto and Suryanto, 2017).

The Ministry of Research, Technology and Higher Education supports Entrepreneurship Campus Centres (*Pusat Kewirausahaan Kampus)*, which offer advisory services, mentoring and lectures to encourage student entrepreneurship. The same Ministry also operates the Student Entrepreneurial Programme (*Programme Mahasiswa Wirausaha*), which offers funding to students who develop a business plan for the commercialisation of creative and/or innovative products.

The Ministry of Education and Culture, on the other hand, has developed the Entrepreneurship Lecture Programme, the aim of which is to nurture entrepreneurial attitudes among students. This programme is structured around five core competences: character; communication and interpersonal skills; creativity and innovation; marketing; and business management. These five core competences are organised in 14 modules, each of which consists of a 150-minute lecture (Ministry of Education and Culture, 2013). The creation of such a structured programme is a positive development which strengthens the consistency of entrepreneurship teaching and learning at the university level.

Another noteworthy programme, still from the Ministry of Education and Culture, is the Business Lecture Programme (*Kuliah Kerja Usaha, KKU/KKN-PP*), a practical course intended to equip students with the ability to apply what they learn to solve social problems at the community level.

On the whole, Indonesia is well advanced in the field of entrepreneurship education thanks to several learning opportunities offered by the Ministry of Research, Technology and Higher Education and the Ministry of Education and Culture. Nonetheless, there could be better co-ordination between the different levels of the education system (from primary to university) to ensure a more strategic approach to entrepreneurial learning objectives and outcomes. Moreover, standardised programmes to train teachers on the contents and methods of entrepreneurship training should be promoted.

The example of the Dutch National Entrepreneurship Education Programme shows how the creation of a national commission on entrepreneurship and education, with membership from all relevant ministries and levels of education, has helped examine entrepreneurship education curriculum and learning outcomes at each education level to ensure a building-block approach (path) to the progression of entrepreneurial attitudes and competencies across levels of education (see Box 5.9).

Entrepreneurship education in Indonesia could also be strengthened in other ways. According to recent academic work, there is still more emphasis on theory than practice; better linkages between incubators and entrepreneurship education opportunities should be developed; and more needs to be done to embed an entrepreneurial culture within the university system (Purwana and Idyastuti, 2017).

Box 5.9. International inspiring practice: National Entrepreneurship Education Programme, the Netherlands

Description of the approach

In 2000, the Dutch government launched the National Entrepreneurship Education Programme as part of its policy to create a more entrepreneurial society. The Ministry of Economic Affairs, in co-operation with the Ministry of Education, Culture and Science, established a broad-based, consultative Commission on Entrepreneurship and Education consisting of 16 people from different fields of education, employer associations, entrepreneurs (male and female) and multicultural organisations to plan the strategic integration of entrepreneurship at all levels of the education system. All levels of education were represented in the membership of the Commission. An independent chair headed the Commission and the Ministry of Economic Affairs served as its secretariat.

The Commission was given a threefold task:

- To create support and awareness of entrepreneurship within the education community.
- To draft proposals for the development, piloting and implementation of activities to foster entrepreneurial skills and enterprise creation within the education system.
- To draft proposals to remove obstacles that prevented an entrepreneurial culture from prospering within the education system.

The Commission was mandated to develop a portfolio of good practices/projects in entrepreneurship, spanning all levels of education from primary school to university, and which would serve as examples that could be easily duplicated by other educational institutions. The ultimate objective was to create a snowball-effect throughout the education system and, at the same time, develop a continual learning path from primary school to secondary school, vocational education and university. To reach this goal the Commission organised a series of meetings with experts and representatives from the different levels of education; completed an inventory of the existing good-practice initiatives that fit in this learning path; and identified barriers faced by schools and universities in promoting entrepreneurship education.

The final outcome was the Dutch "Pulchri" model, which distinguished five phases in the entrepreneurial learning journey.

- *First experiences with entrepreneurship (primary schools)*: Students are introduced to the notion of entrepreneurship as a life option. At this stage students learn through play some general skills, such as working in groups/projects, orientation to production, and research.
- *Consciousness of skills (lower secondary schools):* Students gain an understanding of their own skills and talents.

- *Creative applications and enrichment of experiences (upper secondary schools):* Students are introduced to learning by experience and to elements of competition. This could involve mini-enterprise projects where students from secondary and higher vocational education run their own enterprise over the course of a year supported by a teacher and mentor (often an entrepreneur).
- *Preparation and real start-up:* At this stage, education institutions should raise interest in entrepreneurship. In higher education, this may mean support of a real start-up as part of the regular curriculum.
- *Growth and innovation phase:* In this final phase support for start-up firms becomes more important. Higher education can provide supporting facilities (finance, personnel, knowledge). Co-operation with intermediaries, such as chambers of commerce and former students, can be very useful in supporting transfer of knowledge and the overall enterprise growth.

In order to stimulate the broader application of entrepreneurship projects, the Dutch government approved a Subsidy Scheme on Entrepreneurship to fund small pilot projects (e.g. seminars, training for teachers etc.) and larger development projects (e.g. projects that developed learning instruments and methods linked to the school curriculum).

Success factors

Support for larger development projects linked to the school curriculum was a critical factor of success because it safeguarded the structural place of entrepreneurship in the education system and prevented the risk that projects would only have a temporary effect.

Moreover, the build-up of a portfolio of good practices for every education level, to serve as examples for other institutions, helped ensure the diffusion of entrepreneurship education across the different levels of the education system (i.e. snowball-effect).

Obstacles and responses

The major barriers, as noted by Dutch officials and experts, involved giving entrepreneurship a structural place in the curricula of the different levels of the education system, changing the often negative culture towards entrepreneurship within the education sector (including entrepreneurship as a legitimate area of study), and training teachers who could teach students about entrepreneurship.

Relevance to Indonesia

Indonesia already has a host of programmes and activities supporting entrepreneurship education. The creation of an Entrepreneurship and Education Commission and the subsequent launch of a national entrepreneurship education programme could help promote a more strategic approach to entrepreneurial learning objectives and outcomes.

Sources for further information

Stevenson L. and A. Lundström (2002), Beyond the Rhetoric: Defining Entrepreneurship Policy and Its Best Practice Components, Swedish Foundation for Small Business Research, Stockholm, pp. 296-300.

Social entrepreneurship and corporate social responsibility

Social entrepreneurship has gained momentum in recent years in Indonesia, as shown by the emergence of many social businesses, the establishment of social entrepreneurship study centres on several university campuses, and the formation of the Indonesian Social Entrepreneurship Association (AKSI) in 2009. The government has also begun to emphasise social entrepreneurship development, particularly with the inclusion of a dedicated chapter in the Draft Law on National Entrepreneurship. As of mid-2018, however, there was no shared definition of a social enterprise at national level, although the Draft Law on National Entrepreneurship refers to social entrepreneurship as entrepreneurship which has the vision and mission to solve social problems and/or provide positive changes to the welfare of society and the environment, and that reinvests most of its profits to support its mission. The draft law further states that social entrepreneurship involves the participation and empowerment of communities through business activity and can take the form of foundations, associations and co-operatives.

The Ministry of Social Affairs is the main government institution mandated with social enterprise development, except for co-operatives which may also have social objectives but are under the responsibility of the Ministry of Co-operatives and SMEs. Support for social entrepreneurship is still at a very incipient stage in Indonesia and is mostly driven by donors.

In the Indonesian context, social entrepreneurship can also be tied to the concept of corporate social responsibility (CSR), which is backed by government laws requiring all large businesses to have a CSR strategy and to allocate CSR funds for social causes, including entrepreneurship development. This creates a fertile ground for co-operation between for-profit businesses and social entrepreneurs, as shown, for example, by the environmentally-oriented partnership between *Asgar Muda*, a youth social enterprise foundation based in Garut (West Java), Chevron Corporation and Indonesia Power.

In addition, state-owned enterprises (SOEs) have an obligation to engage in the Partnership Programme with Small Business (PKBL). The PKBL is regulated by the Ministry of SOEs' Regulation 02/MBU/7/2017, which mandates that SOEs should reserve 4% of their after-tax profits to this programme. As part of the PKBL, small businesses benefit from subsidised loans to finance the acquisition of fixed assets or working capital. The programme is also used to support education, training, marketing and promotional activities of small businesses (Fridaus, 2014; Palesangi, 2017). To be eligible for the PKBL, small enterprises must have a maximum net worth not exceeding IDR 200 million (excluding land and buildings) or maximum annual sales of IDR 1 billion; have at least one year of activity; and find traditional bank credit inaccessible.

Programmes for specific target groups

Women's entrepreneurship programmes

The priorities of the National Medium-Term Development Plan 2015-2019 include women's integration in the national labour force, the collection of data allowing gender-based analysis, and the formulation of gender-responsive economic development policies. These objectives are to be achieved mostly through gender mainstreaming, which involves taking into consideration the gender dimension in the design and implementation of most economic development policies,[7] and establishing gender-based policy targets and policy indicators.

In addition, Indonesia also has a number of specific programmes for women entrepreneurs, although they appear to be small in scale and fragmented across different technical ministries. The Ministry of Women's Empowerment and Child Protection organises trade shows and financial literacy training, and supports technology adoption in women-owned businesses. This Ministry also co-operates with the Ministry of Co-operatives and SMEs through an agreement whereby the latter commits to facilitate women's participation in co-operatives and SMEs through improving their access to markets and finance.

The Ministry of Co-operatives and SMEs also runs the Welfare and Healthy Families and Women Programme, a revolving fund that provides financing to women's co-operatives and that has proven an important vehicle for addressing the financial constraints of women-owned micro and small enterprises. The Ministry provides IDR 100 million to each co-operative part of the programme, which in turn lends up to IDR 4 million to each member of the co-operative. Once members repay their loans to the co-operatives, funds are re-used for loans to other members.

Bank Indonesia has also supported women's financial inclusion strategies. Between 2013 and 2016, the Central Bank ran the Women Empowerment Programme to offer financial literacy training for women micro-entrepreneurs. Moreover, many financial institutions, including commercial banks, seek to reach women self-employed through microcredit schemes which use group lending methodologies (World Bank, 2016).

Access to markets is often as important as access to finance. However, there are limited programmes in Indonesia to prepare women-owned SMEs to tap into global supply chains. Two exceptions are the Embroidery and Apparel Cluster Development Pilot Project, initiated by Bank Indonesia, and the Women in Global Business-Indonesia Project, which is a partnership of the Indonesian government with the International Trade Centre and donor funding from Australia.

With respect to the domestic market, Indonesia actively supports the participation of women-owned enterprises in public procurement. Reforms to the procurement system of Indonesia take place within the framework of the Millennium Challenge Account (MCA) Indonesia Procurement Modernisation Project which, among other things, emphasises gender-sensitivity in national procurement practices. Through this project, the Goods and Services Procurement Agency of Indonesia (*Lembaga Kebijakan Pengadaan Barang/Jasa Pemerintah*, LKPP) has sought to make the procurement system more friendly to women-owned businesses (MCA-Indonesia et al., 2014), including by hiring more female procurement officers and by organising workshops to educate local procurement officers on a gender-equitable procurement process and women entrepreneurs on the skills required to access government contracts. One of the main challenges in this process has been that the overwhelming majority of women-owned businesses are informal.

Since Indonesia is in the early stage of implementing gender-sensitive public procurement practices, it could draw inspiration from the experience of the United States, one of the forerunners in this area (see Box 5.10).

Box 5.10. International inspiring practice: Procurement policies and programmes targeting women-owned businesses, United States

Description of the approach

The 1994 Federal Acquisition Streamlining Act was the first to establish a goal (not the mandate) of 5% of the value of all federal prime contracts and subcontracts in each fiscal year to be awarded to women-owned small businesses (WOSBs). This initial initiative, however, had limited success, which led to further legislative changes through the 2000 Small Business Programs Reauthorization Act. The new Act set out the definition of a WOSB (i.e. a minimum of 51% of the business is owned by one or more women); allowed agencies to restrict competition in industries in which WOSBs were under-represented; required WOSBs to provide proof of certification; and directed the Small Business Administration (SBA) to conduct a study of industries where WOSBs were under-represented in federal procurement contracts. In order to implement the procurement provisions of the Reauthorization Act, the SBA established the Office of Federal Contract Assistance for Women Business Owners, which was mandated to work with agencies to increase their contracting to WOSBs.

In 2011, the SBA-administered WOSB Federal Contracting Programme went into effect. Its main aim was to level the playing field for WOSBs to compete for federal contracts and, for the first time, allowed specific set-asides for WOSBs. The programme expanded the number of industries where WOSBs were substantially under-represented and where set-asides were thus required. WOSB set-asides now apply to contracting in more than 92 NAICS (North American Industry Classification System) industry groups. In 2013, the programme also removed previous caps on the contract size falling within the WOSB set-aside limits (USD 6.5 million in manufacturing and USD 4 million for all other contracts).

The aim is for not less than 5% of the value of all federal procurements in each fiscal year to be awarded to WOSBs. This target has been in place since 1994, but was first reached only in 2015 (totalling USD 17.8 billion).

Success factors

The SBA provides regular training workshops to public procurement officers on the WOSB Federal Contracting Programme. To make this possible, it was important to develop a process for women-owned businesses to become certified as valid WOSBs. The list of certified WOSBs is hosted on an SBA platform that can be accessed by public procurement officers when they look for women suppliers.

To educate women about the programme, the SBA Learning Centre has developed a primer for WOSBs on how to compete for federal contracts that can be accessed on its website, and the SBA offers training to women business owners on contracting opportunities and procedures as well as facilitating connections with government buyers around the country.

Obstacles and responses

The full implementation of the procurement programme for women-owned businesses has encountered many obstacles. Initially, there was limited success in achieving the 5% goal due to lack of a specific definition of a WOSB and lack of knowledge about in which sectors WOSBs were under-represented in procurement contracts. This was resolved by setting out the definition of a WOSB (and requiring companies to provide a certification) and undertaking research on the allocation of public procurement contracts by the gender of the business owner.

In addition, further legislation was required to achieve the 5% target. The establishment of the SBA Office of Federal Contract Assistance for Women Business Owners, for example, worked with agencies to increase their contracting to WOSBs, including by introducing rules making it easier for WOSBs to compete for tenders.

Relevance to Indonesia

The US experience indicates that it can take considerable time and effort to raise the level of participation of women-owned businesses in public procurement. The main takeaway is that several actions are needed in order to increase women's participation in the tendering process and their success in securing awards, namely: i) setting a definitional criteria for a women-owned business; ii) establishing a process for certifying that the enterprise meets the definitional requirement; iii) establishing procurement set-asides for which only women-owned businesses can compete; iv) training of public procurement officers in the implementation of the procurement rules; v) training of women entrepreneurs in how to participate in public procurement; vi) promoting the programme widely among women entrepreneurs' networks; vii) organising opportunities for women entrepreneurs to meet with government buyers; and viii) reporting on progress made towards achieving the prescribed quota.

Sources for further information

SBA, "Federal Government Breaks Contracting Record for Women-Owned Small Businesses", SBA Press Release, 2 March, 2016, https://www.sba.gov/content/sba-federal-government-breaks-contracting-record-women-owned-small-businesses/.

Federal Procurement Data System Small Business Goaling Reports (for trends in the awarding of contracts to WOSB), https://www.fpds.gov/fpdsng_cms/index.php/en/reports.html/.

Beede, D. and R. Rubinovitz (2015), *Utilization of Women-Owned Businesses in Federal Prime Contracting*, Report prepared for the Women-Owned Small Business Program of the Small Business Administration (SBA), Office of the Chief Economist, U.S. Department of Commerce, Washington, DC.

In addition to the national government, associations of women entrepreneurs, notably the Indonesian Women's Business Association (IWAPI) with its membership of about 30 000 female entrepreneurs, also play a relevant role in women's entrepreneurship support. For example, IWAPI collaborates with multinational technology companies (Microsoft, Nokia, etc.) to improve the digital literacy, online presence and logistic operations of its members. Women's associations are also active in favouring access to finance for their members, including through the establishment of their own financial institutions, mainly savings and loan co-operatives.

To summarise, there are a number of support programmes for women's entrepreneurship in Indonesia, but these are mostly small in scale and concentrated on women's co-operatives and micro-enterprises. There are also some significant policy gaps. For example, there is no formal mentoring programme for women entrepreneurs, contrary to what is observed in other ASEAN countries (OECD/ERIA, forthcoming; World Bank, 2016). Women are also poorly represented in main supply-chain development initiatives, except for some that have been funded by international donors in sectors where women are predominant (e.g. clothing).

It follows that Indonesia would benefit from a more targeted and comprehensive approach to meet the needs of different types of women-owned SMEs. For example, programmes to support micro-enterprises could focus on improving financial literacy and managerial and workforce capacity; women-owned small businesses could be better assisted by improving access to technology, innovation, and new markets; and support to medium-sized enterprises could prioritise internationalisation and the overall improvement of enterprise competitiveness.

Youth entrepreneurship programmes

About half of the Indonesian population is under the age of 30, pointing to the importance of education and skills policies to support the participation of the Indonesian youth population in the (formal) labour force. For the purposes of youth entrepreneurship policy, youth is defined as the age between 16 and 30 years in Indonesia. Law 40/2009 and Regulation 41/2011 on youth development mandates all levels of government to promote youth entrepreneurship through training, apprenticeships, mentoring and access to capital, further stipulating that local governments are to establish Youth Entrepreneurship Centres to roll out such activities.

The Ministry of Youth and Sports is the main institutional player in this field, delivering its own programmes and co-ordinating those of other ministries (e.g. the National Entrepreneurship Movement of the Ministry of Co-operatives and SMEs). The 2018 budget of this Ministry dedicated to youth entrepreneurship was IDR 47.4 trillion, with programme activities including entrepreneurship workshops, financial support for Youth Entrepreneurship Centres, e-commerce training, youth entrepreneurship fairs, and youth entrepreneur competitions. The two main programmes are the Young Beginner Entrepreneur Programme (*Wirausaha Muda Pemula*, WMP) and the Youth Entrepreneurship Centres (*Sentra Kewirausahaan Pemuda*, SKP).

The Young Beginner Entrepreneur Programme offers non-repayable financial contributions to young people who have run a business for less than 36 months. Applicants need to submit a business development plan, supplemented by budget details and a business analysis. The programme offers annually 1 000 small grants of up to IDR 20 million on a competitive basis, for a total budget of IDR 20 billion. Grants can be used for: purchasing raw materials and equipment; marketing and product promotion; participation in entrepreneurship development training courses; and reducing production costs. The WMP financing may also include access to low-cost loans from the Partnership Programme of State-Owned Enterprises (if the enterprise has at least a one-year track record and is able to show turnover growth).

Youth Entrepreneurship Centres are established locally with support from the central government and support youth entrepreneurship through training, mentoring and networking. These centres can also apply to the Ministry of Youth and Sports for additional funding to implement the Young Beginner Entrepreneur Programme as part of their activities. In 2017, the Ministry funded 34 Youth Entrepreneurship Centres with a total budget of IDR 34 billion.

Entrepreneurship programmes for returning migrants

The National Agency for the Placement and Protection of the Indonesian Migrant Worker (*Badan Nasional Penempatan dan Perlindungan Tenaga Kerja Indonesia*, BNP2TKI) undertakes a wide range of training programmes to equip Indonesian workers with sufficient skills and abilities to work abroad and to help them live independently when they return home. This includes entrepreneurship training so that returning migrants can invest their savings into productive activities in Indonesia. For example, in 2017, the Bandung office of the BNP2TKI organised entrepreneurship training in the Garut regency (West Java province) attended by 50 full-time migrant workers who had worked in the Middle East and Korea. They attended entrepreneurship training for seven days, with a focus on handicraft and livestock businesses. The training was co-ordinated by several government agencies with the involvement of the business sector, co-operatives, banks and local trainers.

Public procurement

Based on Presidential Regulation 16/2018 on the procurement of government goods and services, ministries and government agencies are expected to maximise the offer of government contracts to micro and small businesses (as defined by the 2008 MSME Law) and small co-operatives by reserving for them all government contracts of up to IDR 2.5 billion, except for contracts requiring high technical competences which micro and small enterprises may not be able to meet. Furthermore, the regulation expects companies winning larger bids (above IDR 2.5 billion) to subcontract some of the work to micro and small enterprises.

The Presidential Regulation falls short of setting a target for the percentage of procurement contracts (number or value) to be awarded to micro and small companies. However, although the National Government Procurement Agency (LKPP) does not report data on the share of procurement contracts being awarded to micro and small enterprises, in 2017, 587 014 procurement packages were issued with a value of up to IDR 2.5 billion each (and, thus, *de facto* reserved for micro and small enterprises), totalling IDR 87.7 trillion, while 15 104 procurement packages had a nominal value above IDR 2.5 billion each for a total of IDR 222.4 trillion (LKPP, 2017). Thus, 97.5% of procurement packages were issued to micro and small enterprises, although this only amounted to 28.3% of the total procurement value in 2017.

The government also gives preferential treatment to micro and small enterprises in terms of the percentage of the contract that can be paid in advance: 30% versus 20% for other businesses. Furthermore, the LKPP manages an online vendor directory where SMEs can register. This raises awareness of their businesses among procuring agencies and increases their opportunities to bid for government contracts. As seen earlier, the LKPP is also working to increase the participation of women-owned businesses in the procurement process through gender-sensitive practices and targeted promotion and training (see previous section on women's entrepreneurship programmes).

Overall, Indonesia offers good public procurement opportunities to micro and small businesses (and small co-operatives), although less than 30% of the total value of government contracts is assigned to micro and small companies by the virtue of falling under the legal threshold of IDR 2.5 billion. Moving forward, the government could work with business associations and chambers of commerce to provide guidelines and training to SMEs on how to bid for government contracts and to create opportunities for SMEs to meet with public procurement officials.

Conclusions and policy recommendations

Indonesia has a large number of support measures for SMEs and entrepreneurship, although some of them lack scale and there are overlaps among certain programmes (e.g. business incubators and entrepreneurship training). The largest SME programme is the People's Business Credit Programme (*Kredit Usaha Rakyat*, KUR), a government-backed loan guarantee *cum* interest rate subsidy whose budget has increased considerably after the 2015 reform. Besides traditional debt finance, Indonesia also supports diversification in the sources of enterprise finance, for example through two junior equity markets with less strict listing requirements than the main stock market. National innovation policies mostly consist of grants and advisory services, rather than fiscal measures such as tax credits. In particular, two national roadmap strategies drive the development of business incubators and e-commerce. Science and technology parks and the creative economy are two other important government priorities. Support for business internationalisation includes traditional policies such as export finance (i.e. credit, guarantees and insurances), market and export information, product development and export training, but also new approaches where SMEs can export by partnering with large state-owned enterprises or where SMEs are helped to become suppliers of exporters.

Entrepreneurship and management training (outside the national education system) and entrepreneurship education (within the national education system) are common in Indonesia, although the former lacks common competency standards which could improve the quality and consistency of the training, while the latter would benefit from a more strategic and integrated approach to entrepreneurial learning objectives and outcomes across the different levels of education. The Indonesian government also supports youth entrepreneurship and women's entrepreneurship, although programmes in these two domains are relatively small. Micro and small enterprises also receive preferential conditions in public procurement by having government contracts below IDR 2.5 million reserved for them.

One more general consideration is that most SME government spending in Indonesia is on socially-oriented programmes supporting necessity-based entrepreneurship. For example, KUR's average loan size makes it effectively a subsidised microcredit programme. In addition, several other programmes encourage business creation in traditional sectors of the economy, with many of them specifically targeting socially-disadvantaged groups such as low-income people, the unemployed, migrant workers or people living in rural and border areas. These measures are important in generating a source of revenues for the recipients and their families, but they are unlikely to become a main source of high-quality jobs.

Shifting the attention, and some budgetary resources, from socially-oriented programmes to economically-driven programmes encouraging business growth (e.g. through innovation, internationalisation, business linkages, the upgrading of workforce skills) would further the scale-up of existing SMEs and the generation of more productive and better-paid jobs in the (formal) economy. In fact, especially in low and middle-income countries, earnings are typically higher and social protection is more common in wage employment than in self-employment (Fields, 2014). Moreover, firms which scale up typically generate jobs not only for the high-skilled but also for the low-skilled (Coad et al., 2014). More government spending on programmes that "upgrade" the performance of

SMEs would also be in line with the provisions of Law 20/2008 (MSME Law) which aims to strengthen, among other things, the participation of Indonesian SMEs in economic growth and job creation.

Based on the analysis in this chapter, the following recommendations are offered to strengthen national SME and entrepreneurship programmes.

Recommendations on national SME and entrepreneurship programmes

- Increase spending on programmes that aim to improve SME productivity (e.g. innovation, internationalisation, managerial and workforce skills) by augmenting the overall SME policy budget or, alternatively, by transferring some of the existing resources from other more socially-driven programmes.

Financing programmes

- Consider increasing the focus of the KUR Programme on certain target groups of disadvantaged borrowers, such as first-time borrowers, enterprises in lagging regions, and sectors experiencing more constrained access to finance.
- Monitor possible misuse of the KUR Programme as well as the rate of KUR-backed non-performing loans.
- Consider decentralising the loan evaluation process in the LPDB Agency's Revolving Fund Programme, with the aim of improving capital allocation efficiency and favouring better geographical representation in the programme.
- Support the growth of the domestic venture capital industry through the establishment of a government venture capital fund and investment readiness programmes for growth-oriented SMEs.

Innovation programmes

- Reduce the number of ministries involved in the development of business incubators with the aim of simplifying the co-ordination of the National Roadmap for Incubator Development and increasing the size of existing incubators.
- Ensure that incubators are well integrated into the local entrepreneurial ecosystem by building relationships with external business support service providers, universities, research organisations and sources of equity finance.
- Open up university-based business incubators to applicants outside of the university hosting the incubator with the aim of making the selection process more competitive and improving the quality of tenant companies.
- Consider shifting the focus of the Indonesia Stock Exchange incubator from start-ups to existing high-growth firms, as the latter are typically closer to the stage of an initial public offering (IPO), which is one of the aims of the programme.
- Ensure that the location of science and technology parks is mostly driven by economic considerations, including the presence of a local base of innovative firms and knowledge-based workers.
- Support business accelerators, whose focus is on scaling up existing growth-oriented SMEs.

- Ensure that the targets of digitalisation support measures, such as the One Million id. Domain Programme, are not only met, but are also sustainable after government support comes to an end, and that they generate a real economic impact (e.g. in terms of increased revenues, profits and export at the firm level).
- Consider the development of a new intervention which fosters the adoption of digital technologies in SMEs beyond e-commerce, notably the use of hardware and software programmes supporting the professionalization of small business management.

Internationalisation programmes

- Increase budgetary resources for business internationalisation, including training measures to improve the export-related skills of SMEs and programmes such as export-oriented consortia or co-operatives that enable SMEs to gain direct exposure to export activity.
- Improve the involvement of SMEs in the KURBE Programme (i.e. the Export Oriented People's Business Credit Programme), for example by targeting not only Tier-I but also Tier-II suppliers of large exporters or SMEs which have the potential to become Tier-I suppliers.
- Strengthen existing programmes to improve the participation of Indonesian SMEs in global value chains, including by facilitating co-operation between multinationals and local SMEs.

Entrepreneurship and management training

- Initiate an evaluation of the main entrepreneurship and management training programmes with a view to assessing the outcomes (e.g. rate of business start-ups by trained participants) and identifying best-practice approaches and curricula.
- Expand the Youth Entrepreneurship Apprenticeship Programme to benefit a larger number of apprentices and SMEs. Ensure that businesses offering internships within this programme focus on the learning process of students and possibly on creating employment opportunities for them.

Entrepreneurship education

- Establish a National Commission on Entrepreneurship and Education, represented by relevant ministries and all levels of the education system, to review the entrepreneurship-related curriculum and learning outcomes at each educational level and to ensure a building-block approach (path) to the progression of entrepreneurial attitudes and competencies across the different levels of education.
- Allocate resources to the capacity building and professional development of teachers in the primary and secondary education systems to improve their competencies and abilities in the teaching of entrepreneurship content.

Social entrepreneurship and corporate social responsibility

- Establish government support for the development of social entrepreneurship and social enterprises in the form of dedicated capacity-building actions and access to finance.

- Develop a clear definition of social entrepreneurship and social enterprise in order to substantiate eligibility for government support programmes.

Programmes for specific target groups

- Consider increasing the size of the grant in the Young Beginner Entrepreneur Programme (and as a result the overall budget) to foster the creation of employer enterprises. Consider making job creation one of the requisites of the programme.
- Give stronger attention to supporting growth-oriented women-owned enterprises through appropriate programmes providing mentoring, training and access to domestic and international markets.
- Consider establishing goals or legal set-asides in terms of the proportion of procurement contracts to be awarded to women-owned businesses, whose definition and eligibility requirements should be set by the law.

Public procurement

- Strengthen SME access to public procurement through enhanced information on existing government contract opportunities and through targeted training to increase the ability of SMEs to bid for government contracts.

Notes

[1] Optimal efficiency is reached when capital markets work perfectly, that is, when capital flows to the most productive uses. If credit markets are inefficient, however, capital may flow to less productive activities or may not flow at all. In this case, interest rate subsidies may help redress the situation by channelling resources into more productive uses than would otherwise have been the case.

[2] Information from the ASEAN Co-operation Project Number "IND/SME/11/002/REG", Republic of Indonesia, Jakarta.

[3] "Indonesia Expects Jump in Creative Economy by 2019", Jakarta Post, 15 March 2017. http://www.thejakartapost.com/news/2017/03/15/indonesia-expects-jump-in-creative-economy-by-2019.html

[4] "Creative Economy Agency: Where Are You?", Global Indonesian Voices, 13 May 2017. http://www.globalindonesianvoices.com/26138/creative-economy-agency-where-are-you/

[5] "Indonesia Eximbank Financing Soars by 18.31%", Jakarta Post, 15 March 2017, http://www.thejakartapost.com/news/2017/03/15/indonesia-eximbank-financing-soars-by-18-31.html

[6] Competency-based training enables participants to start and end training programmes at different times and levels, based on the level of acquired competencies. It can involve various training methods and techniques, including on-the-job training, off-the-job training and training through relevant media tools.

[7] Examples include training programmes which are delivered at times suitable to the working hours of women, financing programmes open to sectors where women-owned businesses are most prominent, etc.

References

Agarwal, S. and R. Hauswald (2010), "Distance and private information in lending", *Review of Financial Studies*, Vol. 23, pp. 2757-2788.

Åstebro, T. and N. Bazzazian (2011), "Universities, entrepreneurship and local economic development", in M. Fritsch (ed.), *Handbook of Research on Entrepreneurship and Regional Development*, pp. 252-333, Edward Elgar Press, Cheltenham, UK.

Baygan, G. (2003), "Venture capital policies in Israel", *OECD Science, Technology and Industry Working Papers*, 2003/03, OECD Publishing, Paris.

Beede, D. and R. Rubinovitz (2015), *Utilization of Women-Owned Businesses in Federal Prime Contracting*, Report prepared for the Women-Owned Small Business Program of the Small Business Administration, 31 December, Office of the Chief Economist, U.S. Department of Commerce, Washington, DC.

Coad, A., S. Daunfeldt, D. Johansson and K. Wennberg (2014), "Whom do high-growth firms hire?", *Industrial and Corporate Change*, Vol. 23, N. 1, pp. 293-327, http://dx.doi.org/10.1093/icc/dtt051.

Degryse, H. and S. Ongena (2005), Distance, lending relationship and competition", *Journal of Finance*, Vol. 60, pp. 231-266.

European Commission (2013), *Setting Up, Manage, and Evaluating EU Science and Technology Parks*, Brussels.

European Commission (2002), *Final Report: Benchmarking of Business Incubators*, Brussels

Fields, G. (2014), "Self-employment and poverty in developing countries", *IZA World of Labor*, http://dx.doi.org/10.15185/izawol.60

Fridaus, N. (2014), "Poverty alleviation through social entrepreneurship approach" (*Nur. Pengentasan Kemiskinan Melalui Pendekatan Kewirausahaan Sosial)*, *Jurnal Ekonomi Dan Pembangunan*, Vol. 22, N. 1.

Garcia F., C. Bizzotto, S. Pires and T. Chierighini (2015), *Reference Center for business incubation: a proposal for a new model of operation*, Brazilian Associati on of Science Parks and Business Incubators, http://anprotec.org.br/cerne/menu/english/.

Google & A.T. Kearney (2017), *Indonesia Venture Capital Outlook 2017*, Jakarta

Hermanto, B. and S. Suryanto (2017), "Entrepreneurship ecosystem policy in Indonesia", *Mediterranean Journal of Social Sciences*, Vol. 8, N. 1, pp. 110-115.

Liunir, Z., M. Astuti, I. Widiaty and S. Ana (2017), "Magang Kewirausahaan Sebagai Upaya Peningkatan Manajerial" (Enterprise internships to increase managerial ability of business students), (http://jurnal.upi.edu/file/Liunir.pdf.

LKPP (Lembaga Kebijakan Pengadaan Barang/Jasa Pemerintah) (Goods and Services Procurement Agency of Indonesia) (2017), "Policy of Development MSMEs Business Climate in Procurement of Government Goods and Services" (Kebijakan Pengembangan Iklim Usaha KUMKM Dalam Pengadaan Barang/Jasa Pemerintah).

Mardanugraha E. and B. Yappi (2017), "Principal-agent problem of governmental MSME financing", paper presented at the 2nd International Conference on Indonesian Economy and Development, Universitas Indonesia, Jakarta.

Millennium Challenge Account (MCA)-Indonesia, LKPP and BAPPENAS (2014), *Gender in Government Procurement in Indonesia: Summary of Survey Findings on Access to Procurement, Key Barriers and Trends*, Jakarta.

Ministry of Education and Culture (2013), Entrepreneurship: Learning Module (*Kewirausahaan: Modul Pembelajaran*), Jakarta. https://philarchive.org/archive/FUGACN.

Morduch, J. (1999), "The role of subsidies in microfinance: Evidence from the Grameen Bank". *Journal of Development Economics*, Vol. 60, pp. 229-248.

OECD (2016a), *SME and Entrepreneurship Policy in* 2016, OECD Publishing, Paris, https://doi.org/10.1787/9789264262324-en

OECD (2016b), "Increasing Productivity in Small Traditional Enterprises: Programmes for Upgrading Management Skills and Practices", unpublished report.

OECD (2015), *New Approaches to SME and Entrepreneurship Financing: Broadening the Range of Instruments*, https://doi.org/10.1787/9789264240957-en

OECD (2014), *Italy: Key Issues and Policies,* OECD Studies on SMEs and Entrepreneurship, OECD Publishing, https://doi.org/10.1787/9789264213951-en

OECD (2013), *Mexico: Key Issues and Policies*, OECD Studies on SMEs and Entrepreneurship, OECD Publishing, https://doi.org/10.1787/9789264187030-en

OECD (2012), *OECD Economic Surveys: Indonesia 2012*, OECD Publishing, Paris, https://doi.org/10.1787/eco_surveys-idn-2012-en.

OECD (2010), *OECD Innovation Policy Platform: Technology Incubators*, https://www.oecd.org/innovation/policyplatform/48136826.pdf

OECD/Economic Research Institute for ASEAN and East Asia (ERIA) (forthcoming), *ASEAN SME Policy Index 2018*, OECD Publishing, Paris.

Palesangi, M. (2017), *Pemuda Indonesia Dan Kewirausahaan Sosial* (Indonesian Youth and Social entrepreneurship), Parahyangan Catholic University.

Petersen, M. and R. Rajan, R. (2002), "Does distance still matter? The information revolution in small business lending", *Journal of Finance*, Vol. 57, pp. 2533-2570.

Purwana, D. and U. Idyastuti (2017), "Does entrepreneurial university support entrepreneurship education?", *Asian Journal of Social Sciences and Management Studies*, Vol. , N. 2, pp. 70-75.

Rowter, K. (2016), "Indonesian capital market developments and challenges", *Nomura Journal of Asian Capital Markets*, Vol. 1, N. 1, pp. 9-13.

Stevenson L. and A. Lundström (2002), *Beyond the Rhetoric: Defining Entrepreneurship Policy and Its Best Practice Components*, Swedish Foundation for Small Business Research, Stockholm, pp. 296-300.

World Bank (2017), *Indonesia Economic Quarterly March 2017: Staying the Course*, World Bank, Indonesia office, Jakarta.

World Bank (2016), *Women Entrepreneurs in Indonesia: A Pathway to Increasing Shared Prosperity*, Finance and Markets Global Practice, East Asia Pacific Region, World Bank Indonesia Office, Jakarta.

6. The local dimension of SME and entrepreneurship policy in Indonesia

This chapter presents information on the local dimension of SME and entrepreneurship policy in Indonesia. It includes information on geographical differences in economic and SME activity, the role of local governments in SME policy, existing mechanisms for the tailoring of national policies to the local context, and mechanisms to ensure policy co-ordination among different levels of government. Indonesia features large local variations in wealth, the business environment, SME and entrepreneurship activity, and enterprise access to strategic resources, which reflect the large size of the population and the geographical expanse of the country. A large-scale devolution of powers in the early 2000s has given significant SME policy functions to local governments, which has helped provide the necessary flexibility to target national policies to the local context. Nonetheless, appropriate tailoring of national policies to local business needs and effective policy co-ordination across levels of government are on occasion impaired by the large number of government institutions involved in SME policy and by uneven policy capacities at the local level.

The local context for SME and entrepreneurship policy

This section looks at geographical variations in wealth (GDP per capita), the business environment, business activity, and access to strategic resources (e.g. bank loans and business development services) in Indonesia. It points to strong heterogeneity in economic conditions and SME performance across provinces, which reflects the geographical expanse of Indonesia and calls for the tailoring of national policies to the local context.

Geographical variations in GDP per capita

Indonesia has a population of 261 million people distributed across roughly 1 000 inhabited islands. The distribution of the population is somewhat uneven, with over half (55%) of the population living on the island of Java which also hosts the capital city of Jakarta.

There are strong geographical variations in GDP per capita across the country. For 28 of the overall 34 provinces which comprise Indonesia, GDP per capita varies between IDR 15 million (East Nusa Tenggara) and IDR 48 million (Papua), already a significant range. However, for the top six provinces, this range is even wider, between IDR 72 million in West Papua and IDR 195 million in the Special Capital Region of Jakarta (Figure 6.1). Besides the capital-city effect – Jakarta's GDP per capita is four times higher than the national average – natural resource endowments explain the other peaks, notably oil and gas (East Kalimantan, Riau and Riau Islands), copper and gold (Papua) and palm oil (again Riau and Riau Islands). Indonesia's poorest provinces, on the other hand, are typically remote southern and eastern islands lacking significant natural resources (e.g. Maluku). Indonesia's GDP per capita is also much more dispersed than in other major emerging-market economies (Figure 6.2).

Figure 6.1. GDP per capita across Indonesian provinces, 2015

GDP per capita by province, percentile distribution

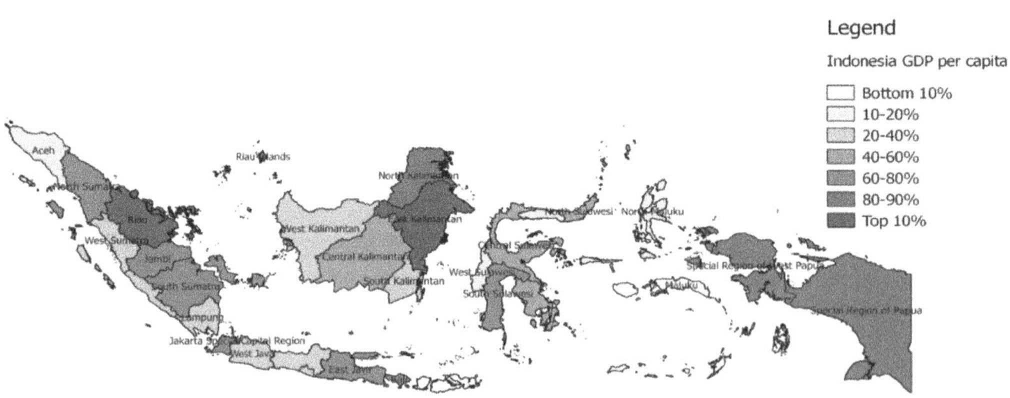

Source: OECD based on Central Bureau of Statistics.

StatLink https://doi.org/10.1787/888933824268

Figure 6.2. GDP per capita distribution in Indonesia compared to other emerging-market economies, 2013

Log of ratio of regional GDP per capita (current local currency) to national average

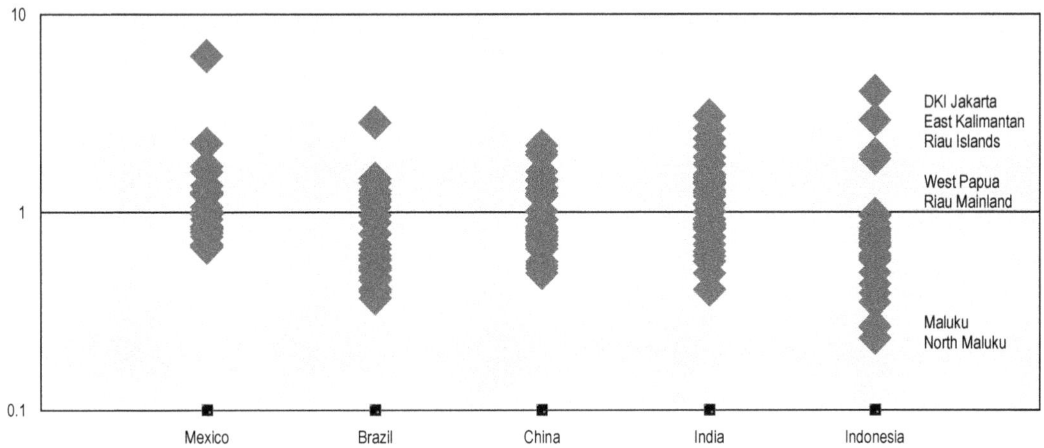

Source: OECD (2016), *OECD Economic Surveys: Indonesia 2016*, OECD Publishing, Paris, https://doi.org/10.1787/eco_surveys-idn-2016-en, based on OECD Regional Database.

StatLink https://doi.org/10.1787/888933824287

Geographical variations in the business environment

Geographical variations in the quality of the business environment have been captured by two subnational World Bank Doing Business surveys in 2010 and 2012. These two surveys benchmarked 14 Indonesian cities and found considerable differences in the burden of business regulations. For example, in 2012, the cost of dealing with construction permits ranged between 132% of annual per capita income in Makassar (South Sulawesi) and 32% in Jambi (Central Sumatra), while the cost of opening a business in relation to income per capita was nearly twice as high in Manado (North Sulawesi) as in Pontianak (Borneo): 31% compared with 18%. The number of days to open a business also changed across provinces, although there was no evident relationship with the incurred costs. At the time of the 2012 survey, for example, it took 42 days to open a business in Pontianak and 34 days in Manado (Figure 6.3).

The quality of the local business environment also includes the efficiency and effectiveness of the local public sector in delivering public services (William, Ritzen and Woolcock, 2006). The Indonesia Governance Index captures the quality of local political office, bureaucracy, civil society and economic society in Indonesia through a composite index (Gismar, Lockman and Hidayat, 2012). This index shows that the quality of local government is best in Yogyakarta and worst in North Maluku, suggesting that it is linked, among other things, to local levels of income. Such heterogeneity is also likely to have an impact on the capacity of local governments to design and implement effective SME and entrepreneurship programmes.

Figure 6.3. Variations in the ease of doing business across Indonesian cities, 2012

Percentage of city per capita income

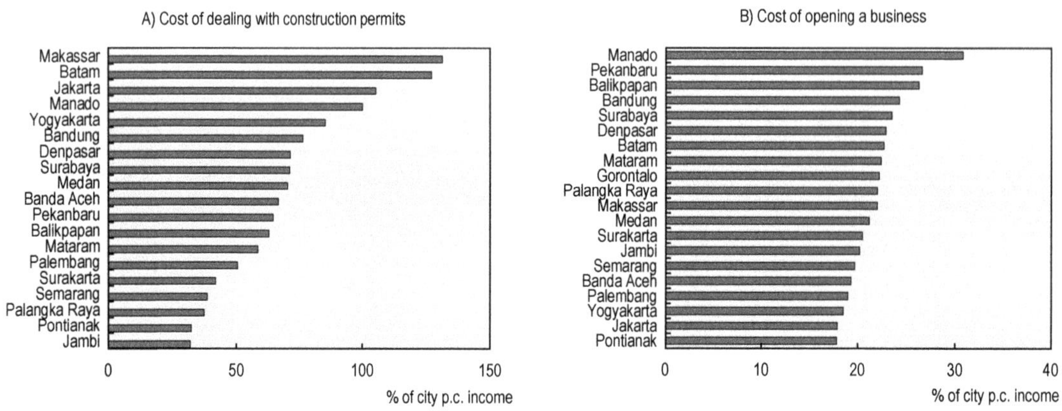

Notes: Data for Jakarta and Surabaya are for 2018; all other data are for 2012.
Source: World Bank (2018), *Doing Business in Indonesia 2018,* and World Bank (2012), *Doing business in Indonesia 2012*, World Bank, Washington DC.

StatLink https://doi.org/10.1787/888933824306

Aware of such heterogeneity in business regulations, the Indonesian government has launched several economic policy reforms to simplify and harmonise business regulations across provinces. For example, the 2016 XII Economic Policy Package specifically aimed to remove regulatory burdens for businesses and improve the ease of doing business. Nevertheless, the Monitoring Committee for the Implementation of Regional Autonomy (KPPOD) has found that despite these efforts there are still many overlaps in regulations which are partly the consequence of the speed at which the decentralisation process has taken place and which has left behind conflicting laws and unclear jurisdictions across different levels of governments (KPPOD, 2016).

Geographical variations in SME and entrepreneurship activity

Geographical differences are also evident in SME and entrepreneurship activity. Figure 6.4, based on information from the annual Micro and Small Manufacturing Industry Survey of the Indonesian Central Bureau of Statistics (BPS), shows substantial variations across Indonesian provinces with respect to industry-based small business density, which is measured as the number of industry-based businesses with 1-19 employees per 1 000 people. The densely populated areas of Central Java, Bali and East Java have the highest ratios (between 21 and 31), while the lowest ratios (2-3 businesses per 1 000 inhabitants) are found in the Special Region of West Papua, Papua, North and East Kalimantan, and Riau. Overall, 25 of the total 34 provinces had ratios below 20 small businesses per 1 000 people in 2015.

Variance in small business density can be influenced by many local factors, such as the presence of large employers, natural resource endowments (since large companies tend to dominate the exploitation of natural resources), whether the province is mostly rural or urban, and the weight of the informal sector.

Figure 6.4. Regional variations in industry small business density, 2015

Number of industry-based businesses with 1-19 employees per 1 000 population

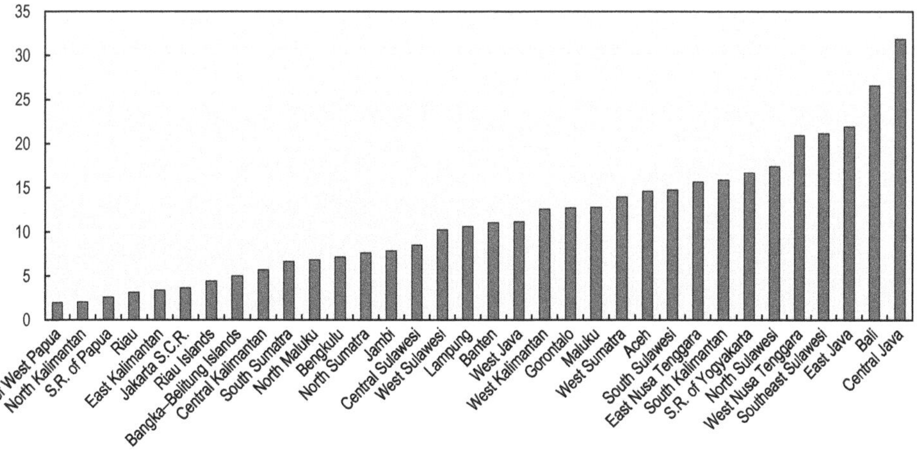

Notes: S.R. stands for Special Region, S.C.R. for Special Capital Region.
Source: OECD calculations based on Central Bureau of Statistics, "Micro and Small Manufacturing Industry Survey" and Population Statistics.

StatLink https://doi.org/10.1787/888933824325

Geographical variations in access to resources: loans and BDS

The BPS "Micro and Small Manufacturing Industry Survey" also provides insights on the access of small manufacturing companies to strategic resources, such as bank loans and business development services (BDS). The extent to which bank loans are the main source of loans ranged from 7% in Banten to 65% in the Special Region of West Papua in 2015. Family loans, and to a lesser degree, loans from individuals replaced bank loans as the main source of finance in certain specific cases, such as Banten, Aceh, South Sumatra and South Sulawesi. Loans from co-operatives were, on the other hand, mostly used in remote provinces such as North Maluku and East Nusa Tenggara (Figure 6.5).

With respect to the main reasons for small businesses not obtaining a loan, these were similar across all provinces. The most commonly reported reason was that a loan was not needed at the time of the survey, followed by procedural difficulties (notably in Java and Tenggara) and high collateral requirements (notably in Java, Bali and Sumatra). However, while the order of importance was similar, the incidence of each motive/barrier changed considerably by province. For example, "procedural difficulties" were mentioned by only 9% of small industrial companies in Bali, but by 26% in North Kalimantan and 53% in Maluku, where it was the single most important barrier to receiving a loan.

Provincial conditions also affect the take-up of BDS, which ranged between 1.5% in the eastern province of Maluku and 14% in the Special Region of Papua. Lack of awareness about BDS was the main reason across all provinces for entrepreneurs and small business owners not using them. Where lack of awareness was less pronounced, procedural difficulties were often pointed out (South Sulawesi and the Special Region of Papua) (Figure 6.6) (see chapter 7 for a more detailed analysis of BDS provision in Indonesia).

Figure 6.5. Source of main loans across Indonesian provinces, 2015

Survey of industry-based businesses with 1-19 employees, Percentage values

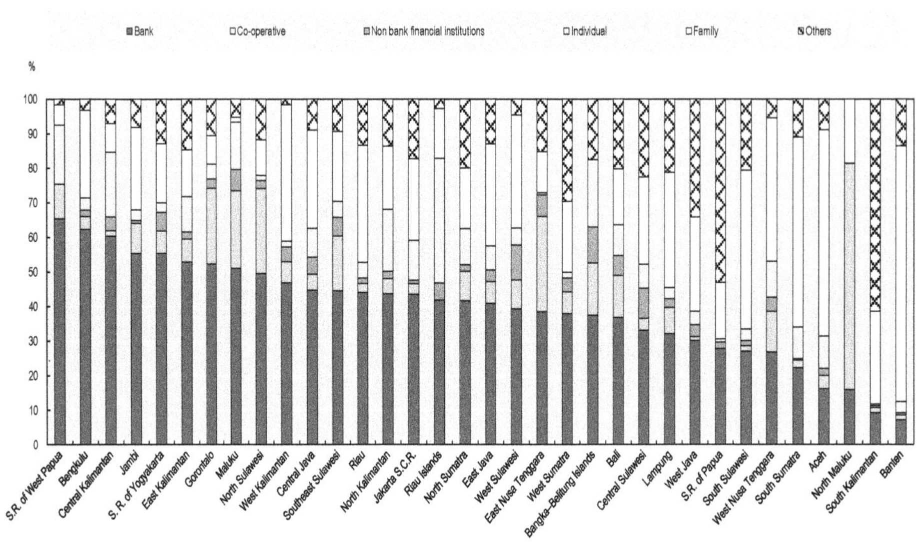

Notes: S.R. stands for Special Region, S.C.R. for Special Capital Region.
Source: Central Bureau of Statistics (BPS), "Micro and Small Manufacturing Industry Survey".

StatLink https://doi.org/10.1787/888933824344

Figure 6.6. Main reasons for not having received BDS across Indonesian provinces, 2015

Survey of industry-based small businesses (1-19 employees), Percentage values

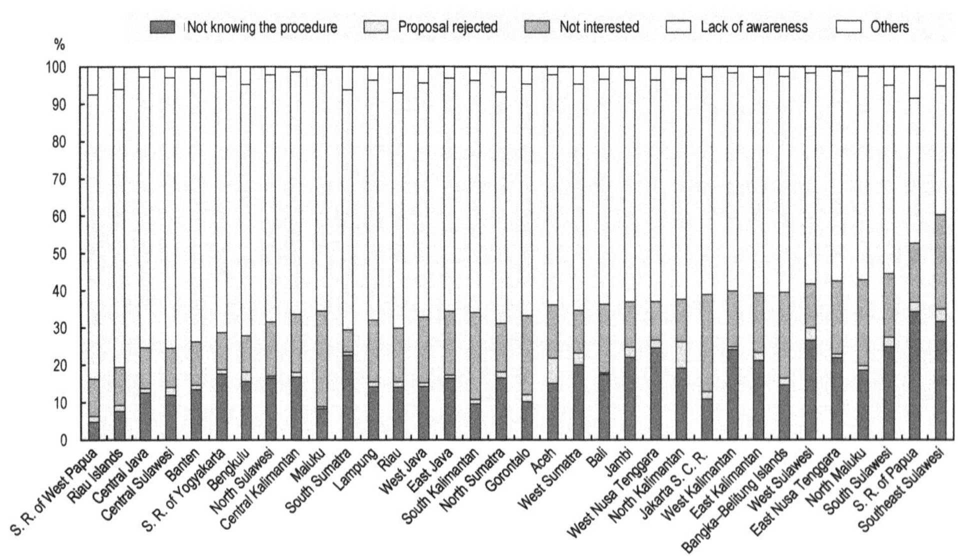

Notes: S.R. stands for Special Region, S.C.R. for Special Capital Region.
Source: Central Bureau of Statistics (BPS), "Micro and Small Manufacturing Industry Survey".

StatLink https://doi.org/10.1787/888933824363

Local government responsibilities in SME policy

Transforming from a long history of centralisation, Indonesia has undertaken a programme of extensive and rapid decentralisation since 1999. Law 22/1999, which was implemented in 2001 and resulted in the so-called "Big Bang" devolution, transferred many functions to subnational governments in all but a few tasks expressly assigned to the central government (defence, justice, police and planning). Because of the decentralisation process, the regional share in total government spending quickly doubled and two-thirds of the central government workforce was transferred to the regions (Hofman and Kaiser, 2002). As of 2012, fiscal transfers from the national government constituted 82% of the revenues at the district level, 66% at the city level and 34% at the provincial level, while own source revenues were 7% at the district level, 18% at the city level and 46% at the provincial level. Decentralisation has also led to a rise in the number of governmental units at all four sub-national tiers of government: provinces, regencies and cities, districts, and villages (Table 6.1).

Table 6.1. Levels of government in Indonesia

Type	Type (Indonesian)	Head of administration (English)	Head of administration (Indonesian)	Number
Central	Central	President (elected)	President	1
Province	Provinsi	Governor (elected)	Gubernur	34
Regency & City	Kabupaten & Kota	Regent & Mayor (elected)	Bupati & Wali kota	416 & 98
District	Kecamatan	Head of district (appointed)	Camat	7 160
Village	Desa & Kelurahan	Chief (elected for village, appointed for Kelurahan)	Kepata dasa / Lurah	83 184

Source: OECD (2016a), *OECD Economic Surveys: Indonesia 2016*, OECD Publishing, Paris, https://doi.org/10.1787/eco_surveys-idn-2016-en, based on Ministry of Home Affairs, Regulation 56/2015.

Following the decentralisation process, local government responsibilities in SME policy have grown to include the fulfilment of regulatory functions (e.g. business licenses and permits) and the design and implementation of support programmes (e.g. access to finance, infrastructure provision, business information and partnership, and trade promotion). One of the consequences of increased local autonomy has, therefore, been stronger variations in regulatory and licensing regimes across provinces.

In addition, a recent law on local government responsibilities (Law 23/2014) assigns the task of supporting specific enterprise sizes to different tiers of government. More specifically, this law provides that:

- The national government is responsible for the development of co-operatives and for providing education, training, and guidance for all SMEs. Furthermore, it is responsible for the development of medium-sized enterprises through other policies beyond education, training and guidance.
- The provincial government is responsible for the development of small enterprises (except for education, training and guidance provision).
- The city/regency government is responsible for the development of micro-enterprises (except for education, training and guidance provision).

While Law 23/2014 makes SME policy a legal obligation for local governments, it lacks a clear rationale by limiting the possibility for local governments to have policies for enterprises of a different size to the one they are responsible for by law. As it stands, this law might cause confusion among policymakers and entrepreneurs and might generate overlaps in certain cases and leave policy gaps in others. Furthermore, there is a risk that, if fully implemented, this law could leave micro and small companies in poorer regions managed and supported by local administrations with lower financial and human resource capacities than those in richer regions, thus widening the development divide among Indonesian provinces and regencies/cities.

At the very local level (i.e. district level), SME development falls within the responsibility of the Heads of District. At this level, whether SME development is a priority and whether national and provincial programmes are properly implemented often depends on the political agenda of the Head of District and the capacity of local government staff, adding a further element of volatility to the breadth and depth of SME policies at the local level.

Although local governments have a high degree of autonomy to tailor national programmes to local circumstances, limited local resources often inhibit the development of adequate policies, especially at the city and district levels. The range of SME and entrepreneurship programmes is, therefore, narrow in some places, and policies supporting the upgrading of SMEs into higher-value added activities are relatively sporadic. Limited local resources also mean that national attempts to simplify the system of business permits and licenses can be resisted at the local level because local governments wish to protect the revenue stream generated from granting such permits.

In addition to a lack of resources, local governments may lack the capacity to properly analyse the local situation and develop and implement appropriate policy responses, especially in less developed regions. The long tradition of centralisation in Indonesia has meant that for a long time local governments did not have the necessity to build the capacity for local economic development planning and policies (Nasution, 2016), although this has partly improved after the main decentralisation reform of the early 2000s. Monitoring and evaluation activities are also uneven and often focused upon counting quantitative inputs, activities and outputs of policies rather than focusing upon outcomes and longer-term impacts.

It follows that some of the generic supply-side policies are insufficiently differentiated and tailored to the local context. Examples include a lack of appropriate local access to finance initiatives for non-trade sectors such as fisheries and forestry in areas where these are key sectors; digitalisation initiatives that are not sufficiently matched to the different stages of business development; and limited export and internationalisation promotion for SMEs at the local level, with the partial exception of major cities (see chapter 5 for more details on national programmes).

Other stakeholders have made progress in tailoring their services to local conditions. The Association of Business Development Services of Indonesia (ABDSI), for example, has focused on developing vocational training, access to seed capital, and provision of equipment in border and under-developed areas, including in primary sectors such as fisheries and forestry. Going forward, business associations and chambers of commerce could become anchor institutions to provide capacity building to local governments, as shown by the example of Germany (see Box 6.1).

Box 6.1. International inspiring practice: Capacity building for local governments by chambers of commerce, Germany

Description of the approach

Several branches of the German Chambers of Commerce and Industry have developed checklists, training seminars and online support materials to help local governments to create a business-friendly environment for entrepreneurs and SMEs in their community, city, or region. The checklist includes questions on whether one-stop shops have been enacted locally, how high quality and transparency in service provision to businesses is secured, and what online services have been established. According to the local branches of the chamber of commerce, this initiative has helped raise awareness in local communities on how policy can stimulate entrepreneurship locally, including how local public officials can facilitate service provision for SMEs and entrepreneurs.

Success factors

Key success factors have been the traditionally close ties of the local chambers of commerce with city and village governments, which have helped to build a relationship of mutual trust, as well as the organisation of inter-communal seminars in which different communities were able to exchange and learn from each other on how to improve the local business climate.

Obstacles and responses

Key challenges have included difficulties in overcoming institutional rigidities such as limited flexibility in the allocation of staff and the lack of available budget to implement certain support measures. These issues were solved in a number of areas through co-operation among smaller municipalities and inclusion of practical implementation aspects in training events and seminars.

Relevance to Indonesia

One of the key issues in local entrepreneurship and SME policy formulation is a lack of capacity on how to create a business-friendly local environment and how to actively support entrepreneurship and SME development locally. The national government could consider a training academy in collaboration with the chambers of commerce to build local government knowledge on key issues related to local economic strategy building, strategic marketing and branding, and business aftercare services.

Sources for further information:

https://www.dihk.de/themenfelder/wirtschaftspolitik (in German)

Mechanisms for tailoring national SME and entrepreneurship programmes to local conditions

Two co-ordination mechanisms ensure that national SME and entrepreneurship policies are tailored to local needs. The first is a bottom-up policy co-ordination process which provides the lower levels of government with the opportunity to express their views. This consultation process has its starting point in each village through regular village council meetings and goes through district, regency/city and finally province to the central government to feed into national policy making. While this mechanism theoretically provides local governments with the possibility to feed into national policy development, it is unclear to what extent it is implemented across provinces. Moreover, as noted earlier, research and analytical capacities to identify local conditions and issues and to inform policy making is uneven across local governments.

The second co-ordination mechanism, of a more top-down nature, ensures that nationally-funded SME programmes are tailored to local circumstances through the setting of national targets that local governments are responsible for delivering. However, such targets tend to focus on the numbers of certain activities rather than on their contents and outcomes, thus reducing the scope for adaptation to local conditions.

In addition, the decentralised governance system of Indonesia has offered substantial autonomy for governments at local levels, which also supports policy tailoring. For example, the national One Village, One Product Programme focuses on targeting support for the development of a product that is unique to its local area. This programme is effective in addressing local conditions through relying on local knowledge, skills, traditions and resources. However, one possible downside is that a similar programme could end up reinforcing economic specialisations in low value-added activities at the expense of promoting upgrading of existing products or the creation of new products.

Clear policy targeting is also evident locally in programmes for specific groups such as women and youth, for sectors and key products (e.g. food, furniture, garments), and for geographical areas, such as lagging and border regions. Combinations of such targeting are also utilised where appropriate (see Box 6.2). The leadership of responsible national ministries is also visible in offering support at the local level. For example, the Ministry of Industry runs the Indonesian Footwear Development Centre, which focuses support on size standardisation, product quality and branding in footwear, and the Bali Creative Industry Centre, which develops competences in animation and ICT, crafts, and fashion.

Box 6.2. Targeting women's empowerment and entrepreneurship at the local level in Papua

Bank Indonesia has implemented a nationwide programme jointly with local governments to increase women's participation in economic activities and in the formal banking system. In Papua, the identified local economic potential mostly involved handicrafts for domestic and export markets. The programme aimed to support women through education, training and individual mentoring on aspects related to business planning, marketing and technology. The programme also encouraged the formation of formal groups of women producers with the aim of enhancing their chances of receiving credit from local banks. Finally, an annual sales exhibition is organised in Jakarta that brings products for sale from all 46 areas where the programme has been operating.

Mechanisms for co-ordinating national-local SME and entrepreneurship programmes

The main policy co-ordinating mechanisms in Indonesia work in a top-down fashion. At the central level, the Ministry of National Development Planning (BAPPENAS) prepares Long-Term, Medium-Term and Annual National Development Plans, based on priorities set out at the Presidential level. These plans provide broad economic policy directions and inform the work of all technical ministries, each of which prepares a "Strategic Plan" to fulfil its mandate. Co-ordinating Ministries, notably the Co-ordinating Ministry for Economic Affairs in the case of SME policy, also play an important role in the co-ordination of the work of technical ministers (see chapter 4 for more details on the governance of national SME policy).

Local governments at province, regency/city, and district levels each have Medium-Term Development Plans that are used to adapt the national plans to local conditions. In addition, the elected governors have the possibility to introduce their own local priorities following their election. Annual co-ordination meetings are held between national and local-level stakeholders that involve national and local government and the private and civic sectors. Quarterly regional meetings are also used for information exchange, technical co-ordination and programme adjustment activities.

National technical ministries collaborate with the local level either directly or through their local representative offices. For example, the national Ministry of Co-operatives and SMEs, in the framework of the Integrated Business Services Centres (see chapter 7), has encouraged local governments to use existing buildings to provide services to SMEs and entrepreneurs so as to reduce the need for national government funding. On this occasion, local governments have also been asked to engage and lever in resources from other local stakeholders including banks, universities, and research centres.

Joint working between national ministries and local governments has also led to policy innovations in certain cases, for example on gender empowerment (see Box 6.3).

Box 6.3. Gender budgeting and the home industry programme in Cilegon city, Banten province

In 2016, the gender budgeting and home industry programme was piloted in a three-year Memorandum of Understanding between the Ministry of Women's Empowerment and Child Protection and the city of Cilegon in the province of Banten. Cilegon is a relatively poor area in the national context; identified local issues included high levels of migrant flows and people trafficking. The aim of the programme was, first, to provide greater gender transparency in the local government budgeting process and, second, to develop a programme to support women's home-based business start-ups. The programme was match funded by the national Ministry and the local government on a phased basis, reducing from 100% national funding in Year 1 to 20% in Year 3 and 100% local funding in Year 4.

Identified as a longstanding issue, co-ordination between the national and local levels in Indonesia is complicated by the large number of national and subnational governmental units involved in SME policy and by uneven policy capacity at the local level (Budiharsono, 2014; OECD, 2016a). Other key problems identified by different ministries include the need for a better understanding of SME and co-operative development issues at the local level; reducing duplication and clarifying roles and responsibilities, especially for programme implementation; increasing the funding and incentives for programmes that stimulate productivity improvement; and enhancing monitoring and evaluation (see, for example, Burger et al., 2015).

Mechanisms for co-ordination among local governments and their partners in SME and entrepreneurship policy

Horizontal co-ordination – i.e. co-ordination among local governments and between local governments and other local stakeholders – is central to aligning and integrating local activities in support of SMEs and entrepreneurship. At the provincial level, the Forums of Economic and Resource Development, which include the provincial government, business associations, academics, and other service providers, are a key co-ordination mechanism (Phelps and Wijava, 2016). The forums, which are present in many provinces, bring together policy makers and key local stakeholders and also involve the regency/city and district governments.

Cluster Consultation Forums have also been utilised to engage the government with SMEs, cutting across government geographical boundaries and levels. Examples include industrial, agricultural and tourism clusters, such as footwear in Cibaduyut (Western Java) and ceramics in Plered (Special Region of Yogyakarta). Cluster forums support information and knowledge exchange and the targeting of policy support for SMEs and entrepreneurs working within the cluster.

Formal co-operation between local governments, however, has been limited by the lack of appropriate regulations to govern it (Budiharsono, 2014). Provincial governments have highlighted the lack of a legal basis for certain kinds of collaborative activities and joint projects.

Intermediary institutions are used in other national contexts to support co-ordination between local governments and other local stakeholders in the public, private and civic sectors. These institutions can be set up with the explicit objective of bringing partners together, facilitating dialogue, building capacity, and aligning policy and programme objectives, expenditure and activities. They can be jointly funded by the partners and can have a specific policy focus, as shown by the example of the Japanese *Kosetsushi* Centres focusing their support on innovation and technology upgrading (see Box 6.4).

Box 6.4. International inspiring practice: *Kosetsushi* Centres and other similar organisations, Japan

Description of the approach

Japan's local public technology centres (*Kosetsushi* Centres) help SMEs through technology consulting and, increasingly, by acting as a network hub for more general knowledge transfer. They focus mainly on manufacturing, food industry and design, and have inspired other similar local intermediary organisations to support SME innovation in Japan.

For example, Sasebo City in the prefecture of Nagasaki works closely with West Kyushu Techno-Consortium based at one of the technology colleges in the city. The consortium was established in 2006 to connect surrounding municipalities in the North of the Nagasaki Prefecture with other public and private actors, including the local foundation for industrial promotion, *Kosetsushi* Centres, industry, universities and other technical colleges in the area. The consortium aims to develop innovative technology and enhance skills for local development.

Another example is the Fukui Prefecture which established the Open Innovation Promotion Organisation in 2016. This organisation aims to facilitate and co-ordinate a programme which encourages R&D-centred collaboration among university, industry, government and financial institutions. The prefecture government responds to R&D needs of local SMEs not only through local networks and intermediaries, including the *Kosetsushi* Centres, but also by mobilising networks with national research institutes and large corporations beyond the local jurisdiction.

Success factors

The nature and functions of local innovation support mechanisms for SMEs have changed over the years in Japan both at prefecture and city/municipality levels. *Kosetsushi* Centres have existed since the late 19th century and have been funded by local authorities. They have played an important role in the Japanese innovation system through supporting local technological innovation, particularly providing consulting services for local manufacturing SMEs. In recent years, the scope of *Kosetsushi* Centres has shifted from only providing R&D-oriented support to a more "needs-driven" intermediary function facilitating networking and knowledge transfer among local SMEs (Nobuya and Akira, 2016). These centres are also building broader collaborative relationships with universities, sometimes connecting beyond local authority jurisdictions.

Obstacles and responses

The rise of the intangible economy has meant a growing importance of intangible assets beyond R&D. To respond to this major shift, the *Kosetsushi* Centres have moved from being R&D centres to hubs of knowledge transfer which work on both technological and non-technological innovation. Furthermore, job mobility of local public officers, which is common in Japan, helps co-ordination among local governments, the *Kosetsushi* Centres and other local stakeholders even when formal local co-ordination mechanisms are not in place.

Relevance to Indonesia

Indonesian SMEs face problems in adopting new technologies for improving productivity. While local programmes have been developed in some provinces, strong institutions and arrangements to align and co-ordinate initiatives aimed at supporting technology innovation in small enterprises are relatively sporadic. The Japanese *Kosetsushi* Centres, and similar other initiatives, could be a model for local government engagement with local partners from industry and universities to support SME innovation at the local level.

Sources for further information

Fukui prefecture: http://www.yuchi.pref.fukui.jp/en/fukui/1300-4m.html.
Nishi Kyushu Techno consortium:
http://www.sasebo.ac.jp/~kikaku/yoran/16youran/pages/35.html.
Nobuya, F. and G. Akira (2016), *Problem Solving and Intermediation by Local Public Technology Centers in Regional Innovation Systems*, first report on a branch-level survey on technical consultation, http://www.rieti.go.jp/en/

Conclusions and policy recommendations

Indonesia is characterised by large geographical variations in wealth, the quality of the business environment, SME and entrepreneurship activity and enterprise access to strategic resources (e.g. loans and business support services). A devolution process started in the early 2000s has helped provide the necessary flexibility to target policy to local needs; however, there are still challenges both with regard to the tailoring of national SME and entrepreneurship policies to the local context and to ensuring effective policy co-ordination across levels of government. Both are made difficult by the large number of national and subnational institutions involved in SME policy and by uneven policy capacity at the local level.

Furthermore, the recent law on the role of local government in SME policy (Law 23/2014) is a source of complexity by giving policy responsibility for firms of different sizes to different levels of government. This law is difficult to implement and, if fully implemented, would likely leave SMEs in poorer provinces and regencies/cities supported by subnational governments with poorer resources and capacities.

Based on this analysis the following recommendations are offered to strengthen the local dimension of SME and entrepreneurship policy in Indonesia.

Policy recommendations on the local dimension of SME and entrepreneurship policy

- Build capacity among local policy makers to develop local SME and entrepreneurship policies, including through information and awareness raising, training and guidance material, and mentoring and peer learning networks between stronger and weaker local governments.
- Encourage local-level reviews of the range of SME programmes in place to ensure an appropriate policy mix, which should also include programmes aimed at upgrading SME productivity through the use of new technologies, workforce training and/or managerial skills upgrading.
- Match quantity with quality targets for SME and entrepreneurship policy outcomes at the local level. This will require changing targets from focusing solely on the total numbers of SMEs and entrepreneurs created and/or sustained to a wider focus on their quality in relation to indicators such as value added, wage levels and employment.
- Consider amending Law 23/2014 where it assigns responsibility for the development of specific business size classes to specific levels of government (micro-enterprises to regencies or cities, small enterprises to provinces, and medium-sized enterprises to the national level) since this is a source of complexity and risks widening the development divide between more and less prosperous regions.
- Further streamline business regulation procedures and limit the negative impact of administrative fragmentation caused by the increase in the number of local government units.
- Develop and enhance mechanisms to improve co-ordination between government institutions at national and local levels, and among local governments, through more regular co-ordination meetings and policy dialogue on SME and entrepreneurship policies.
- Strengthen policy monitoring and evaluation systems and better align national and local-level monitoring and evaluation approaches and activities.

References

Brunori, D. (2003), *Local Tax Policy: A Federalist Perspective*, Urban Institute Press, Washington DC.

Budiharsono, S. (2014), *Local Economic Development: The Indonesia Experience*, https://de.slideshare.net/budiharsonos/local-economic-development-the-indonesian-experiences.

Burger, N., C. Chazali, A. Gaduh, A. Rothenberg, I. Tjandraningsih and S. Weilant (2015), *Reforming Policies for Small and Medium Enterprises in Indonesia*, RAND Corporation and Tim Nasional Percepatan Penanggulangan Kemiskinan (TNP2K), Jakarta, Indonesia.

Gismar, A., I. Lockman and L. Hidayat (2012), *Towards A Well-Informed Society and Responsive Government* , Executive Report Indonesia Governance Index 2012, The Partnership For Governance Reform, *Kemitraan Bagi Pembaruan Tata Pemerintahan*), http://www.kemitraan.or.id/igi/index.php/data/publication/factsheet/275-igi-executive-report.

Hofman, B. and K. Kaiser (2002), "The Making of the Big Bang and its Aftermath: A Political Economy Perspective", paper presented at the conference "Can Decentralization Help Rebuild Indonesia?", Atlanta, 1-3 May 2002, http://www1.worldbank.org/publicsector/decentralization/March2004Course/Hofman2.pdf.

KPPOD (Monitoring Committee for the Implementation of Regional Autonomy) (2016), *Evaluation of the Implementation of the Economic Policy Package on Regulatory Reform across Indonesian Regions*, (in Indonesian), KPPOD Publishing, Jakarta, https://www.kppod.org/backend/files/laporan_penelitian/eodb-reformasi-kemudahan-berusaha.pdf.

Nasution, A. (2016), "Government decentralization program in Indonesia", *ADBI Working Paper 601*, Asian Development Bank Institute, Tokyo, https://www.adb.org/sites/default/files/publication/201116/adbi-wp601.pdf.

Nobuya, F. and G. Akira (2016), *Problem Solving and Intermediation by Local Public Technology Centers in Regional Innovation Systems*, first report on a branch-level survey on technical consultation, http://www.rieti.go.jp/en/.

OECD (2016a), *OECD Economic Surveys: Indonesia 2016*, OECD Publishing, Paris, https://doi.org/10.1787/eco_surveys-idn-2016-en.

OECD (2016b), *Open Government in Indonesia*, OECD Public Governance Reviews, OECD Publishing, Paris, http://dx.doi.org/10.1787/9789264265905-en.

Phelps, N. and H. Wijaya (2016), "Joint action in action? Local economic development forums and industry cluster development in Central Java, Indonesia", *International Development Planning Review*, Vol. 38, N. 4, pp. 425-448, http://dx.doi.org/10.3828/idpr.2016.24.

Strickland, T. (2016), "Funding and financing urban infrastructure: a UK-US comparison", Newcastle University, Doctor of Philosophy Dissertation, https://theses.ncl.ac.uk/dspace/bitstream/10443/3148/1/Strickland%2C%20T.%202016.pdf.

William, E., J. Ritzen and M. Woolcock (2006), "Social cohesion, institutions, and growth", *Economics and Politics*, Vol. 18, N. 2, pp. 103-120, http://dx.doi.org/10.1111/j.1468-0343.2006.00165.x.

World Bank (2012), *Doing business in Indonesia 2012*, World Bank, Washington DC, http://www.doingbusiness.org/~/media/WBG/DoingBusiness/Documents/Subnational-Reports/DB12-Indonesia.p.

7. Business development services for SMEs and entrepreneurship

This chapter assesses the system of business development services (BDS) in Indonesia. It presents information on the demand for such services by small businesses, describes the evolution and current offer of BDS in Indonesia, and analyses in detail the recent initiative of the Integrated Business Services Centres for Co-operatives and SMEs (PLUT-KUMKM Centres). There are currently a large number of BDS programmes run by different ministries in Indonesia. The Ministry of Co-operatives and SMEs is working to improve the standardisation of BDS and to consolidate the supply of BDS nationwide through the PLUT-KUMKM Centres. This initiative can help rationalise the offer of government-supported BDS, especially if it succeeds in building further synergies with other existing similar programmes.

Introduction

The concept of "business development services" (BDS) refers to services aimed at enhancing the productivity and competitiveness of SMEs through the upgrading of managerial and technical skills, access to markets, new or improved technologies, and appropriate financing mechanisms (see Box 7.1). Micro and small enterprises often cannot afford such services at market rates, leading many governments in OECD and non-OECD countries to offer subsidised BDS.

Government-supported BDS can be administered directly by public agencies, private-sector organisations (e.g. chambers of commerce and business associations), NGOs or a combination of the three (Storey, 2003). The services offered often include business diagnostics, information and advice, and coaching and mentoring, which can be delivered in physical spaces (e.g. one-stop shops and business services centres) or online (Mole, 2018).

Box 7.1. Definition of business development services

Business development services can be defined as "…services that improve the performance of the enterprise, its access to markets, and its ability to compete (…)". They include a wide array of business services, both strategic and operational. Operational services are those needed for day-to-day operations, such as information and communications, management of accounts and tax records, and compliance with labour laws and other regulations. Strategic services can help the enterprise to identify and service markets, design products, set up facilities, and seek financing" (Committee of Donor Agencies for Small Enterprise Development, 2001).

The demand for BDS by Indonesian small enterprises

Survey data from the Central Bureau of Statistics (BPS) offer an insight into the demand and use of BDS and training services by Indonesian small industry-based companies (1-19 employees). In 2014 and 2015, only 4.5% and 4.2% of these companies had received business advisory services respectively (Table 7.1). Between 61% and 65% of the surveyed enterprises reported that they had not made use of such services due to a lack of awareness, while another 16% indicated that they did not know how to access these services. The government could seek to remedy this through awareness-raising campaigns on existing BDS programmes and opportunities and through ensuring that these services are available nationwide through physical government offices, mobile support centres or partnership arrangements with private-sector BDS organisations.

For the small proportion of small industry-based enterprises that used business advisory services, government programmes were the most used singular source, followed by BDS provided by co-operatives and banks. As shown in chapter 6, there is also variation in the use of business advisory services across Indonesian provinces.

Table 7.1. Proportion of industry-based small enterprises receiving business advisory services, 2014 and 2015

Survey of industry-based businesses with 1-19 employees

	2014		2015	
	Number of SMEs	%	Number of SMEs	%
Total number of SMEs	3 505 064	100%	3 668 879	100%
Received business advisory support	159 475	4.5%	153 884	4.2%
Did not receive business advisory support	3 505 064	95.5%	3 515 787	95.8%
Reasons for not having received business advisory support		Of the 95.5%		Of the 95.8%
Did not know about the service	2 047 987	61.2%	2 269 425	64.6%
Did not know the procedures for accessing it	536 076	16.0%	555 605	15.8%
Not interested	556 231	16.6%	520 318	14.8%
Request for assistance was rejected	41 003	1.2%	47 079	1.3%
Other	164 292	4.9%	119 909	3.4%
Percentage who received business advisory support (4.5% in 2014 and 4.2% in 2015) organised by:		Of the 4.5%		Of the 4.2%
Government programme	54 464	33.0%	63 532	40.7%
Co-operatives	34 929	21.2%	35 303	22.6%
Bank	23 989	14.5%	26 429	16.9%
Private	12 714	7.7%	10 307	6.6%
NGO	5 219	3.2%	3 104	2.0%
Other (e.g. chamber, business association, etc.)	33 683	20.4%	17 519	11.2%

Source: Central Bureau of Statistics (BPS), "Micro and Small Manufacturing Industry Survey".

StatLink https://doi.org/10.1787/888933824382

The same BPS survey also reveals that in 2015 only 4.3% of the 3.66 million industry-based small businesses undertook any form of workforce training (Table 7.2). Similarly to business advisory services, government programmes were the most common source of workforce training.

Table 7.2. Proportion of industry-based small enterprises receiving training, 2015

Survey of industry-based businesses with 1-19 employees

	Number of SMEs	%
Total number of SMEs	3 668 879	100%
Have never received training	3 512 434	95.7%
Have received training	156 439	4.3%
Source of training for the 4.3% of SMEs that received training:		Of the 4.3%
Government programme	96 550	60.4%
Themselves	22 578	14.9%
Private sector	20 186	12.6%
NGO	10 015	6.3%
Other	10 441	6.5%

Source: Central Bureau of Statistics (BPS), "Micro and Small Manufacturing Industry Survey".

StatLink https://doi.org/10.1787/888933824401

The evolution and current offer of BDS programmes in Indonesia

Private-sector BDS

The Indonesian government's first BDS policy in the 1990s consisted in subsidising the activity of private-sector BDS consultants working with SMEs, with the long-term goal of helping the rise of local BDS markets. In this first phase, the government would provide a small amount of initial operational capital to private-sector consultants willing to offer professional services to SMEs, which were in turn encouraged to get together to receive the technical assistance. This approach reflected the general principles for donor interventions in BDS for small enterprises, notably that sustainable BDS would be best achieved if delivered by the private sector on a user-pay basis (Committee of Donor Agencies for Small Enterprise Development, 2001).

From the early 2000s, however, the Indonesian government grew unsatisfied with this approach. The quality of the consultants was uneven and often unpredictable, thus causing strong heterogeneity in the quality of services across the country. Furthermore, most consultants were based in large urban areas, leaving SMEs in many parts of Indonesia underserved or unserved. Finally, in a system where only part of the services cost was covered by the government, most consultants preferred working with larger SMEs which could pay more, thus leaving smaller SMEs underserved.

SME Business Clinics

As a result, in 2006, the Ministry of Trade launched the so-called SME Business Clinics to provide free training and advisory services to SMEs in areas such as business management and access to markets, capital, raw materials and technology. The initial phase of this project was funded by the Ministry of Trade with the involvement of many other government and non-government institutions (e.g. the Ministry of Co-operatives and SMEs, Bank Indonesia, Bank Rakyat Indonesia and the Chamber of Commerce and Industry) in its implementation. Since the very beginning, this policy initiative partnered closely with local governments, which were expected to fund the activities of SME Business Clinics after the initial period of central government support. SME Business Clinics still exist today, but they are mostly operated at the local level by local governments and universities.

The Ministry of Industry's Sentra Programme and SMI Technical Services Units

In the mid-2000s, the Ministry of Industry also started to encourage the creation of self-help groups, called SMI *Sentras*, to upgrade managerial skills in small and medium industry-based enterprises (SMIs). A *"Sentra"* is a group of at least five SMIs, in a certain geographic region, with similar raw material needs, production processes or end products, which come together to receive technical assistance facilitated by external consultants recruited by the Ministry of Industry. The technical assistance focuses on human resources capabilities, technology development and market development.

In 2016, there were more than 7 400 *Sentra* groups in Indonesia involving around 37 000 SMIs, with each SMI field consultant working with six *Sentra* groups. The Ministry of Industry plans to further expand this programme, with budget allocations of IDR 245 billion in 2016 (for new SMI *Sentras* in 191 districts) and IDR 531.5 million in 2017 (for new SMI *Sentras* in 14 districts). Proposals for the new SMI *Sentra* must come from district governments, with the requirement that property used for the *Sentra* is government-owned.

The Ministry of Industry also operates 40 Small and Medium Industry (SMI) Technical Services Units through a network of about 500 technology extension workers. These workers proactively reach out to SMEs in their respective local areas to offer free consulting and technical assistance in technology-related areas such as product development, intellectual property acquisition, design and product marketing, standard certification and energy use management.

The Ministry of State-Owned Enterprises' Creative Houses

A more recent development has been the creation of so-called Creative Houses by the Ministry of State-Owned Enterprises (SOEs). These facilities, started in 2016, are a corporate social responsibility initiative of the Ministry of SOEs, targeting SMEs with technical guidance and assistance in product development, access to finance, marketing and promotion, and skills development. The ambition of the Ministry of SOEs is to have 545 of these facilities all over Indonesia.

Other initiatives

Other ministries and agencies operate programmes that provide BDS to SMEs, although these tend to be more limited in scope and number. For example, the Ministry of Youth and Sports operates about 60 Youth Entrepreneurship Centres to provide training and advisory services to clusters of young entrepreneurs (similar to the *Sentra* model). The Ministry of Manpower runs 22 Productivity Centres and the Business Advisory Programme, both of which target entrepreneurs and small business owners from disadvantaged social groups. Since 2015, the Financial Services Authority (*Otoritas Jasa Keuangan*, OJK) has established Centres for Education, Consumer Services and Financial Access for SMEs (PELAKU) at its regional branch offices. In 2017, the PELAKU Centres operated in 14 OJK branches, although the final objective is to have one in each of the 35 regional offices. The main activity of the PELAKU Centres is to facilitate access to credit and other sources of finance through dissemination of information on financial services and bank requirements.

The experience of the Integrated Business Services Centres for Co-operatives and SMEs (PLUT-KUMKM Centres)

In 2013, the Ministry of Co-operatives and SMEs launched the "Integrated Business Services Centres for Co-operatives and SMEs" (PLUT-KUMKM Centres), the main objective of which is to provide comprehensive, integrated and affordable (free) BDS to SMEs and co-operatives through a network of local one-stop shops. The centres aim to cover seven key business competencies: management advice; product quality and intellectual property; legal affairs; access to finance; marketing and promotion; ICT adoption; and business networks. A key principle of these centres is that their staff and consultants will reach out to small business owners in their workplaces, similarly to the Ministry of Industry's SMI Technical Services Units and their extension workers.

In 2017, there were 51 PLUT-KUMKM Centres in operation, which had offered assistance to nearly 200 000 entrepreneurs and small business owners. The goal is to have 200 such centres by the end of 2019, which requires additional funding and which still might not be enough to guarantee a widespread presence of the centres across the country.

By way of comparison, the Brazilian Micro and Small Enterprise Agency (SEBRAE) operates a network of 700 SME Support Service Centres for a population of 207 million, while Canada, with its small population of 36 million dispersed over a very large territory, has a network of 240 federally-funded Community Business Development Centres.

The PLUT-KUMKM Centres build on a close collaboration between the Ministry of Co-operatives and SMEs, provincial governments and, in some cases, local authorities (regencies and cities). The Ministry has issued technical guidelines on the design (e.g. the centres must have a front office, a consulting room, a training room and a networking room), organisational structure and technical responsibilities of the centres to ensure homogeneity in services delivery across the country. Furthermore, it has produced a Standard Operating Procedures Manual to give guidance to provincial and regency/city governments on how to operate a PLUT-KUMKM Centre. At the local level, the operations of the centres are managed by the department of the provincial government responsible for SME empowerment. Provinces have, sometimes, decided to build more than one centre to reach locations beyond the provincial capital. In such cases, the main provincial PLUT-KUMKM Centre co-ordinates and supervises the work of the centres located elsewhere within the same province.

The original aim of the national government was to meet the initial costs of each PLUT-KUMKM Centre, including the construction of the facilities intended to host the centres and the operational costs of the centres for the first three years of operations. However, due to budget constraints, only 5 of the 90 requests from provinces could be approved in 2017. As a result, since 2018, provinces submitting proposals for the PLUT-KUMKM Centres must agree to meet the costs related to the physical facility of the centre, possibly by renovating an existing public building, with the central budget only covering operational costs (i.e. the cost of the staff giving advice and training) for the first three years. Eventually, it is expected that provincial and local governments will fund the operations of the PLUT-KUMKM Centres through their own budgets.

Besides the close partnership between the central government and the provincial/local governments, the PLUT-KUMKM initiative rests on the involvement of private-sector organisations with strong BDS expertise. This has the advantage of leveraging existing private-sector expertise and creating a local demand for BDS.

The main private-sector organisation involved in the operations of the PLUT-KUMKM Centres is the Association of Business Development Services Indonesia (ABDSI), whose members account for 40% of the approximately 300 consultants/advisors in the existing 51 centres. Together with ABDSI, the Ministry of Co-operatives and SMEs has developed a four-level (i.e. beginner, intermediate, advanced and master) competency standard for BDS providers leading to a national qualification. The development of the competency standard has been informed by a review of experiences in other countries and has benefited from the collaboration of the Ministry of Manpower.

An essential component in the management of the certification programme will be the establishment of a national certification body. ABDSI is in the process of creating a Professional Certification Institute that could play this role. The Pelita Harapan University also has experience certifying small business counsellors under an agreement with the Asia-Pacific Economic Co-operation (APEC) and could also provide valuable inputs into this process.

The Ministry of Co-operatives and SMEs also collaborates with ABDSI to reach out to parts of the country lacking a PLUT-KUMKM Centre and to gather information on the profile of SME clients visiting and using the services of the centres. This latest development could permit the collection of useful information for the monitoring and evaluation of the activities of the PLUT-KUMKM Centres. Data collected from each PLUT-KUMKM Centre should, however, go beyond simply counting the number of users to report on their characteristics (e.g. gender, sector of activity, stage of business development, etc.), types of services received, and level of satisfaction with the information and assistance received. This information should be collected from each PLUT-KUMKM Centre into a centralised electronic system to make aggregate analysis possible.

Other third-party organisations also participate more occasionally in the operations of the PLUT-KUMKM Centres. For example, some of the centres have installed SME Digital Villages in partnership with Telkom Indonesia to improve the quality of market access for co-operatives and SMEs, while the Chamber of Commerce and Industry (KADIN) delivers training courses on small business management in some of the centres.

Moving forward, it will be important to increase the number of PLUT-KUMKM Centres to better reflect the geographical expanse and population size of Indonesia, although this could also partly be achieved through better integration of the PLUT-KUMKM Centres with other similar government programmes, such as the Creative Houses of the Ministry of SOEs and the SMI Technical Services Units of the Ministry of Industry. Stronger collaborations with other stakeholders of the national entrepreneurial ecosystem, such as universities, should also be developed. The case study of the *Negosyo* Centres from the Philippines provides an example of how another ASEAN country has built an integrated BDS offer nationwide through a single visible entry point for small business owners and entrepreneurs (see Box 7.2)

Box 7.2. International inspiring practice: *Negosyo* Centres, Philippines

Description of the approach

The *Negosyo* Centres (NCs) were established under the Republic Act 10644 of 2014 (also known as the "Go *Negosyo* Act") in order to enhance the contribution of SMEs and new entrepreneurs to economic growth and social cohesion. The Act stipulates that the NCs are governed by the Micro, Small and Medium Enterprise Development (MSMED) Council under the oversight of the Department of Trade and Industry (DTI), and that they should be established in every province, city and municipality through public-private partnerships.

The main tasks of the NCs involve the provision of: i) assistance with business registration, including co-ordination with the respective local government units (LGUs); ii) business information, including on training opportunities, financial institutions and government support programmes; iii) business advisory services, including free one-on-one advice and the organisation, together with the local chambers of commerce, of a mentoring programme for future and existing entrepreneurs.

NCs are classified into three operating models. "Full-Service Centres" have 3-5 business counsellors and administrative support staff and cover the whole range of activities. "Advanced Centres" are staffed with 2-3 business counsellors and need the support of the DTI or a Full-Service Centre in order to execute certain programmes and activities. "Basic Centres" are staffed with one business counsellor and mainly disseminate business-related information and provide assistance in the processing of documentation.

By the end of 2017 there were 789 NCs in the Philippines, 691 of which were located in local government offices (87%), 76 in DTI regional offices (10%) and the remaining 3% in universities or NGOs. The majority of the NCs are Basic Centres (352, i.e. 45% of the total), 35% are Advanced Centres (275) and 20% are Full-Service Centres (162). As of end-2017 the NCs employed 1 682 people (average of 2.1 persons per centre) and had assisted a total of approximately 636 000 clients, about half of whom with business registration, 15% with management training support, and 2% with access to finance-related services. Based on information from government documents (Multi-Phase Plan of 2014-2022), the DTI plans to establish an additional 526 centres by the end of 2022.

To establish an NC, local stakeholders, including the local DTI office, the LGU, the business community, academia and the financial services sector, meet to discuss and identify their individual roles and responsibilities, which are formalised in a legal agreement. Thereafter, the different representatives participate in a Learning Workshop offered by DTI covering the operational details related to managing an NC. In cases where an LGU already operates a business development centre, it can apply to the DTI to upgrade it into an NC to offer a wider and more consistent range of services.

The NCs operate based on a co-funding arrangement by which the host cities and municipalities provide the physical space and the DTI assumes responsibility for the basic equipment and the training components of the programme.

Success factors

A critical success factor in the NC Programme has been co-ordination and collaboration with the local level of government and the private sector, for example to secure subscription plans to advanced network connectivity (e.g. Quickbooks Online and Microsoft Office 365 Accounts).

The existence of a co-ordinating body for the NCs at the DTI, the "*Negosyo* Centre Programme Management Unit" (NC-PMU), has also played an important role. In addition to overseeing the establishment of new NCs, the NC-PMU holds monthly meetings and workshops with the NC co-ordinators to monitor developments and ensure that the operations of all centres comply with national standards.

Furthermore, good internet connectivity has also proven crucial. For example, the use of cloud-based software enables all NCs and the NC-PMU to store, manage and transmit large amounts of information across regions and has enabled the creation of the *Negosyo* Centre Monitoring System at the NC-PMU.

Obstacles and responses

Ensuring the competences of the staff working in the NCs has proven the main challenge. In this respect, the "Go *Negosyo* Act" stipulates that DTI business counsellors and staff working in the NCs must undergo the Small Business Counselling Course (SBCC) training which covers modules on business diagnostics, strategic marketing, operations management, financial management, and investment promotion. As of December 2017, 2 800 NC staff and business counsellors had participated in the SBCC training.

Relevance to Indonesia

The *Negosyo* Centres illustrate the benefits of building a single visible entry point for the supply of government BDS nationwide at a moment when the Indonesian government is seeking to reduce the current fragmentation in its offer of BDS programmes. Other interesting insights from the experience of the *Negosyo* Centres relate to the development of an online platform for managing information and data, the emphasis on performance reporting and monitoring, and the value of developing partnerships with private-sector suppliers of business management tools.

Sources for further information

The Department of Trade and Industry (DTI) website at: http://www.dti.gov.ph/programs-projects/negosyo-center/

It will also be important that the national BDS offer reach rural and remote regions, as these often have specific support needs (Best et al., 2004). This could be done through Mobile SME Support Centres, such as those in use in Canada and Kazakhstan (see Box 7.3), or through emulating the practice of SEBRAE's SME Support Service Centres, which offer a virtual platform for entrepreneurs to access training and counselling services online. In this endeavour, the Ministry of Co-operatives and SMEs should work in collaboration with the Ministry of Villages, Disadvantaged Regions and Transmigration.

Box 7.3. Mobile Entrepreneur Support Centres, Kazakhstan

Kazakhstan's Ministry of National Economy operates a "single window" network of Entrepreneurship Support Centres in partnership with the offices of the National Chamber of Entrepreneurs. To address the needs of SMEs in rural villages, the government of Kazakhstan has created Mobile Entrepreneur Support Centres as an integral component of the Entrepreneurship Support Centres. These mobile units make regularly scheduled visits to rural areas to provide initial advice and information to aspiring and existing entrepreneurs, as well as to disseminate information and handouts on government programmes.

Source: OECD (forthcoming), *SME and Entrepreneurship Policy in Kazakhstan 2018*, OECD Publishing, Paris.

With respect to the everyday operations of the centres, it would be recommended that PLUT-KUMKM staff be aware of other national and local government support programmes and local private-sector BDS specialists to be able to perform effective referral services. This task would be facilitated by the mapping of existing support programmes and by making the information available on an online portal accessible to PLUT-KUMKM staff (see also chapter 4 and the example of the Canada Business Network).

Finally, the Indonesian government could encourage the clients of the PLUT-KUMKM Centres to complete a diagnostic assessment of their current strengths and weaknesses to identify the areas in greatest need of improvement. This diagnosis would allow the staff of the centres to better tailor programme assistance to the needs of the businesses, including referrals to consultancy advice and technical assistance in areas not covered by the centres. In this field, Indonesia could benefit from the experience of Malaysia, where the national SME agency (SME Corp. Malaysia) has developed SME diagnostic assessment tools tailored to micro-enterprises (M-CORE) and small and medium-sized enterprises (SCORE) (see Box 7.4).

Box 7.4. International inspiring practice: SME diagnostic assessment tools, Malaysia

Description of the approach

SME Corporation Malaysia (SME Corp.), the SME Agency of Malaysia, has developed two diagnostic tools to assess the capabilities, performance and needs of SMEs: the "SME Competitiveness Rating for Enhancement" (SCORE) and the "Micro-Enterprise Competitiveness Rating for Enhancement" (M-CORE).

SME Competitiveness Rating for Enhancement (SCORE): this online tool enables individual SMEs to assess themselves against seven criteria: financial performance; business performance; management capability and human resources; production capability; technical capability; technology adoption; and quality system/certification. The assessment leads to a 1-5 star-rating which reflects the quality of the business. Upon request of the company, the assessment can be verified by a qualified SME Corp. auditor through an onsite visit. The final assessment report, prepared by the SME Corp. auditor, includes a spider diagram of the firm's performance against the seven criteria and recommendations for improvement, including the type of assistance needed. The auditor can also work with the enterprise to develop an Action Plan outlining how to implement the suggested actions.

M-CORE (Micro-Enterprise Competitiveness Rating for Enhancement): this is a separate diagnostic tool that assesses the capabilities and competitiveness of micro-enterprises, *i.e.* businesses with less than five full-time employees or less than MYR 300 000 in turnover. The tool assesses performance in four key business areas: business performance; financial capability; operations; and management.

Micro-enterprises achieving a qualifying rating of Level 1 and above in the M-CORE assessment are eligible to participate in the Micro-Enterprise Enrichment and Enhancement Programme, an integrated approach to strengthen the core business of micro-enterprises and build their capacity. To qualify for assistance, micro-enterprises must be registered and hold a valid business license (i.e. they must be formal businesses), meet the full definition of a micro-enterprise, be in operation for at least six months and be operating on a full-time basis. The application can be submitted online. The programme's capacity-building components include:

- Skills upgrading: short-term courses provided by training centres appointed by SME Corp. Malaysia and focusing on entrepreneurship training (e.g. branding, packaging, etc.).
- Advisory services: consulting from business counsellors and members of the SME Corp.'s SME Expert Advisory Panel.
- Facilitating access to finance: advisory services from various financial institutions on how to increase the chances of receiving external finance.

Success factors

One of the main benefits of the SCORE and M-CORE tools is the identification of support services that are better matched to individual business needs. For example, for SMEs with a star-rating of 3 or below, SME Corp. concentrates on improving their capacities and abilities through business advisory services, while the 4 and 5-star rated SMEs are more likely to receive support in the form of participation in supply chains and international trade missions.

Obstacles and responses

A main challenge has been to build a cadre of trained auditors able to deliver the back-up support to SMEs completing the online SCORE assessment tool. This was addressed by delivering a training programme to selected consultants in the SCORE methodology, which includes SME site visits to gather additional inputs (through interviews and observations) for the assessment.

One quality of the SCORE tool is to enable SMEs to benchmark themselves again the industry average. This required building an electronic database to collect information on the performance results of all SMEs completing the SCORE assessment form.

Relevance to Indonesia

An SME diagnostic assessment tool could allow the PLUT-KUMKM Centres to better assess the strengths and weaknesses of their SME clients and tailor the intervention accordingly to the areas in greatest need of improvement.

Sources for further information

Business Advisory and Support Division, SME Corp. Malaysia, Kuala Lumpur. Email: sekretariatscore@smecorp.gov.my
SCORE Programme and description at: http://www.score.gov.my.

Conclusions and policy recommendations

There are many BDS programmes and models in Indonesia, such as the SME Business Clinics originally created by the Ministry of Trade; the Ministry of Industry's SMI *Sentra* and SMI Technical Services Units; the Ministry of SOEs' Creative Houses; and more than 1 000 independent private-sector BDS consultants, some of whom are members of the Association of Business Development Services Indonesia (ABDSI). The Ministry of Co-operatives and SMEs is seeking to standardise and consolidate the supply of BDS nationwide through the Integrated Business Services Centres for Co-operatives and SMEs (PLUT-KUMKM Centres), which is a positive development given the large number of programmes providing similar BDS at the national level. In a large country like Indonesia, it will also be important that the BDS offer reach rural and peripheral areas, for example through the deployment of mobile support centres.

A parallel challenge relates to improving the quality and standardisation of the services offered by government-supported BDS centres. In this respect, the implementation of national competency standards through training programmes and the related certification of qualified BDS managers and consultants will be a priority.

Based on the analysis in this chapter, the following recommendations are offered to strengthen the BDS system of Indonesia.

Recommendations on the national business development services (BDS) system

- Improve the take-up of BDS among SMEs by raising local awareness about the existence of such services and by ensuring that BDS are available across the whole country.
- Consolidate the offer of BDS in Indonesia through the integration, co-location and merger of some of the existing government-backed BDS programmes into the new PLUT-KUMKM Centres.
- Develop mobile business development services centres operating out of the PLUT-KUMKM centres to serve the needs of SMEs and entrepreneurs in more remote districts.
- Fully implement the national competency standard for business advisors through the development of a national training programme and the establishment of a certification body to attest the qualifications of professionals completing the training.
- Develop a diagnostic tool enabling SMEs to assess their performance and business counsellors to tailor the nature of advisory and consultancy services, based on the results of the diagnostic assessment.
- Ensure that business counsellors attached to the PLUT-KUMKM Centres are fully aware of existing government support programmes and local BDS consultants to be able to provide appropriate referral services to SME clients.
- Convene an annual conference for managers and business advisors of the PLUT-KUMKM Centres for the purpose of competency enhancement, sharing of good practices, and exchange of information and experience.

- Enhance the monitoring and evaluation system of the PLUT-KUMKM Centres by collecting and assessing data from users on their characteristics, types of services received, and level of satisfaction with the assistance received. Implement an electronic system to centralise this information for the purposes of aggregate analysis.

References

Best, R., S. Ferris and C. Wheatley (2004), *A Guide to Strengthening Business Development Services in Rural Areas*, USAID, Washington DC, https://www.crs.org/sites/default/files/tools-research/guide-to-strengthening-business-development.pdf

Committee of Donor Agencies for Small Enterprise Development (2001), *Business Development Services for Small Enterprises: Guiding Principles for Donor Intervention*, World Bank Group, Washington DC, https://www.enterprise-development.org/wp-content/uploads/BDS-Guiding-Principles-2001-English.pdf.

Mole, K. and J. Capellaras (2018), "Take-up and variation of advice for new firm founders in different local contexts", *Journal of Environment and Planning: Politics and Space*, Vol.36, Issue 1.

OECD (forthcoming), *SME and Entrepreneurship Policy in Kazakhstan 2018*, OECD Publishing, Paris.

Storey, D. (2003), "Entrepreneurship, small and medium sized enterprises and public policies", in D. Audretsch and Z. Acs (eds.), The Handbook of Entrepreneurship, pp. 473-511, Kluwer Publishing House, London.

ORGANISATION FOR ECONOMIC CO-OPERATION AND DEVELOPMENT

The OECD is a unique forum where governments work together to address the economic, social and environmental challenges of globalisation. The OECD is also at the forefront of efforts to understand and to help governments respond to new developments and concerns, such as corporate governance, the information economy and the challenges of an ageing population. The Organisation provides a setting where governments can compare policy experiences, seek answers to common problems, identify good practice and work to co-ordinate domestic and international policies.

The OECD member countries are: Australia, Austria, Belgium, Canada, Chile, the Czech Republic, Denmark, Estonia, Finland, France, Germany, Greece, Hungary, Iceland, Ireland, Israel, Italy, Japan, Korea, Latvia, Lithuania, Luxembourg, Mexico, the Netherlands, New Zealand, Norway, Poland, Portugal, the Slovak Republic, Slovenia, Spain, Sweden, Switzerland, Turkey, the United Kingdom and the United States. The European Union takes part in the work of the OECD.

OECD Publishing disseminates widely the results of the Organisation's statistics gathering and research on economic, social and environmental issues, as well as the conventions, guidelines and standards agreed by its members.

OECD PUBLISHING, 2, rue André-Pascal, 75775 PARIS CEDEX 16
(85 2018 22 1 P) ISBN 978-92-64-30625-7 – 2018

www.ingramcontent.com/pod-product-compliance
Ingram Content Group UK Ltd.
Pitfield, Milton Keynes, MK11 3LW, UK
UKHW051501290926
15471UKWH00008B/1350

9 789264 306257